24シーンのミニドラマで口からすらすら

日常英会話。
ほんとに使える表現 500

はじめに

本書は、英語の自然な日常会話に欠かせない、たくさんの典型的なフレーズや表現に慣れ親しんでもらうことを目的につくられました。24回のスキットからなる主人公のミユキとジョーとその家族や友人たちの物語を通して、読者のかたがたにはネイティブスピーカーが日常的に使っている英語の表現を頭の中で覚えるだけではなく、自然に使えるように「吸収」していってもらえるのではないかと思います。同時に、日本と他の国々との文化的な相違点や類似点に対する見方を養い、異なった背景をもつ人たちとのコミュニケーションをより効果的に進めていくストラテジーも身につけることができるように工夫しました。

　先にキーフレーズを決めて、それをスキットに入れ込むのではなく、まず物語があって、そこにキーフレーズが自然に「現れる」ようにしてあります。いいかえれば、ミユキやジョーやアナたち登場人物の会話は、実生活で使われている自然なことばで書かれているということです。ですから、キーフレーズは登場人物たちの会話の中で、自然に「発生」したものです。つまり、本書に出てくるキーフレーズは、ネイティブスピーカーの会話の中で実際にひんぱんに使われる表現であり、登場人物たちの置かれたそれぞれの状況において、ごく自然に用いられている表現なのです。

もちろん、表現の選定にはきちんとした指針を設けています。可能なかぎり最も役に立つ表現を選ぶため、英語学習者はどんな状況でネイティブスピーカーと知り合い、そのときに最も必要とされる英語の表現は何だろう、と頭を悩ませました。誰かに初めて会ったら、当然、まずあいさつをし、自己紹介をして、相手に少し質問をします。食べ物や飲み物をすすめたり、相手を家に招待したりするかもしれません。お互いのことが少しずつわかるようになり、友だちになってくると、意見を述べたり、どう感じているかを話したり、冗談をいったりするなど、会話の内容も多岐にわたるようになります。また同時に、レストランで食事をしたり、海外旅行に行ったり、パーティーに参加したり主催したりなどと、英語に関わるさまざまな社会的状況に身をおくことにもなるでしょう。

　そこで生まれたのが、友情から始まる物語というアイデアでした。生涯にわたって続く（と筆者は信じています）友情の、その最初の1年目の物語です。ミユキが外資系企業で仕事を始めるところからスタートします。ミユキと上司のジョーや各国から来ている同僚たちが出会い、交流が深まり、そこから新しい友情（きわめて特別な友情（！）も含めて）の輪が広がっていきますが、そのすべてが英語で行われます。ミユキやその家族が英語に自信をもつようになっていくのと同時に、読者のみなさんもだんだん英語に自信がもてる

はじめに

ようになるはずです。また、言語や文化に関係なく、楽しみや苦しみ、悩みや喜びを分かち合う登場人物たちの物語そのものも楽しんでいただければと思います。

　物語を読み進めていく中でひとつ覚えておいていただきたいのは、ミユキやその家族は自然な方法で新しい英語の表現を学んでいくということです。もちろん言語習得においては学習と努力も重要な部分ですが、英語を学ぶ上ではコミュニケーションがポイントになります。英語の会話の中で、新しい表現を無理に使う必要はありません。それらの表現がさまざまな状況（本書のほかに、映画やテレビ、実際の生活の中でも）で話されるのを耳にしていくうちに、それらを使っている自分に気づくようになるでしょう。

　コミュニケーションは友情のようなもので、ときには努力を必要としますが、ほとんどの場合は自然に生じるものです。

　この「物語」の構造は、セクションごとの最後に設けられた練習にも反映させています。まずやっていただきたいことは、英語の音に慣れるために会話を聞き、シャドーイングを通じて、本書の 24 のスキットの会話をまねていただくことです。英語の音は日本語とはかなり異なります。カラオケでも初めての歌は一度聞いただけでは、上手に歌えませんよね？　何度も聞いてやっと自分でも歌えるようになるわけです。英会話も同じです。まずは何度も聞いてみて

ください。

　慣れたところで今度は応用編。ネイティブスピーカーと会話しているつもりで、相手の問いに答えてみてください。解答例はありますが、あくまでも参考として載せています。最初は速くて聞き取れなくても、慣れるまで聞いてから臨んでみましょう。ご自分に当てはまる答えを考えてみてください。後半は、相手にこちらから問いかけをします。ネイティブスピーカーの友人や同僚らと実際に会話しているつもりで、楽しんで挑戦してみてください。表現が自然にすらすらと出てくるようになればしめたものです。

　英語にかぎらず外国語は、状況に沿った意味のある会話のやりとりの中で習得されるものだと考えます。ですからシャドーイングだけでなく、本書の会話のやりとりの練習もぜひ積極的に行ってみてください。

　読者のみなさんが、本書の物語を通して表現を身につけ、英語を使って友情の輪を広げていかれることを願ってやみません。

　では、いっしょに温かな友情に満ちた物語の世界への一歩を踏み出しましょう。

2008年10月1日
キャスリーン・フィッシュマン
坂本光代

CONTENTS

はじめに…………2
本書の構成と使い方…………10
CDトラック表…………14

Chapter 1　April…………16
Skit A　新しい職場で「はじめまして」…………17
＜場面・状況＞　新しい職場での1日目
＜表現のテーマ＞　職場での紹介の仕方と自己紹介
Exercises…………23

Skit B　春うらら。公園でお花見…………25
＜場面・状況＞　公園でお花見
＜表現のテーマ＞　プライベートな場面での紹介の仕方と自己紹介
Exercises…………31
Chapter 1 重要表現リスト…………33

Chapter 2　May…………34
Skit A　カフェで上司からアドバイス…………35
＜場面・状況＞　ジョーが社内カフェでミユキの話を聞く
＜表現のテーマ＞　飲食店での定番やりとり／YesとNoを使い分ける／本音を打ち明ける／誘う
Exercises…………41

Skit B　カフェテリアでランチトーク…………43
＜場面・状況＞　カフェテリアで同僚3人がランチ
＜表現のテーマ＞　ジョークを交えたやりとり／誘う
Exercises…………49
Chapter 2 重要表現リスト…………51

Chapter 3　June……… 52

Skit A　オープンハウスに招かれて………53
＜場面・状況＞　ジョーとアナの家でホームパーティー
＜表現のテーマ＞　パーティーにおける定番のやりとり
Exercises…………59

Skit B　ジョーの家族を家に招いて　61
＜場面・状況＞　ミユキの家にジョーの家族を招く
＜表現のテーマ＞　お客を迎える／訪問する
Exercises　　 67
Chapter 3 重要表現リスト 69

Chapter 4　July………70

Skit A　イタリアンレストランで初デート………71
＜場面・状況＞　レストランでミユキとリチャードが初デート
＜表現のテーマ＞　レストランでの定番のやりとり／感想・意見をいう
Exercises…………77

Skit B　男同士が居酒屋で！………79
＜場面・状況＞　居酒屋でジョーがタケシにアドバイス
＜表現のテーマ＞　アドバイスを求める／アドバイスをする
Exercises…………85
Chapter 4 重要表現リスト…………87

Chapter 5　August………88

Skit A　ロサンゼルス空港に到着………89
＜場面・状況＞　ロサンゼルス空港で入国審査後、出迎えを受ける
＜表現のテーマ＞　入国審査でのやりとり／出迎える／出迎えを受ける
Exercises…………95

Skit B　素晴らしき友情に乾杯！…………97
＜場面・状況＞　野球合宿の試合終了後の懇親会
＜表現のテーマ＞　ほめる／別れる
Exercises…………103
Chapter 5 重要表現リスト…………105

Chapter 6　September………106

Skit A　小学生にアメリカでの異文化体験を語る…………107
＜場面・状況＞　タケシが小学生を前に教室で簡単なスピーチをする
＜表現のテーマ＞　インフォーマルなスピーチのスタートから終了まで
Exercises…………113

Skit B　器作りもラクじゃない…………115
＜場面・状況＞　陶芸教室で作品を作る
＜表現のテーマ＞　ほめる／励ます／いらだつ
Exercises…………121
Chapter 6 重要表現リスト…………123

Chapter 7 October……124

Skit A 熟年夫婦、オーストラリアを旅する…………125
＜場面・状況＞　ミユキの両親がオーストラリアを旅行する
＜表現のテーマ＞　旅行などで使える、覚えておくと便利なことば
Exercises…………131

Skit B 温泉、サイコー！…………133
＜場面・状況＞　ふた組のペアが箱根の温泉に行く
＜表現のテーマ＞　感動を表す／意見を述べる
Exercises…………139
Chapter 7 重要表現リスト…………141

Chapter 8 November……142

Skit A 一筋縄でいかない電話での応対…………143
＜場面・状況＞　顧客からの電話にうまく応対できない
＜表現のテーマ＞　電話での基本応答
Exercises…………149

Skit B うれしくも気がかりな誕生日…………151
＜場面・状況＞　リチャードの誕生日をミユキが祝うが……
＜表現のテーマ＞　自分の気持ちを表す
Exercises…………157
Chapter 8 重要表現リスト…………159

Chapter 9 December……160

Skit A 初めての海外出張——トロントで商談…………161
＜場面・状況＞　トロント出張でホテルを相手に商談する
＜表現のテーマ＞　質問する／ほめる／感想を述べる
Exercises…………167

Skit B 男性陣、テレビの前に集合！…………169
＜場面・状況＞　テレビの前で男3人がアメフト観戦
＜表現のテーマ＞　ジョーク／非難する／応援する／断る
Exercises…………175
Chapter 9 重要表現リスト…………177

Chapter 10 January……178

Skit A ミユキの家に全員集合！…………179
＜場面・状況＞　ミユキの家で新年会を開く
＜表現のテーマ＞　質問する／驚く／喜ぶ／お礼をいう
Exercises…………185

Skit B 日本料理はどうですか？…………187
＜場面・状況＞　老舗の料亭で本社の副社長をもてなす
＜表現のテーマ＞　接待でのやりとり
Exercises…………193
Chapter 10 重要表現リスト…………195

Chapter 11　February……………196

Skit A 両家の両親、ゴタイメ〜ン…………197
＜場面・状況＞　ミユキとリチャードの両親が初めて対面する
＜表現のテーマ＞　初対面のあいさつ／紹介する／スモールトーク
Exercises…………203

Skit B 結婚披露パーティー、始まる…………205
＜場面・状況＞　ミユキとリチャードの結婚式当日
＜表現のテーマ＞　祝う／感謝の気持ちを伝える
Exercises…………211
Chapter 11 重要表現リスト…………213

Chapter 12　March……………214

Skit A 花見をしながら送別会…………215
＜場面・状況＞　花見をしながらジョーとアナの送別会
＜表現のテーマ＞　お礼をいう／質問をする／写真を撮る／別れを惜しむ
Exercises…………221

Skit B ミユキの昇進と新人登場！…………223
＜場面・状況＞　ミユキは昇進し新人が入社する
＜表現のテーマ＞　総まとめ
Exercises…………229
Chapter 12 重要表現リスト…………231

コラム

握手…………24	さまざまな英語…………132
花見…………32	愛情の表し方…………140
チップ…………42	謝罪に対する意識…………150
ジョーク…………50	バレンタインデー…………158
ハウスパーティー…………60	気持ちを伝える…………168
座る位置…………68	スポーツTV観戦…………176
デート…………78	クリスマスとお正月…………186
お客さんと店員さんの関係…………86	お酒の席…………194
夫婦別姓…………96	結婚とお墓…………204
ほめる…………104	結婚式 & gift registry…………212
小学校のスクールランチ…………114	写真…………222
先生の呼び方…………122	happy hour & 割り勘…………230

本書の構成と使い方

　本書は Hit the Road Travel という外資系の旅行会社に入った塚沢ミユキという28歳の女性と、アメリカ人の上司のジョーを中心に、同僚やその家族たちが経験するさまざまな出来事を、4月から翌年の3月までの1年間、24のシーンのスキット (Skit) の中で展開します。

　本書の構成は以下のようになります。

Skit の
ストーリーについてと
表現について

Skit にすんなり入っていけるように、登場人物やストーリーの背景について説明します。

章のトビラ

Skit で扱う表現のテーマは複数になることもあります。

Skit の表現のテーマを中心に解説します。また、Skit の中でその他の注目すべき表現や会話のやりとりについても解説を加えます。

Skit 本書の中核をなすミニドラマです。

Chapter 1 April Skit A

Track 02

新しい職場で「はじめまして」

Joe: Morning!
Staff members: Morning!/Hi, Joe.
Miyuki: Ah! Good morning. My name is…
J: Hello! You must be our new assistant travel consultant, Miyuki… Tsukazawa.
M: Yes, Tsukazawa. Please call me Miyuki.
J: Thank you! Good idea!
Welcome to Hit the Road Travel, Miyuki. I'm Joe Valeriani. I'm in charge of the North America/Australia/New Zealand Division.
M: It's nice to meet you, Mr. Valeriani.
J: Oh, please call me Joe.
M: Thank you! Good idea! But… it's OK? To call…?
J: Is it OK to call me by my first name? Of course! We all use first names here—even the president, Akiko… uh… See? I don't even remember her last name!
M: It's Ito.
J: I was just kidding.
M: Uh…
J: I mean I was joking. I didn't really forget her name.
M: Oh! I see!
J: So, Miyuki, have you ever worked in an international office before?
M: Um… at a British bank… for one year. But my department… all Japanese. I didn't speak English in my job.
J: I see. And I heard you worked at an advertising company before you came here?
M: Yes, in the market research department. My main job was… *anketo*.
J: *Anketo*… Oh, surveys?
M: Yes! Surveys.
J: Was that interesting?
M: Uh… no.
J: I like your honesty, Miyuki.
M: I'm sorry my English is poor.
J: Nonsense! It's good! And you'll be using English every day here, so it will get better and better. Now, let me introduce you to the others. Excuse me, everyone. Can I have your attention? This is Miyuki Tsukazawa, our new assistant travel consultant.
Others: Hi, Miyuki! / Welcome! / Nice to meet you!
M: It's nice to meet you. Please call me Miyuki.
Dave: I was planning to!
J: Don't mind Dave. He's always kidding.
M: Kidding… Oh, joking!
J: See? Your English is getting better already!

語注 — You must be…: ～さんですね / in charge of…: ～を担当する / call…by one's first name: ～を名前で呼ぶ / See?: ほらね / I was kidding.: ふざけていたのよ / department: 部門、課 / advertising company: 広告代理店 / survey: 調査 / poor: 下手な / Nonsense!: とんでもない! / Can I have your attention?: ちょっといいですか（注目を集めるとき）/ Don't mind…: ～を気にするな

色のついた英文は、次の「ポイント解説」で説明しています。

ポイント解説

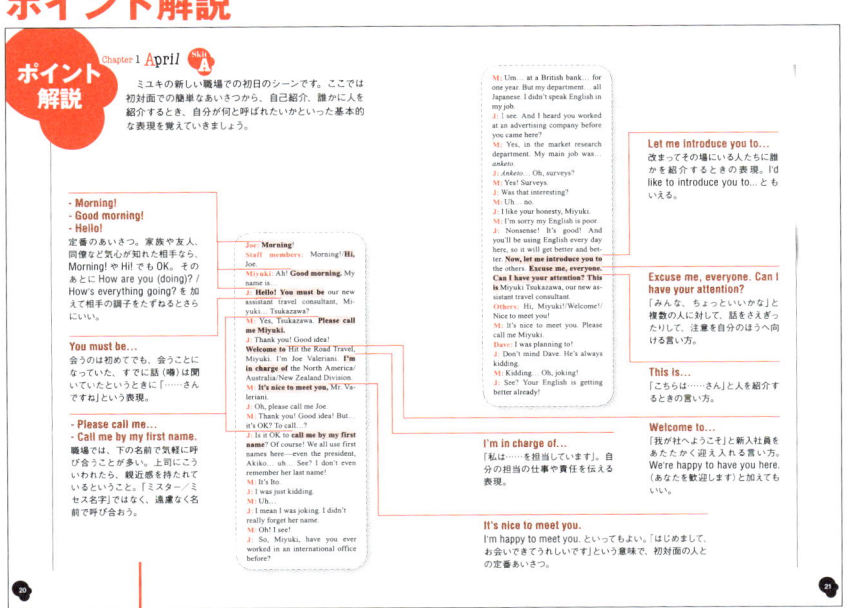

Chapter 1 April Skit A

ミユキの新しい職場での初日のシーンです。ここでは初対面での簡単なあいさつから、自己紹介、誰かに人を紹介するとき、自分が何と呼ばれたいかといった基本的な表現を覚えていきましょう。

- Morning!
- Good morning!
- Hello!

定番のあいさつ。家族や友人、同僚など気心が知れた相手なら、Morning! や Hi! でも OK。そのあとに How are you (doing)? / How's everything going? を加えて相手の調子をたずねるときにいい。

You must be…

会うのは初めてでも、会うことになっていた、すでに話（噂）を聞いていたというときに「……さんですね」という意味。

- Please call me…
- Call me by my first name.

職場では、下の名前で気軽に呼び合うことがあります。上司にこういわれたら、親近感を持たれているということ。「ミスター／ミセス名字」ではなく、遠慮なく名前で呼び合おう。

I'm in charge of…

「私は……を担当しています」。自分の担当の仕事や責任を伝える表現。

It's nice to meet you.

I'm happy to meet you. といってもよい。「はじめまして、お会いできてうれしいです」という意味で、初対面の人との定番あいさつ。

Let me introduce you to…

改まってその場にいる人たちに誰かを紹介するときの表現。I'd like to introduce you to… ともいえる。

Excuse me, everyone. Can I have your attention?

「みんな、ちょっといいかな」と複数の人に対して、話をさえぎったりして、注意を自分のほうへ向ける言い方。

This is…

「こちらは……さん」と人を紹介するときの言い方。

Welcome to…

「我が社へようこそ」と新入社員をあたたかく迎え入れる言い方。We're happy to have you here. (あなたを歓迎します) と加えてもいい。

Skit の中で、特に気をつけてほしい表現の使い方や関連表現などを解説します。

訳

対照用の英文

Joe: Morning!
Staff members: Morning!/Hi, Joe.
Miyuki: Ah! Good morning. My name is…
J: Hello! You must be our new assistant travel consultant, Miyuki… Tsukazawa?
M: Yes, Tsukazawa. Please call me Miyuki.
J: Thank you! Good day?
Welcome to Hit the Road Travel, Miyuki. I'm Joe Valeriani. I'm in charge of the North America/Australia/New Zealand Division.
M: It's nice to meet you, Mr. Valeriani.
J: Oh, please call me Joe.
M: Thank you! Good idea! But…it's OK? To call…?
J: Is it OK to call me by my first name? Of course! We all use first names here—even the president, Akiko… uh… See? I don't even remember his last name!
M: It's Ito.
J: I was just kidding.
M: Uh…
J: I mean I was joking. I didn't really forget her name.
M: Oh! I see!
J: So, Miyuki, have you ever worked in an international office before?
M: Um… at a British bank… for one year. But my department… all Japanese. I didn't speak English in my job.
J: I see. And I heard you worked at an advertising company before you came here?
M: Yes, in the market research department. My main job was… ankeeto.
J: Ankeeto…Oh, surveys?
M: Yes! Surveys.
J: Was that interesting?
M: Uh… no.
J: I like your honesty, Miyuki.
M: I'm sorry my English is poor.
J: Nonsense! It's good! And you'll be using English every day here, so it will get better and better. Now, let me introduce you to the others. Excuse me, everyone. Can I have your attention? This is Miyuki Tsukazawa, our new assistant travel consultant.
Others: Hi, Miyuki!/Welcome!/Nice to meet you!
M: It's nice to meet you. Please call me Miyuki.
Dave: I was planning to!
M: Don't mind Dave. He's always kidding.
M: Kidding… Oh, joking?
J: See? Your English is getting better already!

Skitの訳

ジョー：おはよう。
社員たち：おはようございます。/やあ、ジョー。
ミユキ：あ、おはようございます。私は…
ジ：やあ、新しいアシスタント・トラベル・コンサルタントのミユキ…ツカザワさんだね。
M：はい、ツカザワです。「ミユキ」で結構です。
ジ：ありがとう。それはいいね。ミユキ、ヒット・ザ・ロード・トラベルへようこそ。私はジョー・ヴァレリアーニ。北米/オーストラリア/ニュージーランド部門を担当しているんだ。
ミ：ヴァレリアーニさん、はじめまして。
ジ：ジョーでいいよ。
ミ：ありがとうございます。いいですね。でも、…、かまわないですか。
ジ：私を下の名前で呼んでいいかって？ もちろん。ここではみんな下の名前で呼び合うんだよ。なにしろ社長のアキコ…えっと…ほら、私は彼の名字さえ覚えてないよ。
ミ：「イトウ」さんです。
ジ：ちょっと「キッディング」しただけだよ。
ミ：え…
ジ：つまり冗談だよ。本当に彼女の名字を忘れたわけじゃない。
ミ：なるほど。
ジ：それでミユキ、これまでに国際企業で働いたことは？
ミ：えっと、1年間イギリスの銀行で……。でもその部署は全員日本人だし、仕事では英語は話しませんでした。
ジ：そうか。それとここに来る前は広告代理店で働いていたって聞いたけど？
ミ：はい、マーケット・リサーチ部で。私の仕事は……、アンケートと。
ジ：アンケート……ああ、「サーベイ」だね。
ミ：そうです、「サーベイ」です。
ジ：おもしろかった？
ミ：その……いいえ。
ジ：正直でいいね、ミユキ。
ミ：英語が下手ですいません。
ジ：とんでもない。うまいよ。それにここではこれから毎日英語を使うことになるんだから、どんどん上手くなるよ。それじゃあ、みんなに紹介しよう。みんな、ちょっといいかな。新しいアシスタント・トラベル・コンサルタントのミユキ・ツカザワさんだ。
社員たち：やあ、ミユキ、ようこそ。/はじめまして。
ミ：はじめまして。ミユキと呼んでください。
デーブ：そのつもりだったよ！
ミ：デーブのことは気にしないで。彼はいつも「キッディング」するんだ。
ミ：「キッディング」？ ああ、冗談のことですね。
ジ：ほらね、もう英語が上達してるよ。

Exercises

Chapter 1 April Exercises

Part A Track 02

①リスニング、②パラレル・リーディング(音を聞きながらテキストを音読)、③プロソディ・シャドーイング(音の再現)、④コンテンツ・シャドーイング(意味を意識)で会話を再現してみましょう。下記の Key Phrases を意識しながら、最低でも7回は会話を聞いてみましょう。

Key Phrases:
- Morning! -Good morning! -Hello!
- You must be…
- Please call me…
  - Call me by my first name.
- Welcome to…
- I'm in charge of…
- It's nice to meet you.
- Let me introduce you to…
- Excuse me, everyone. Can I have your attention?
- This is…

Part B

相手の問いやコメントに対して、自分なりの答えを考えてみましょう。

1) Andrea: Hello! You must be our new marketing assistant.
   You: _____
2) Andrea: Welcome to Seattle. I'm A
   You: _____
3) Andrea: How was your flight?
   You: _____

今度は相手に質問してみましょう。

4) 初対面の人とあいさつします。
   You: _____
   Andrea: Nice to meet you. I'm Andorea Larson.
5) 相手の仕事をたずねてみましょう。
   You: _____
   Andrea: I'm a sales manager at a small company in Vermont.
6) 相手をファーストネームで呼んでよいかの確認をしましょう。
   You: _____
   Andrea: Sure, please do. Everyone calls me Andrea.

Exercisesの解答例と訳

Exercisesの解答例と訳

1) Yes. Nice to meet you. My name is (Derek Smith.)
2) Nice to meet you. I'm (Eric.)
3) It was good, thank you. I couldn't sleep much, but it was OK.
4) Hello. My name is (Toru Sato.)
5) What do you do?
6) My I call you Andrea? / Do you mind if I call you Andrea?

問題と答えの訳
1) アンドレア：こんにちは！ あなたが新しい営業部のアシスタントですね。
   あなた：はい、はじめまして。私の名前は（デレック・スミス）です。
2) アンドレア：シアトルへようこそ。私はアンドレアといいます。
   あなた：はじめまして。私は（エリック）です。
3) アンドレア：飛行機はどうでしたか。
   あなた：良かったです。ありがとう。/ よく眠れませんでしたが、大丈夫です。
4) あなた：こんにちは。私の名前は（サトウ・トオル）です。
   アンドレア：はじめまして。私はアンドレア・ラーソンといいます。
5) あなた：お仕事は何をしていますか。
   アンドレア：バーモントの小さな会社で営業部長をしています。
6) あなた：アンドレアと呼んでもいいですか。/「アンドレア」と呼んでもかまいませんか。
   アンドレア：もちろん、そうしてください。みんな私をアンドレアと呼んでいますから。

コラム 握手

日本人と欧米人では握手に対する意識がちがうようです。日本はお辞儀の文化ですから、初めて会った人には、まずお辞儀をするのが習慣になっていますが、アメリカなどの英語圏の国では握手をします。アメリカは人と会ったときに、だれもが握手をするわけではありませんが、ビジネスの場面では握手をするのが一般的です。以前はビジネス・シチュエーションでは、女性が手を差し出したら握手をするといわれていましたが、最近では男女を問わず握手をすることが一般的となっているようです。
日本人は握手に慣れていないため、指先だけを持ったり、軽く手に触れるだけということがありますが、そのような握手をすると欧米人は失礼な印象を与えることになります。握手をするときは、相手の目を見て、しっかりと手を握りましょう。同時に自分の名前を言ったり、"Nice to meet you." などと軽くあいさつをするなおかまいません。ただし、あまり強くギュッとしめつけすぎないように。また、欧米人は別れ際にもよく握手をします。その際にも、"(It was) Nice meeting you." というのがあまり文句なので、ぜひ覚えておきましょう。

この Skit の内容に関連があるコラムです。日本と異なる生活習慣について社会的文化的背景の理解を深めます。

章末の重要表現リスト

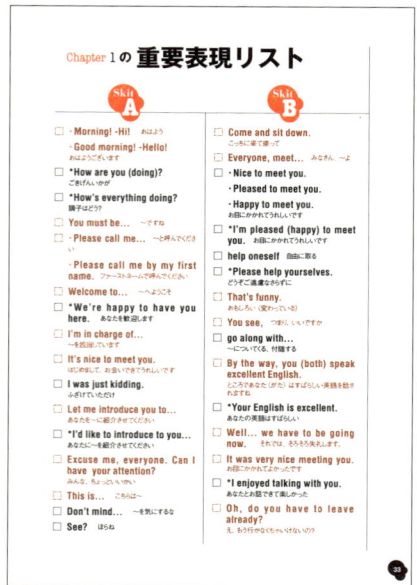

Chapter 1の重要表現リスト

Skit A
- ☐ Morning! -Hi! おはよう
  - Good morning! -Hello! おはようございます
- ☐ *How are you (doing)? ごきげんいかが？
- ☐ *How's everything doing? 調子どう？
- ☐ You must be… …ですね
- ☐ Please call me… …と呼んでください
  - Please call me by my first name. ファーストネームで呼んでください
- ☐ Welcome to… …へようこそ
- ☐ *We're happy to have you here. あなたを歓迎します
- ☐ I'm in charge of… …を担当している
- ☐ It's nice to meet you. はじめまして、お会いできて嬉しいです
- ☐ I was just kidding. 冗談でいっただけ
- ☐ Let me introduce you to… あなたを…に紹介させてください
- ☐ *I'd like to introduce to you… あなたに…をご紹介いたします
- ☐ Excuse me, everyone. Can I have your attention? みなさん、ちょっといいですか
- ☐ *I enjoyed talking with you. あなたとお話できて楽しかったです
- ☐ This is… こちらは…
- ☐ Don't mind… …を気にしない
- ☐ See? ほらね

Skit B
- ☐ Come and sit down. こっちに来て座って
- ☐ Everyone, meet… みなさん、…よ
- ☐ Nice to meet you.
  - Pleased to meet you. お目にかかれてうれしいです
- ☐ *I'm pleased (happy) to meet you. お会いできてうれしいです
- ☐ help oneself 自由に取る
- ☐ *Please help yourselves. どうぞご遠慮なくどうぞ
- ☐ That's funny. おもしろい（変わっていますね）
- ☐ You see, でね、でしょう？
- ☐ go along with… …についていく、付随する
- ☐ By the way, you (both) speak excellent English. ところであなた（がた）はすばらしい英語を話されますね
- ☐ *Your English is excellent. あなたの英語はすばらしい
- ☐ Well… we have to be going now. それでは、そろそろ失礼します
- ☐ It was very nice meeting you. お会いできてよかったです
- ☐ *I enjoyed talking with you. あなたとお話できて楽しかったです
- ☐ Oh, do you have to leave already? え、もう行かなくちゃいけないの？

Exercisesについて

各 **Skit** の終わりには **Exercises** が用意されています。**Exercises** は **Part A**、**Part B** のふたつのパートに分かれます。**Part A** は **Skit** の英文と音声を用いたリスニング、シャドーイングの練習、**Part B** はリスニングプラス発話練習となります。**Exercises** を始める前に、テキストで英文、重要表現、訳などをチェックしておいてください。

なお、**Part B** の音声は、コスモピアの下記サイトから無料でダウンロードできます。

http://www.cosmopier/phrases500_exercises

◆Part Aについて

Part A の **Exercises** は 4 段階に分けてあります:
- **Step 1** テキストを見ないで、音に注意しながらの **リスニング**
- **Step 2** テキストを見ながら音声を聞いて発話する **パラレル・リーディング**
- **Step 3** 音を再現しながらの **プロソディ・シャドーイング**
- **Step 4** 意味を意識した **コンテンツ・シャドーイング**

Step 1 では、聞くことのみに集中します。英語の流れ、アクセントの強弱、イントネーションの高低、英語特有の音などにも注意して聞いてみましょう。

Step 2 では、テキストを見ながら CD を聞いて口を動かす練習をしてみてください。

Step 3 のプロソディ・シャドーイングでは、聞きながら自分でも音を再現してみます。シャドーイングをするのが難しいと感じる人は、再度 **Step 2** のパラレル・リーディングに戻ってください。慣れてきたら、特にチャンク（意味のかたまり）を意識しながらシャドーイングをして、音を再現してみましょう。

Step 4 のコンテンツ・シャドーイングは最後の段階です。英文の意味を把握しながらの再現となります。発話ごとに自分が何をいっているのか、意識して再現してみましょう。

◆Part B について

Part B は、短いダイアローグ（会話）形式をとっています。前半では、まず相手の問いに対して答えてみます。解答例が一番最後に挙げてありますが、もちろんまったく同じである必要はありません。実践することを仮定して、自分に当てはまる言い回しを使って答えてみましょう。例えば、**What do you do?**（お仕事は何をしていますか）という問いに対し、**I work at a company.**（会社に勤めています）ではなく、自分が実際所属している会社名で答えてみましょう。

Part B 後半は、自分の問いに対し、相手が答えてくれます。まずは、相手の答えを見てからどのような質問が最適か、**Key Phrases** を参考にしながら質問してみましょう。こちらも解答例は用意されていますが、まったく同じである必要はありません。

Part B の会話例は上記サイトから無料でダウンロードできますので、ぜひ上記 **Step 4** のコンテンツ・シャドーイングを実践してみてください。相手の音声も注意深く聞き、再現してみるのです。相手との会話のやりとりを楽しむようにいってみてください。

発音は、英会話能力のひとつの重要ポイントではありますが、一番大切なのは、相手のいうことを正しく理解し、またこちらのいっていることを相手に正確に理解してもらうことです。小声でもごもご躊躇しながら話していては、せっかくの会話が続きません。はっきりと自信をもって発話しましょう。

章末の重要表現リスト

章の終わりには **Skit A**、**Skit B** ごとの重要表現のリストがあります。色文字の英文は「ポイント解説」に取り上げた表現、スミ文字の英文は **Skit** 中にある英文で語注などで取り上げた表現、＊のついた表現は **Skit** の中には出てこないけれども、解説の中で重要表現の関連表現として紹介されている表現です。

CDトラック表

Track		内容	ページ
1		オープニング	–
2	Chapter 1 April Skit A	新しい職場で「はじめまして」	18
3	Chapter 1 April Skit B	春うらら。公園でお花見	26
4	Chapter 2 May Skit A	カフェで上司からアドバイス	36
5	Chapter 2 May Skit B	カフェテリアでランチトーク	44
6	Chapter 3 June Skit A	オープンハウスに招かれて	54
7	Chapter 3 June Skit B	ジョーの家族を家に招いて	62
8	Chapter 4 July Skit A	イタリアンレストランで初デート	72
9	Chapter 4 July Skit B	男同士が居酒屋で！	80
10	Chapter 5 August Skit A	ロサンゼルス空港に到着	90
11	Chapter 5 August Skit B	素晴らしき友情に乾杯！	98
12	Chapter 6 September Skit A	小学生にアメリカでの異文化体験を語る	108
13	Chapter 6 September Skit B	器作りもラクじゃない	116
14	Chapter 7 October Skit A	熟年夫婦、オーストラリアを旅する	126
15	Chapter 7 October Skit B	温泉、サイコー！	134
16	Chapter 8 November Skit A	一筋縄ではいかない電話の応対	144
17	Chapter 8 November Skit B	うれしくも気がかりな誕生日	152
18	Chapter 9 December Skit A	初めての海外出張——トロントで商談	162
19	Chapter 9 December Skit B	男性陣、テレビの前に集合！	170
20	Chapter 10 January Skit A	ミユキの家に全員集合！	180
21	Chapter 10 January Skit B	日本料理はどうですか？	188
22	Chapter 11 February Skit A	両家の両親、ゴタイメ～ン	198
23	Chapter 11 February Skit B	結婚披露パーティー、始まる	206
24	Chapter 12 March Skit A	花見をしながら送別会	216
25	Chapter 12 March Skit B	ミユキの昇進と新人登場！	224
26		エンディング	–

A Year in English

1年間 24 シーンのミニドラマ

Make Friends with English!

Chapter 1
April

Skit A		
場面・状況	**新しい職場での1日目**	
表現の テーマ	**職場での紹介の仕方と自己紹介**	

Skit B		
場面・状況	**公園でお花見**	
表現の テーマ	**プライベートな場面での 紹介の仕方と自己紹介**	

Chapter 1 April

Skit A

ストーリーについて

　ミユキ Miyuki は 28 歳。いままで外資系の銀行や広告代理店で働いてきましたが、今度アメリカに本拠地を置く大手旅行代理店の日本支店に転職することになりました。そして、きょうが新しい職場での初日。彼女の部署の同僚はほとんどが外国人。ある程度は英語を話すことができるものの、これから毎日彼らと英語で話さなければならないと思うとミユキは少々不安です。幸いなことに、アメリカ人である上司のジョー Joe はフレンドリーで話しやすそうです。

ここで扱う表現について

　この章では、あいさつや自己紹介を中心とした基本的なスキットをご紹介します。初対面の人とどうやって言葉を交わすか、どのように自分のことを相手に紹介するか、どのようなあいづちをうって相手に理解していることを示すか、どのように会話をつなげるかなどのヒントが随所にあります。

　初対面の人との会話では、日常会話でよく用いる Good morning. や Hello、My name is... などの基本表現のほかに、自己紹介で使う It's nice to meet you. や他の人を紹介するときに用いる Let me introduce you to... など独特の表現が用いられます。日本語に直訳するとそれぞれ「お会いできて光栄です」、「……さんをご紹介します」とぎこちない表現になってしまいますが、意味的には「はじめまして」、「……さんです」といった日本語表現と似ています。なお、日本語の会話ではあえて主語「私 (I)」をつけないことが多いのですが、英語では名前の前に、I'm をつけて自分の名前を伝えます。

　英語の発音は高低が日本語よりもはっきりとしています。イントネーションに注意しながら聞いてみましょう。また、日本語のように一語一句はっきりと発音するのではなく、音によって強弱があります。発音すべき音とそうでない音とのちがいを意識しながら会話を聞いてみてください。

　ここでは、表現を用いるタイミングや表現に対する受け答え方などの使い方に注目し習得しましょう。

Chapter 1 April

Skit A

Track 02

新しい職場で「はじめまして」

Joe: **Morning**!
Staff members: Morning! / **Hi,** Joe.
Miyuki: Ah! **Good morning.** My name is…
J: **Hello! You must be** our new assistant travel consultant, Miyuki… Tsukazawa?
M: Yes, Tsukazawa. **Please call me** Miyuki.
J: Thank you! Good idea! **Welcome to** Hit the Road Travel, Miyuki. I'm Joe Valeriani. **I'm in charge of** the North America/Australia/New Zealand Division.
M: **It's nice to meet you,** Mr. Valeriani.
J: Oh, please call me Joe.
M: Thank you! Good idea! But… it's OK? To call…?
J: Is it OK to **call me by my first name**? Of course! We all use first names here—even the

You must be…:
〜さんですね

in charge of…:
〜を担当する

Call… by one's first name:
〜を名前で呼ぶ

president, Akiko… uh… See? I don't even remember her last name!
M: It's Ito.
J: I was just kidding.
M: Um…
J: I mean I was joking. I didn't really forget her name.
M: Oh! I see!
J: So, Miyuki, have you ever worked in an international office before?
M: Um… at a British bank… for one year. But my department… all Japanese. I didn't speak English in my job.
J: I see. And I heard you worked at an advertising company before you came here?
M: Yes, in the market research department. My main job was… *anketo*.
J: *Anketo*… Oh, surveys?
M: Yes! Surveys.
J: Was that interesting?
M: Uh… no.
J: I like your honesty, Miyuki.
M: I'm sorry. My English is poor.
J: Nonsense! It's good! And you'll be using English every day here, so it will get better and better. Now, **let me introduce you to** the others. **Excuse me, everyone. Can I have your attention? This is** Miyuki Tsukazawa, our new assistant travel consultant.
Others: Hi, Miyuki! / Welcome! / Nice to meet you!
M: It's nice to meet you. Please call me Miyuki.
Dave: I was planning to!
J: Don't mind Dave. He's always kidding.
M: Kidding… Oh, joking!
J: See? Your English is getting better already!

See?:
ほらね

I was kidding.:
ふざけていただけ

department:
部門、課

advertising company:
広告代理店

survey:
調査

poor:
下手な
Nonsense!:
とんでもない！

Can I have your attention?:
ちょっといいですか
（注目を集めるとき）

Don't mind…:
～を気にするな

Chapter 1 April Skit A

ポイント解説

ミユキの新しい職場での初日のシーンです。ここでは初対面での簡単なあいさつから、自己紹介、誰かに人を紹介するとき、自分が何と呼ばれたいかといった基本的な表現を覚えていきましょう。

- Morning!
- Hi!
- Good morning.
- Hello!

定番のあいさつ。家族や友人、同僚など気心が知れた相手なら、Morning! や Hi! でも OK。そのあとに How are you (doing)? / How's everything going? を加えて相手の調子をたずねるとさらにいい。

You must be…

会うのは初めてでも、会うことになっていた、すでに話（噂）は聞いていたというときに「……さんですね」という表現。

- Please call me…
- Call me by my first name.

職場では、下の名前で気軽に呼び合うことが多い。上司にこういわれたら、親近感を持たれているということ。「ミスター／ミズ名字」ではなく、遠慮なく名前で呼び合おう。

Joe: Morning!
Staff members: Morning! / **Hi, Joe.**
Miyuki: Ah! **Good morning.** My name is…
J: Hello! You must be our new assistant travel consultant, Miyuki… Tsukazawa?
M: Yes, Tsukazawa. **Please call me** Miyuki.
J: Thank you! Good idea! **Welcome to** Hit the Road Travel, Miyuki. I'm Joe Valeriani. **I'm in charge of** the North America/Australia/New Zealand Division.
M: It's nice to meet you, Mr. Valeriani.
J: Oh, please call me Joe.
M: Thank you! Good idea! But… it's OK? To call…?
J: Is it OK to **call me by my first name**? Of course! We all use first names here—even the president, Akiko… uh… See? I don't even remember her last name!
M: It's Ito.
J: I was just kidding.
M: Um…
J: I mean I was joking. I didn't really forget her name.
M: Oh! I see!
J: So, Miyuki, have you ever worked in an international office before?

M: Um… at a British bank… for one year. But my department… all Japanese. I didn't speak English in my job.
J: I see. And I heard you worked at an advertising company before you came here?
M: Yes, in the market research department. My main job was… *anketo*.
J: *Anketo*… Oh, surveys?
M: Yes! Surveys.
J: Was that interesting?
M: Uh… no.
J: I like your honesty, Miyuki.
M: I'm sorry. My English is poor.
J: Nonsense! It's good! And you'll be using English every day here, so it will get better and better. Now, **let me introduce you to** the others. **Excuse me, everyone. Can I have your attention? This is** Miyuki Tsukazawa, our new assistant travel consultant.
Others: Hi, Miyuki!/Welcome!/Nice to meet you!
M: It's nice to meet you. Please call me Miyuki.
Dave: I was planning to!
J: Don't mind Dave. He's always kidding.
M: Kidding… Oh, joking!
J: See? Your English is getting better already!

Let me introduce you to…

改まってその場にいる人たちに誰かを紹介するときの表現。I'd like to introduce you to... ともいえる。

Excuse me, everyone. Can I have your attention?

「みんな、ちょっといいかな」と複数の人に対して、話をさえぎったりして、注意を自分のほうへ向ける言い方。

This is…

「こちらは……さん」と人を紹介するときの言い方。

Welcome to…

「我が社へようこそ」と新入社員をあたたかく迎え入れる言い方。We're happy to have you here.（あなたを歓迎します）と加えてもいい。

I'm in charge of…

「私は……を担当しています」。自分の担当の仕事や責任を伝える表現。

It's nice to meet you.

I'm happy to meet you. といってもよい。「はじめまして、お会いできてうれしいです」という意味で、初対面の人との定番あいさつ。

Joe: Morning!
Staff members: Morning! / Hi, Joe.
Miyuki: Ah! Good morning. My name is…
J: Hello! You must be our new assistant travel consultant, Miyuki… Tsukazawa?
M: Yes, Tsukazawa. Please call me Miyuki.
J: Thank you! Good idea! Welcome to Hit the Road Travel, Miyuki. I'm Joe Valeriani. I'm in charge of the North America/Australia/New Zealand Division.
M: It's nice to meet you, Mr. Valeriani.
J: Oh, please call me Joe.
M: Thank you! Good idea! But…it's OK? To call…?
J: Is it OK to call me by my first name? Of course! We all use first names here—even the president, Akiko… uh… See? I don't even remember her last name!
M: It's Ito.
J: I was just kidding.
M: Um…
J: I mean I was joking. I didn't really forget her name.
M: Oh! I see!
J: So, Miyuki, have you ever worked in an international office before?
M: Um… at a British bank… for one year. But my department… all Japanese. I didn't speak English in my job.
J: I see. And I heard you worked at an advertising company before you came here?
M: Yes, in the market research department. My main job was… anketo.
J: Anketo…Oh, surveys?
M: Yes! Surveys.
J: Was that interesting?
M: Uh… no.
J: I like your honesty, Miyuki.
M: I'm sorry. My English is poor.
J: Nonsense! It's good! And you'll be using English every day here, so it will get better and better. Now, let me introduce you to the others. Excuse me, everyone. Can I have your attention? This is Miyuki Tsukazawa, our new assistant travel consultant.
Others: Hi, Miyuki!/Welcome!/Nice to meet you!
M: It's nice to meet you. Please call me Miyuki.
Dave: I was planning to!
J: Don't mind Dave. He's always kidding.
M: Kidding… Oh, joking!
J: See? Your English is getting better already!

ジョー：おはよう。
社員たち：おはようございます。／やあ、ジョー。
ミユキ：あ、おはようございます。私は……
ジョー：やあ。新しいアシスタント・トラベル・コンサルタントのミユキ……ツカザワさんだね。
ミユキ：はい、ツカザワです。「ミユキ」で結構です。
ジョー：ありがとう。それはいいね。ミユキ、ヒット・ザ・ロード・トラベルへようこそ。私はジョー・ヴァレリアーニ、北米／オーストラリア／ニュージーランド部門を担当しているんだ。
ミユキ：ヴァレリアーニさん、はじめまして。
ジョー：ジョーでいいよ。
ミユキ：ありがとうございます。いいですね。でも……、かまわないんですか。
ジョー：私を下の名前で呼んでいいかって？　もちろん。ここではみんな下の名前で呼び合うんだよ。なにしろ社長のアキコ……えっと……ほらね。彼女の名字さえ覚えてないよ。
ミユキ：「イトウ」さんです。
ジョー：ちょっと「キッディング」しただけだよ。
ミユキ：えーと……
ジョー：つまり冗談だよ。本当に彼女の名字を忘れたわけじゃない。
ミユキ：なるほど。
ジョー：それでミユキ、これまでに国際企業で働いたことは？
ミユキ：えーと、1年間イギリスの銀行で……。でも私の部署は全員日本人で、仕事では英語は話しませんでした。
ジョー：そうか。それとここにくる前は広告代理店で働いてたって聞いたけど。
ミユキ：はい、マーケット・リサーチ部で。私の仕事は……えーとアンケート……
ジョー：アンケート……ああ、「サーベイ」だね。
ミユキ：そうです。「サーベイ」です。
ジョー：おもしろかった？
ミユキ：その……いいえ。
ジョー：正直でいいね、ミユキ。
ミユキ：英語が下手ですいません。
ジョー：とんでもない。うまいよ。それにここではこれから毎日英語を使うことになるんだから、どんどんうまくなるよ。それじゃあ、みんなに紹介しよう。みんな、ちょっといいかい。新しいアシスタント・トラベル・コンサルタントのミユキ・ツカザワさんだ。
社員たち：やあ、ミユキ。／ようこそ。／はじめまして。
ミユキ：はじめまして。ミユキと呼んでください。
デーブ：そのつもりだったよ！
ジョー：デーブのことは気にしないで。彼はいつも「キッディング」するんだ。
ミユキ：「キッディング」？　ああ、冗談のことですね。
ジョー：ほらね。もう英語が上達してるよ。

Chapter 1
April

Exercises

Part A `Track 02`

①リスニング、②パラレル・リーディング(音を聞きながらテキストを音読)、③プロソディ・シャドーイング（音の再現）④コンテンツ・シャドーイング（意味を意識）の順で会話を再現してみましょう。下記の Key Phrases を意識しながら、最低でも７回は会話を聞いてみましょう。

Key Phrases:
- -Morning! -Hi! -Good morning. -Hello!
- You must be…
- -Please call me… -Call me by my first name.
- Welcome to…
- I'm in charge of…
- It's nice to meet you.
- Let me introduce you to…
- Excuse me, everyone. Can I have your attention?
- This is…

Part B

相手の問いやコメントに対して、自分なりの答えを考えてみましょう。

1) **Andrea:** Hello! You must be our new marketing assistant.
   You: _____

2) **Andrea:** Welcome to Seattle. I'm Andrea.
   You: _____

3) **Andrea:** Have you ever worked for a publishing company?
   You: _____

今度は相手に質問してみましょう。

4) 初対面の人とあいさつします。
   You: _____
   Andrea: Nice to meet you. I'm Andrea Larson.

5) 相手の仕事をたずねてみましょう。
   You: _____
   Andrea: I'm a sales manager at a small company in Vermont.

6) 相手をファーストネームで呼んでよいのか確認しましょう。
   You: _____
   Andrea: Sure, please do. Everyone calls me Andrea.

Exercises の解答例と訳

1) Yes. Nice to meet you. My name is (Derek Smith.)
2) Nice to meet you. I'm (Eric.)
3) No, I haven't. But I wanted to be an editor when I was younger.
4) Hello. My name is (Toru Sato.)
5) What do you do?
6) My I call you Andrea? / Do you mind if I call you Andrea?

問題と答えの訳

1) アンドレア：こんにちは！　あなたが新しい営業部のアシスタントですね。
   あなた：はい、はじめまして。私の名前は（デレック・スミス）です。
2) アンドレア：シアトルへようこそ。私はアンドレアといいます。
   あなた：はじめまして。私は（エリック）です。
3) アンドレア：これまで出版社に勤めたことはありますか。
   あなた：いいえ、ありません。でも若いころは編集者になりたいと思っていました。
4) あなた：こんにちは。私の名前は（サトウ・トオル）です。
   アンドレア：はじめまして。私は　アンドレア・ラーソンといいます。
5) あなた：お仕事は何をしていますか。
   アンドレア：バーモントの小さな会社で営業部長をしています。
6) あなた：アンドレアと呼んでもいいですか。／アンドレアと呼んでもかまいませんか。
   アンドレア：もちろん、そうしてください。みんな私をアンドレアと呼んでいますから。

コラム

握　手

　日本人と欧米人では握手に対する意識がちがうようです。日本はお辞儀の文化ですから、初めて会った人には、まずお辞儀をするのが習慣になっていますが、アメリカなどの英語圏の国ではまず握手をします。アメリカでは人と会ったときに、だれもが握手をするわけではありませんが、ビジネスの場面では握手をするのは一般的です。以前はビジネス・シチュエーションでは、女性のほうが手を差し出したら握手をするといわれていましたが、最近では男女を問わず握手をすることが一般的となっているようです。

　日本人は握手に慣れていないため、指先だけを持ったり、軽く手に触れるだけということがありますが、このような握手をすると欧米人には失礼な印象を与えることになります。握手をするときは、相手の目を見て、しっかりと手を握りましょう。同時に自分の名前をいったり、"Nice to meet you." などと軽くあいさつするとなおよいでしょう。ただし、あまり強くギュッとしめつけすぎないように。なにごともすぎたるは及ばざるがごとしです。

　また、欧米人は別れ際にもよく握手をします。その際には、"(It was) Nice meeting you." というのが決まり文句なので、ぜひ覚えておきましょう。

Chapter 1 April

Skit B

ストーリーについて

　ミユキの上司であるジョーの妻、アナ Anna と娘のエミリー Emily は、お花見にやってきたところです。ジョーの一家は 2 年前にサンフランシスコから東京へ引っ越してきました。ジョーは合気道に熱中し、アナは日本の陶芸を習っています。また、アナは先生としてインターナショナルスクールで 5 年生を教えています。

　この日の近所の公園でのお花見は、アナの友人で同僚のレナ Lena が企画しました。

ここで扱う表現について

　前回の Chapter 1 Skit A では、職場での自己紹介の表現を練習しました。ここでは、プライベートな場面での自己紹介の仕方を学びます。

　Hello. よりも Hi、Thank you. よりも Thanks. がよく使われるなど、一般的に表現が多少短くなります。「はじめまして」の I'm pleased to meet you. や I'm happy to meet you. の I'm もここでは省略されて Pleased (Happy) to meet you. となっています。微妙な差ですが、このような表現を用いることで他者との距離感は縮まり、親密でカジュアルな会話となります。

　前回ジョーがミユキを社員の前で紹介したときには、Let me introduce you to... といいましたが、カジュアルな場では Meet... といったり、また身内や友人を紹介するときは、This is my wife, ...（こちらが私の妻の……です）というようにシンプルに This is... を使います。

　また、会話の続け方にも注目してください。人に食べ物をすすめるときに、よく使われる表現のひとつに Please help yourselves. があります。直訳すると「みなさん、どうぞご自由に」となりますが、「どうぞ遠慮なさらずに」といったほうが日本語でふだん使う表現に近いかもしれません。

　受け答えにも注目してみましょう。受け答えのひとつに「本当？ (Really?)」というのがありますね。これは、日本語と同じような使い方となります。

　このスキットで、職場で使うほど堅苦しくない、気軽な表現法を習得しましょう。

Chapter 1 **April**

Skit B

Track 03

春うらら。公園でお花見

Anna and Emily: Hi, Lena!
Lena: Oh, hello, you two! **Come and sit down. Everyone, meet** Anna and Emily. Anna and I teach at the same school. And Emily goes to our school.
A and E: Hi!
Others: Hello! / Nice to meet you. / *Konnichiwa!*
A: Look, honey, aren't the cherry blossoms beautiful?
E: Uh-huh. They're like pink clouds!
L: There's lots to eat. Please help yourselves!
A: Thanks! We've brought some food, too.
Takako: Um… hello. My name is Takako. This is my husband, Hideo.
Hideo: Pleased to meet you.
A: Happy to meet you, too!
T: And this is our daughter, Mai. Say hello, Mai.
Mai: Hello.
E: How old are you, Mai? I'm seven.

There's lots to…: 〜するものがたくさんある
help oneself: （遠慮なく）自由に取る

M: I'm six.

L: I didn't know Mai spoke English!

T: She goes to a children's English class. And on Monday she'll start first grade.

E: But school starts in September.

A: Our school starts in September because it's an international school. Japanese schools start in April.

E: Really? **That's funny.**

H: You see, in Japan, spring is the time to start new things. In April we start school and we start new jobs… so cherry blossoms go along with new experiences and new friends.

E: Are you sad when the cherry blossoms go away?

T: A little… but that's why they are so… oh, what's the word?

H: So special. We know they're only here for a little while.

T: But we know that we will see them again next year.

A: By the way, you both speak excellent English. Have you lived overseas?

H: We both lived in England when we were students. That's where we met.

T: But Hideo's English is better than mine.

H: No, Takako's English is better.

M: My English is better!

後で……

H: Well… we have to be going now. It was very nice meeting you.

E: Oh, do you have to leave already?

A: Don't worry, honey. I'm sure we'll see Mai and her mom and dad again.

E: Like the cherry blossoms?

T: That's right! But sooner, we hope! Goodbye!

That's funny.:
おもしろい

You see,…:
いいですか

go along with…:
〜と同時に起きる、〜に付随する

go away:
散る

We have to be going now.:
そろそろ失礼します

Chapter 1 April — Skit B

ポイント解説

ミユキの上司ジョーの妻のアナは、娘や親しい人たちといっしょにお花見をします。カジュアルな雰囲気の中での初対面のあいさつやグループに招き入れる表現、退席するときの応答表現などを見ていきましょう。

Come and sit down.

「こっちに来て座って」。パーティーやピクニック、会合などでやって来た人に声をかけるときの表現。こう声をかけられれば、いわれたほうは緊張がほぐれ、グループに入りやすくなる。

Everyone, meet…

新しい人をみんなに紹介する場合には、Let me introduce you to… のかわりに、Everyone, meet Anna and Emily.（みんな、アナとエミリーよ）などというと、カジュアルな雰囲気になる。

Anna and Emily: Hi, Lena!
Lena: Oh, hello, you two! **Come and sit down. Everyone, meet** Anna and Emily. Anna and I teach at the same school. And Emily goes to our school.
A and E: Hi!
Others: Hello! / Nice to meet you. / *Konnichiwa!*
A: Look, honey, aren't the cherry blossoms beautiful?
E: Uh-huh. They're like pink clouds!
L: There's lots to eat. Please help yourselves!
A: Thanks! We've brought some food, too.
Takako: Um… hello. My name is Takako. This is my husband, Hideo.
Hideo: Pleased to meet you.
A: Happy to meet you, too!
T: And this is our daughter, Mai. Say hello, Mai.
Mai: Hello.
E: How old are you, Mai? I'm seven.
M: I'm six.
L: I didn't know Mai spoke English!
T: She goes to a children's English class. And on Monday she'll start first grade.
E: But school starts in Septem-

ber.
A: Our school starts in September because it's an international school. Japanese schools start in April.
E: Really? **That's funny.**
H: You see, in Japan, spring is the time to start new things. In April we start school and we start new jobs… so cherry blossoms go along with new experiences and new friends.
E: Are you sad when the cherry blossoms go away?
T: A little… but that's why they are so… oh, what's the word?
H: So special. We know they're only here for a little while.
T: But we know that we will see them again next year.
A: By the way, you both speak excellent English. Have you lived overseas?
H: We both lived in England when we were students. That's where we met.
T: But Hideo's English is better than mine.
H: No, Takako's English is better.
M: My English is better!

H: Well… we have to be going now. It was very nice meeting you.
E: Oh, do you have to leave already?
A: Don't worry, honey. I'm sure we'll see Mai and her mom and dad again.
E: Like the cherry blossoms?
T: That's right! But sooner, we hope! Goodbye!

That's funny.

funny には、「おもしろい」という意味のほかに「変わってる」という意味もある。イントネーションを上げると「おもしろい」、下げると「変」という意味に。

You see,…

何かを説明するときに、まず You see,「つまり」「いいですか」といって相手の注意を引きながら話を始めることができる。

By the way, you both speak excellent English.

ホスト側が来客に「おふたりとも英語がお上手ですね」などとコメントして、会話に引き込む配慮が見られる。Your English is excellent. ともいえる。相手をほめることも会話をスムーズにする秘訣。

Well… we have to be going now. It was very nice meeting you.

We have to be going now. は「そろそろ失礼します」といったていどの意味。言い出しにくいときは、Well…（それじゃあ）を前につけるとよい。I enjoyed talking with you.（あなたとお話しできて楽しかった）も使える。

Oh, do you have to leave already?

「もういかなくちゃいけないの？」とホストや他のゲストが残念そうな気持ちを伝える表現。Already?、So early?（もう？）と簡潔にいってもいい。このように相手との別れを惜しむのも礼儀のひとつ。

Anna and Emily: Hi, Lena!
Lena: Oh, hello, you two! Come and sit down. Everyone, meet Anna and Emily. Anna and I teach at the same school. And Emily goes to our school.
A and E: Hi!
Others: Hello! / Nice to meet you. / Konnichiwa!
A: Look, honey, aren't the cherry blossoms beautiful?
E: Uh-huh. They're like pink clouds!
L: There's lots to eat. Please help yourselves!
A: Thanks! We've brought some food, too.
Takako: Um… hello. My name is Takako. This is my husband, Hideo.
Hideo: Pleased to meet you.
A: Happy to meet you, too!
T: And this is our daughter, Mai. Say hello, Mai.
Mai: Hello.
E: How old are you, Mai? I'm seven.
M: I'm six.
L: I didn't know Mai spoke English!
T: She goes to a children's English class. And on Monday she'll start first grade.
E: But school starts in September.
A: Our school starts in September because it's an international school. Japanese schools start in April.
E: Really? That's funny.
H: You see, in Japan, spring is the time to start new things. In April we start school and we start new jobs… so cherry blossoms go along with new experiences and new friends.
E: Are you sad when the cherry blossoms go away?
T: A little… but that's why they are so… oh, what's the word?
H: So special. We know they're only here for a little while.
T: But we know that we will see them again next year.
A: By the way, you both speak excellent English. Have you lived overseas?
H: We both lived in England when we were students. That's where we met.
T: But Hideo's English is better than mine.
H: No, Takako's English is better.
M: My English is better!

H: Well… we have to be going now. It was very nice meeting you.
E: Oh, do you have to leave already?
A: Don't worry, honey. I'm sure we'll see Mai and her mom and dad again.
E: Like the cherry blossoms?
T: That's right! But sooner, we hope! Goodbye!

訳

アナとエミリー：ハイ、レナ。
レナ：あら、ハローおふたりさん。こっちにきて、座って。みなさん、アナとエミリーよ。アナと私は同じ学校で教えているの。エミリーも私たちの学校に通っているのよ。
アナとエミリー：ハイ。
友人たち：ハロー。／はじめまして。／コンニチハ。
アナ：ねえ見て、サクラがきれいじゃない。
エミリー：本当。まるでピンクの雲みたいね。
レナ：食べるものがいっぱいあるわよ、どうぞ自由に取って。
アナ：ありがとう。私たちも食べるもの持ってきたのよ。
タカコ：えーと……ハロー。私の名前はタカコです。こちらは夫のヒデオです。
ヒデオ：はじめまして。
アナ：こちらこそはじめまして。
タカコ：そしてこれが娘のマイです。マイ、ごあいさつしなさい。
マイ：ハロー。
エミリー：マイ、歳はいくつ？　私は7歳よ。
マイ：私は6歳。
レナ：マイが英語を話すなんて知らなかったわ。
タカコ：彼女は子どもの英語教室に通ってるんです。月曜日から彼女は1年生になります。
エミリー：でも学校は9月に始まるでしょ。
アナ：私たちの学校はインターナショナルスクールだから9月に始まるの。日本の学校は4月から始まるのよ。
エミリー：本当？　おもしろい。
ヒデオ：あのね、日本では、春は新しいことを始めるときなんだよ。4月に学校が始まったり、新しい仕事が始まったり……だから桜には新しい経験と新しい友だちがつきものなんだ。
エミリー：桜がなくなっちゃうと寂しくなるの？
タカコ：少しね……でも、だから桜はすごく……ああ、何ていうんだったかしら。
ヒデオ：すごく「スペシャル」なんだ。みんな、桜が咲いているのはほんの短い間だけだってわかっているから。
タカコ：でも、来年もまた見ることができるっていうこともわかっているけど。
アナ：ところで、おふたりとも英語を話すのが上手ですね。海外に住んでいたことはありますか。
ヒデオ：私たちふたりとも学生のときにイギリスに住んでいました。そこで出会ったんです。
タカコ：でもヒデオのほうが私より英語がうまいんです。
ヒデオ：いや、タカコのほうがうまいよ。
マイ：私の英語のほうが上手よ。

ヒデオ：え〜と、そろそろ失礼します。お会いできてとてもよかったです。
エミリー：えー、もう行かなくちゃいけないの？
アナ：大丈夫よ。きっとまたマイとマイのお母さんとお父さんに会えるわよ。
エミリー：桜みたいに？
タカコ：その通り。でもきっともっと早くにね。さようなら。

Chapter 1
April

Exercises

Part A `Track 03`

①リスニング、②パラレル・リーディング(音を聞きながらテキストを音読)、③プロソディ・シャドーイング (音の再現) ④コンテンツ・シャドーイング (意味を意識) の順で会話を再現してみましょう。下記の Key Phrases を意識しながら、最低でも7回は会話を聞いてみましょう。

Key Phrases:
- Come and sit down.
- Everyone, meet…
- That's funny.
- You see,…
- By the way, you (both) speak excellent English.
- Well… we have to be going now.
- It was very nice meeting you.
- Oh, do you have to leave already?

Part B

相手の問いかけや語りかけに対して、自分なりの答えを考えてみましょう。

1) **Bob:** There's lots to eat. Please help yourselves!
   You: _____
2) **Bob:** Hello. My name is Bob. This is my wife, Deborah.
   You: _____
3) **Bob:** By the way, you speak excellent English. Have you lived overseas?
   You: _____

今度は相手の応答にふさわしい語りかけをしてみましょう。

4) 日本の学校が始まる時期をいってみましょう。
   You: _____
   Bob: I see. American schools start in September.
5) 桜の花は美しいですね。
   You: _____
   Bob: Yes. They're like pink clouds, aren't they?
6) そろそろ失礼しなければならない時間になってきました。
   You: _____
   Bob: Oh, do you have to leave already?

Exercisesの解答例と訳

1) Thank you. We brought something, too.
2) Nice to meet you. I'm (Miranda.)
3) No, I've never lived abroad. / Yes, I lived in California for six months.
4) Japanese schools start in April.
5) Aren't the cherry blossoms beautiful?
6) I'm afraid we have to be going now.

問題と答えの訳

1) ボブ：食べ物はたくさんあります。ご自由にとってください。
   あなた：ありがとう。私たちも食べ物を持ってきたんですよ。
2) ボブ：こんにちは。私の名前はボブです。こちらは私の妻デボラです。
   あなた：はじめまして。私は……です。
3) ボブ：ところで、あなたは英語がとても上手ですね。海外に住んだことがあるのですか。
   あなた：いいえ、一度も海外に住んだことはありません。／はい、カリフォルニアに6カ月ほど住みました。
4) あなた：日本の学校は4月に始まります。
   ボブ：なるほど。アメリカの学校は9月に始まります。
5) あなた：サクラってきれいじゃないですか。
   ボブ：ピンク色の雲みたいですね。
6) あなた：申しわけないですが、私たちはもう行かなくては。
   ボブ：おや、もう行かなくてはならないのですか。

コラム　花見

　日本では春に桜の花見をすることが国民的行事となっていますが、アメリカやカナダにはそのような習慣はありません。それは国土が広大だからというのも大きな理由でしょう。たとえばアメリカはアラスカからハワイまで広がり、それぞれの地域に特有の季節があり異なる花が咲きます。チューリップ・フェスティバルなど地域特有の花を見たり、アメリカ北部では10月頃から紅葉 (autumn leaves) を楽しむことはありますが、国中が一斉に花見をする季節などというものはないのです。

　また、欧米では花を見ることそのものを楽しむことはあっても、日本の花見のように大勢で飲食するということはほとんどありません。一般的に北米では、公園などの公共の場では飲酒が禁止されています。

　そういった事情を知らずに、セントラルパークなどでお酒を飲みながら花見をしてしまう日本人がたまにいるそうなので、気をつけましょう。

Chapter 1 の 重要表現リスト

Skit A

- ☐ ・Morning! ・Hi!　おはよう
  ・Good morning! ・Hello!
  おはようございます
- ☐ *How are you (doing)?
  ごきげんいかが
- ☐ *How's everything doing?
  調子はどう?
- ☐ You must be...　〜ですね
- ☐ ・Please call me...　〜と呼んでください
  ・Please call me by my first name.　ファーストネームで呼んでください
- ☐ Welcome to...　〜へようこそ
- ☐ *We're happy to have you here.　あなたを歓迎します
- ☐ I'm in charge of...
  〜を担当しています
- ☐ It's nice to meet you.
  はじめまして、お会いできてうれしいです
- ☐ I was just kidding.
  ふざけていただけ
- ☐ Let me introduce you to...
  あなたを〜に紹介させてください
- ☐ *I'd like to introduce to you...
  あなたに〜を紹介させてください
- ☐ Excuse me, everyone. Can I have your attention?
  みんな、ちょっといいかい
- ☐ This is...　こちらは〜
- ☐ Don't mind...　〜を気にするな
- ☐ See?　ほらね

Skit B

- ☐ Come and sit down.
  こっちに来て座って
- ☐ Everyone, meet...　みなさん、〜よ
- ☐ ・Nice to meet you.
  ・Pleased to meet you.
  ・Happy to meet you.
  お目にかかれてうれしいです
- ☐ *I'm pleased (happy) to meet you.　お目にかかれてうれしいです
- ☐ help oneself　自由に取る
- ☐ *Please help yourselves.
  どうぞご遠慮なさらずに
- ☐ That's funny.
  おもしろい(変わっている)
- ☐ You see,　つまり、いいですか
- ☐ go along with...
  〜についてくる、付随する
- ☐ By the way, you (both) speak excellent English.　ところであなた(がた)はすばらしい英語を話されますね
- ☐ *Your English is excellent.
  あなたの英語はすばらしい
- ☐ Well... we have to be going now.　それでは、そろそろ失礼します。
- ☐ It was very nice meeting you.
  お目にかかれてよかったです
- ☐ *I enjoyed talking with you.
  あなたとお話できて楽しかった
- ☐ Oh, do you have to leave already?　え、もう行かなくちゃいけないの?

May

Chapter 2

Skit A	
場面・状況	ジョーが社内カフェでミユキの話を聞く
表現のテーマ	飲食店での定番やりとり／YesとNoを使い分ける／本音を打ち明ける／誘う
Skit B	
場面・状況	カフェテリアで同僚３人がランチ
表現のテーマ	ジョークを交えたやりとり／誘う

Chapter 2 May

Skit A

ストーリーについて

　ミユキがヒット・ザ・ロード・トラベルで働き始めてから１カ月がたちました。デーブ Dave やジェニファー Jennifer をはじめ、親切な同僚に恵まれ、ミユキはいままでになく仕事に楽しみをおぼえてきました。上司のジョーは、ミユキに仕事の様子はどうか、何か困ったことはないか話を聞くために社内カフェにやってきました。

ここで扱う表現について

　ここでは、許可、依頼、お詫び、招待、感謝などのさまざまな表現に加えて、カフェやレストランなどの飲食店で交わす定番表現を学びます。

　ここで注意すべきところは、英語と日本語のイエス、ノーの使い方のちがいです。Do you mind sitting in the sunshine?（日差しの当たる所に座ってもいいですか？）というジョーの問いに対して、ミユキはまず Yes. と答えていますが、すぐ I mean, no. と言い直していますね。これは Yes. と答えてしまうと、Yes, I do mind.（ええ、私は嫌です）となるからです。Do you mind...? に対して「いいえ、かまいませんよ」といいたければ答えは No(, I don't mind). となります。

　「さて、本題に入りますが」というときのジョーの表現 So... tell me. に注目してください。直訳だと「で、いって」となりますが、このままではおかしな表現ですね。でも英語ではよく使われる表現のひとつです。ここで彼は、ミユキが職場でどうしているか、困ったことはないか、などを聞き出そうとしています。ミユキが It's really interesting.（とてもおもしろいです）といったのに対して、ジョーは That's great. と返していますね。That's good. でももちろんいいのですが、great を使うことで、ジョーの「それはよかった」という気持ちがよりいっそう伝わってきます。ミユキの That would be great. も同様です。

　それから「実は……」と本音を切り出すとき、冒頭に使う表現のひとつに Actually があります。ここではミユキが自分の自信のなさをジョーに打ち明けています。他にも Honestly speaking（正直にいうと）や Frankly（率直にいうと）などがあります。

Chapter 2 May

Skit A

Track 04

カフェで上司からアドバイス

Joe: Is this table OK, Miyuki? **Do you mind sitting** in the sunshine?
Miyuki: Yes. I mean, no—I like sunshine. **It's a beautiful day today.**
Waiter: Hello. **Can I take your order?**
J: Have you decided?
M: Um… **iced coffee, please.**
J: And **I'll have a cappuccino.**
W: OK… thank you.
J: So… tell me, Miyuki—how's everything going? Do you enjoy the work?
M: Yes! It's really interesting. Dave and Jennifer are teaching me so much.
J: That's great. Are there any problems?
M: Well… sometimes there's too much information. When I research hotels or tours, it's hard to… oh, I don't know how to say it…
J: Narrow it down? I'll give you some guidelines.
M: Oh, that would be great. Thank you.
J: No problem. Anything else?

Do you mind -ing…?: 〜してもかまいませんか？
I mean: つまり
Can I take your order?: ご注文をうかがってもいいですか？

So… tell me さてと、それじゃあ
How's everything going?: どんな調子ですか？
guidelines: やり方
narrow… down: 絞り込む
That would be great.: それはいいですね、それは助かります
No problem.: 大丈夫、かまわないよ
Anything else?: 他には？

M: Actually… I'm still worried about my English.

J: Don't worry! You communicate very well. **But I do want to mention something.** When you speak on the phone, you often hesitate.

M: I'm nervous about making mistakes.

J: It's OK to make mistakes, as long as the meaning is clear. Anyway, overall you're making excellent progress.

M: Really? That's good to hear!

W: Here you are.

M: Thank you. … The waiter speaks English, too. I feel like I'm in another country.

J: Speaking of other countries, have you traveled overseas?

M: Yes, to America—Los Angeles, San Francisco and New York. I liked San Francisco best.

J: You're not saying that because I'm from San Francisco?

M: Yes. I mean, no! Well, maybe. By the way… may I ask you a question?

J: Sure.

M: What brought you to Japan?

J: Well, my wife and I are very interested in Japanese culture, so we decided to come here to live. That reminds me—next month we're having an open house party in our new place. **Would you like to come?**

M: Oh, **I would love to.** Thank you!

J: You're welcome. Please feel free to bring a friend—or a date.

M: A date? Um… can you recommend somebody?

J: Let's see… how about Dave?

Dave: Hiya, slackers! See you back at the salt mines!

J: Umm… maybe not.

M: Salt mines?

---

be worried about…: 〜を心配する
I do want to mention something.: ひとつだけいわせてください
hesitate: 遠慮する
be nervous about…: 〜を心配する
It's OK to…: 〜してもかまわない
as long as…: 〜の限り
overall: 全体的に
make progress: 上達する
That's good to hear.: それはいい知らせだ
feel like…: 〜のような感じがする
Speaking of…: 〜といえば
By the way: ところで
What brought you to…?: どうして〜に来たのですか
That reminds me: そういえば
Would you like to…?: 〜したいですか
I would love to.: ぜひしたいです
Please feel free to…: 遠慮なく〜してください
date: 付き合っている相手
recommend: すすめる
Let's see…: そうですね（考えている様子）
How about …?: 〜はどうですか
slacker: 怠け者
back at the salt mines: 職場に戻る

ポイント解説

Chapter 2 May — Skit A

上司のジョーはカフェで、ミユキと仕事の状況などを話します。ここではカフェでの注文のしかたや、本音を語るときの言い方、本題に入るときの言い方など、さまざまな表現を学んでいきましょう。

Joe: Is this table OK, Miyuki? **Do you mind sitting** in the sunshine?

Miyuki: Yes. I mean, no—I like sunshine. **It's a beautiful day today.**

Waiter: Hello. **Can I take your order?**

J: Have you decided?

M: Um… **iced coffee, please.**

J: And **I'll have a cappuccino.**

W: OK… thank you.

J: So… tell me, Miyuki—how's everything going? Do you enjoy the work?

M: Yes! It's really interesting. Dave and Jennifer are teaching me so much.

J: That's great. Are there any problems?

M: Well… sometimes there's too much information. When I research hotels or tours, it's hard to… oh, I don't know how to say it…

J: Narrow it down? I'll give you some guidelines.

M: Oh, that would be great. Thank you.

Do you mind sitting…?

Do you mind …ing? のかたちで「……してもかまいませんか」と相手にていねいに許可を求めるときの定番表現。「かまいませんよ、いいですよ」といいたいときには No, I don't mind. と答えればよい。

It's a beautiful day today.

会話をスタートさせるには、天気のことなどお互いが共有でき、あまりシリアスでないトピックを持ち出すのが無難。

Can I take your order?

レストランやカフェなどのウェイターの「ご注文は？」という定番文句。Are you ready to order? もよく使われる。

- Iced coffee, please.
- I'll have a cappuccino.

注文するときは最後に please をつけると印象がいい。同様に「私は……にします」という意味で I'll have… や、さらにていねいな I'd like (to have)… もよく使われる。

So… tell me…

「さて、本題に入りますよ」というときに切り出す発言。よく使われる言い方なので、CD で言い方のタイミング、抑揚などをしっかり身につけてほしい。

J: **No problem.** Anything else?
M: **Actually…** I'm still worried about my English.
J: Don't worry! You communicate very well. **But I do want to mention something.** When you speak on the phone, you often hesitate.
M: I'm nervous about making mistakes.
J: It's OK to make mistakes, as long as the meaning is clear. Anyway, overall you're making excellent progress.
M: Really? That's good to hear!
W: **Here you are.**
M: Thank you. … The waiter speaks English, too. I feel like I'm in another country.
J: Speaking of other countries, have you traveled overseas?
M: Yes, to America—Los Angeles, San Francisco and New York. I liked San Francisco best.
J: You're not saying that because I'm from San Francisco?
M: Yes. I mean, no! Well, maybe. By the way… may I ask you a question?
J: Sure.
M: What brought you to Japan?
J: Well, my wife and I are very interested in Japanese culture, so we decided to come here to live. That reminds me—next month we're having an open house party in our new place. **Would you like to come?**
M: Oh, **I would love to.** Thank you!
J: You're welcome. Please feel free to bring a friend—or a date.
M: A date? Um… can you recommend somebody?
J: Let's see… how about Dave?
Dave: Hiya, slackers! See you back at the salt mines!
J: Umm… maybe not.
M: Salt mines?

No problem.

直訳では「問題ない」だが、「大丈夫ですよ」、「気にしないで」といった意味。ここでは、「どういたしまして」のようなニュアンスも含まれている。

Actually…

「実は……」と本音を打ち明けるときなどの前置きに使う。Honestly speaking、Frankly (speaking) といってもよい。

But I do want to mention something.

ほめたり、良い点をいったあとに「でもひとつだけいわせてください」と指摘するときの表現。動詞 want のまえに do をつけて強調している。

Here you are.

ウェイターが注文のものや、ビル（請求書）を持ってきたときの「どうぞ」。Here you go. はさらにくだけた言い回し。Thank you. で返す。

- Would you like to come?
- I would love to.

パーティーやイベント、家などに誘うときの表現。「きたいですか？」よりも「いらっしゃいませんか？」のニュアンス。I would (I'd) love to. は、快く「ぜひうかがいます」という返事。

Joe: Is this table OK, Miyuki? Do you mind sitting in the sunshine?
Miyuki: Yes. I mean, no—I like sunshine. It's a beautiful day today.
Waiter: Hello. Can I take your order?
J: Have you decided?
M: Um… iced coffee, please.
J: And I'll have a cappuccino.
W: OK… thank you.
J: So… tell me, Miyuki—how's everything going? Do you enjoy the work?
M: Yes! It's really interesting. Dave and Jennifer are teaching me so much.
J: That's great. Are there any problems?
M: Well… sometimes there's too much information. When I research hotels or tours, it's hard to… oh, I don't know how to say it…
J: Narrow it down? I'll give you some guidelines.
M: Oh, that would be great. Thank you.
J: No problem. Anything else?
M: Actually… I'm still worried about my English.
J: Don't worry! You communicate very well. But I do want to mention something. When you speak on the phone, you often hesitate.
M: I'm nervous about making mistakes.
J: It's OK to make mistakes, as long as the meaning is clear. Anyway, overall you're making excellent progress.
M: Really? That's good to hear!
W: Here you are.
M: Thank you. … The waiter speaks English, too. I feel like I'm in another country.
J: Speaking of other countries, have you traveled overseas?
M: Yes, to America—Los Angeles, San Francisco and New York. I liked San Francisco best.
J: You're not saying that because I'm from San Francisco?
M: Yes. I mean, no! Well, maybe. By the way… may I ask you a question?
J: Sure.
M: What brought you to Japan?
J: Well, my wife and I are very interested in Japanese culture, so we decided to come here to live. That reminds me—next month we're having an open house party in our new place. Would you like to come?
M: Oh, I would love to. Thank you!
J: You're welcome. Please feel free to bring a friend—or a date.
M: A date? Um… can you recommend somebody?
J: Let's see… how about Dave?
Dave: Hiya, slackers! See you back at the salt mines!
J: Umm… maybe not.
M: Salt mines?

ジョー： ミユキ、ここのテーブルでもいいかな？　日が当たる所でも気にしない？
ミユキ： はい……つまり、気にしません。日光は好きですから。きょうはいいお天気ですね。
ウェイター： いらっしゃいませ。ご注文をうかがいましょうか？
ジョー： 決まった？
ミユキ： えーと……アイスコーヒーをお願いします。
ジョー： それと僕はカプチーノで。
ウェイター： かしこまりました。ありがとうございます。
ジョー： それじゃあミユキ、どんな調子だか教えてくれないか。仕事はおもしろい？
ミユキ： はい！　本当に楽しいです。デーブとジェニファーがいろんなことを教えてくれています。
ジョー： それはよかった。何か困ったことはあるかい？
ミユキ： そうですね……たまに情報がありすぎて困ります。ホテルやツアーを調べていると、大変……どういったらいいのかわかりません。
ジョー： 絞り込むことが？　やり方を教えるよ。
ミユキ： それは助かります。ありがとうございます。
ジョー： 大丈夫。他には？
ミユキ： 実は……まだ自分の英語が不安です。
ジョー： 心配ないよ！　よくコミュニケーションをとってるよ。でもひとついいたいことがあるんだ。電話で話すとき、君はよく遠慮がちになる。
ミユキ： 間違いを犯すことが、心配なんです。
ジョー： 間違えてもいいんだよ、意味がはっきりと伝わっているのなら。とにかく、全体的に君はすごく上達してるよ。
ミユキ： 本当ですか？　うれしいです。
ウェイター： ヒア、ユー、アー（どうぞ）。
ミユキ： サンキュー……あのウェイターさんも英語を話すんですね。別の国にいるみたい。
ジョー： 別の国といえば、海外には行ったことはある？
ミユキ： はい、アメリカはロサンゼルス、サンフランシスコ、ニューヨークへ。サンフランシスコが一番よかったです。
ジョー： 別に僕がサンフランシスコ出身だからそういっているわけじゃないよね？
ミユキ： はい。じゃなくて、いいえ！　まあ、そうかもしれません。ところで、ひとつ質問をしてもいいですか？
ジョー： どうぞ。
ミユキ： 何がきっかけで日本にいらしたのですか？
ジョー： そうだな、妻と私は日本文化にとても興味があって、それでここにきて住むことにしたんだ。そういえば、来月、新居公開パーティをするんだ。君もこないかい？
ミユキ： わあ、是非行きたいです。ありがとうございます！
ジョー： どういたしまして。遠慮なく友達、それかお相手を連れてきていいよ。
ミユキ： お相手？　えーと……どなたかご紹介いただけますか？
ジョー： そうだな……デーブはどうかな？
デーブ： やあ、怠け者さんたち！　（ソルト・マイン）オフィスで会おう！
ジョー： うーん……やめたほうがいいかも。
ミユキ： ソルト・マイン？

Chapter 2
May

Exercises

Part A Track 04

①リスニング、②パラレル・リーディング(音を聞きながらテキストを音読)、③プロソディ・シャドーイング（音の再現）④コンテンツ・シャドーイング（意味を意識）の順で会話を再現してみましょう。下記の Key Phrases を意識しながら、最低でも7回は会話を聞いてみましょう。

Key Phrases:
- Do you mind…-ing?
- It's a beautiful day today.
- Can I take your order?
- -Iced coffee, please.
  -I'll have a cappuccino.
- So… tell me…
- No problem.
- Actually…
- But I do want to mention something.
- Here you are.
- -Would you like to come?
  -I would love to.

Part B

相手の質問に対して、自分なりの答えを考えてみましょう。

1) **Cynthia:** Do you mind sitting in the sunshine?
   You: _____
2) **Waiter:** Can I take your order?
   You: _____
3) **Cynthia:** How's everything going?
   You: _____

今度は相手の応答にふさわしい語りかけをしてみましょう。

4) 相手に質問したいことがあります。
   You: _____
   Cynthia: Sure, ask me anything.
5) 相手はオーストラリアについて語っていますね。
   You: _____
   Cynthia: Yes—Sydney, Melbourne, Brisbane and Perth. I liked Perth the best.
6) 日本で何をしたかったのかを答えています。
   You: _____
   Cynthia: I wanted to learn about Japanese culture.

Exercises の解答例と訳

1) No, that's fine. / I'd rather sit in the shade, if that's OK.
2) I'd like (a bagel sandwich.)
3) Everything is going great. / Well, not so great.
4) May I ask you something?
5) Have you been to Australia?
6) What brought you to Japan?

問題と答えの訳

1) シンシア：日があたる席でも気にしませんか。
   あなた：はい、結構ですよ。／もしよければ日かげのほうに座りたいです。
2) ウェイター：ご注文をうかがいましょうか。
   あなた：（ベーグルサンドウィッチ）をください。
3) シンシア：調子はどうですか。
   あなた：すべて順調です。／そうよくはありません。
4) あなた：質問してもいいですか。
   シンシア：もちろん。何でも聞いてください。
5) あなた：オーストラリアに行ったことはありますか。
   シンシア：ええ、シドニー、メルボルン、ブリスベンとパースに。なかでもパースが一番好きです。
6) あなた：日本に来たきっかけは何ですか。
   シンシア：日本の文化について学びたかったんです。

コラム

チップ

日本人が海外に行ったときに困る習慣のひとつが、レストランやホテルなどで規定料金とは別に支払う心付け、チップです。一般的に北米のチップの相場は、レストランでは飲食代の15〜20%、ホテルのベッドメイキングが一泊1〜2ドル、ベルボーイに荷物を運んでもらったときには2ドル程度です。

レストランで食事をすませた後にチップを置かずに去ろうとすると、あからさまに嫌な顔をされたり、時には呼び止められたりすることもあります。その大きな理由はウエーターやウエートレスの時給は一般的に低く、チップからの収入が彼らの収入の大半であるからです。

チップの額はサービスに対する心付けなので、接客があまりよくないときには、意図的に額を減らして10%しか置いていかないという人もいます。

クレジットカードで支払う場合には、ふたつの方法があります。ひとつは、カードで飲食費とチップの両方を支払う方法です。請求書にチップの金額を書き込む欄があるので、見落とさないように気をつけてください。チップの欄は、しばしば "service" とか "gratuity" などと書かれているので注意しましょう。支払いの金額にチップを含めず、飲食代だけカードで払い、チップは現金で置いていくという手もあります。

Chapter 2 May

Skit B

ストーリーについて

　アナとレナは、彼女たちが教えているインターナショナルスクールのカフェテリアでランチをしています。ふたりの友人で同僚の教師のリチャード Richard も彼女たちに加わります。そこへ学校の経営者であるコバヤシ氏が何か知らせを持ってやってきます。

ここで扱う表現について

　冗談好きのリチャードと、レナとアナの楽しい会話です。英語では特にユーモアが大切。ウィットに富んだユーモアをいえたら会話も広がります。ここでは、まずい食事だと知りながら、リチャードがあえて I can't wait to try this.（食べるのが楽しみだな）といいます。その後は、Oh, wow... this is... good! といっていますがこれはもちろん大ウソ。レナとアナをびっくりさせるためにわざと事実とは反対のことをふざけていっています。仰天したふたりが You're kidding!（冗談でしょ！）と返すわけですが、そこで初めて本当のこと It's terrible.（これはひどい）といって笑いを誘っています。

　一方、その前にコバヤシ氏に How do you like the food?（食事はどう？）と聞かれている場面では、Oh... very good. / Yummy! と答えるレナとアナ。冗談を交わす会話のテンポ、相手によっての受け答えのちがいのニュアンスを CD の音声から聞き取ってください。日本人と比べてイギリス人やアメリカ人は場の空気を読まず、物事をはっきりいうと思われがちですが、そんなことはありません。相手の心情を配慮している会話にも注目しましょう。

　ここではジョーの妻のアナがリチャードをパーティーに誘っています。前回の Would you like to come? という丁寧な誘いに対し、気兼ねない相手には Can you come?（来れる？）とカジュアルに尋ねましょう。

Chapter 2 May

Skit B

Track 05

カフェテリアでランチトーク

Lena: Hmm… this pasta's a bit overcooked, isn't it? It's like one solid noodle.
Anna: I got stir-fried… something. I'm not sure what.
L: I heard there's a new cook. Let's hope it's a temporary situation.
A: Hey, Richard. **Why don't you join us?**
Richard: Sure—thanks. Let's hope what's a temporary situation?
L: That tie you're wearing.
R: Hey! This was a gift from my girlfriend—well, my ex-girlfriend. We broke up last week.
L: Because of the tie?
A: **I'm sorry to hear that.** How long were you together?
R: Almost five weeks.

a bit: ちょっと
overcooked: 調理されすぎている
solid: かたまりの
stir-fried: 炒められた
Let's hope…: 〜であることを願おう
temporary situation: 当面のこと
Why don't you join us?: こっちにいらっしゃいよ
Sure.: もちろん
ex-girlfriend: 元彼女
break up: 別れる
I'm sorry to hear that.: それは残念ね

Kobayashi: Hello, everyone.

A: Hi, Mr. Kobayashi!

R: How're you doing, Kobayashi-*san*?

K: Fine, thanks. **Sorry to disturb you.** I'm distributing these notices about the new school regulations.

L: New regulations? I don't like the sound of that.

K: Don't worry—just some small changes. **By the way,** how do you like the food?

A: Oh… very good. /**L:** Yummy!

K: Great! I'll tell the new cook! Well, goodbye! Enjoy your lunch.

L: Oh, we will.

A: Have you heard about the new cook, Richard?

R: Uh-huh. I can't wait to try this… curry? Oh, wow… this is… good!

A and L: You're kidding!

R: Yes. It's terrible.

A: Oh, Richard, we're having an open house party on June 8th—a Sunday. **Can you come?**

R: Party?! Hey, **I'm there!** But… isn't it rude to talk about the party in front of Lena?

L: Oh, very funny. I was invited **ages ago**. Well… ten minutes ago.

A: So what does that notice say?

R: Let's see… "New school regulations. Number 1. Faculty and staff must wear name tags at all times."

A and L: Name tags? … Oh, well.

R: "Number 2. Faculty members may not bring their lunch to school. They must purchase their lunch at the cafeteria every day."

A: Every day? / **L:** Oh, no!

R: Ha ha! **Just kidding!**

A and L: Oh, Richard!

Sorry to disturb you.: ちょっと失礼
distribute: 配布する
notice(s): お知らせ
regulation(s): 規則
I don't like the sound of that.: あまりいい話ではなさそうね
How do you like…?: 〜はどうですか？

Have you heard about…?: 〜のことは聞いた？
I can't wait to…: 〜をするのが楽しみだ

terrible: まずい

I'm there!: 絶対行くよ
Very funny.: おもしろくない
ages ago: とっくに

faculty: 教職員
name tag: 名札
at all times: 常に

purchase: 購入する

Just kidding!: 冗談だよ

ポイント解説

Chapter 2 May Skit B

カフェテリアでランチをするシーンです。全体がジョークに満ちた会話ですが、表現としては会話に誘うひとことや途中から会話に入る表現、相手の話に対するあいづち、話題を変える表現などを学びましょう。

Why don't you join us?
ばったり出くわした人を会話に引き込むための「いっしょにどう？」という表現で、覚えておくと便利。ここではSure—thanks.（ああ、ありがとう）と返しているが、都合が悪い場合は、I would love to, but...「そうしたいのですが、でも……」と好意的に断るのがマナー。

I'm sorry to hear that.
失恋や失敗、事故などよくないニュースを聞いたとき、返事に戸惑う前にまず「それはお気の毒に」という相手を気づかう表現。

Sorry to disturb you.
会話に入り込むときや、何か作業をしている人に話しかけるときには、「お邪魔をしてごめんなさい」「ちょっと失礼」と前置きをしてから話を始める。

By the way,
「ところで……」と話題を変えるときの言い回し。

Lena: Hmm… this pasta's a bit overcooked, isn't it? It's like one solid noodle.
Anna: I got stir-fried… something. I'm not sure what.
L: I heard there's a new cook. Let's hope it's a temporary situation.
A: Hey, Richard. **Why don't you join us?**
Richard: Sure—thanks. Let's hope what's a temporary situation?
L: That tie you're wearing.
R: Hey! This was a gift from my girlfriend—well, my ex-girlfriend. We broke up last week.
L: Because of the tie?
A: **I'm sorry to hear that.** How long were you together?
R: Almost five weeks.
Kobayashi: Hello, everyone.
A: Hi, Mr. Kobayashi!
R: How're you doing, Kobayashi-*san*?
K: Fine, thanks. **Sorry to disturb you.** I'm distributing these notices about the new school regulations.
L: New regulations? I don't like the sound of that.
K: Don't worry—just some small changes. **By the way,** how do you like the food?
A: Oh… very good. /**L:** Yummy!

K: Great! I'll tell the new cook! Well, goodbye! Enjoy your lunch.
L: Oh, we will.
A: Have you heard about the new cook, Richard?
R: Uh-huh. I can't wait to try this… curry? Oh, wow… this is… good!
A and L: You're kidding!
R: Yes. It's terrible.
A: Oh, Richard, we're having an open house party on June 8th—a Sunday. **Can you come?**
R: Party?! Hey, **I'm there!** But… isn't it rude to talk about the party in front of Lena?
L: Oh, very funny. I was invited **ages ago**. Well… ten minutes ago.
A: So what does that notice say?
R: Let's see… "New school regulations. Number 1. Faculty and staff must wear name tags at all times."
A and L: Name tags? … Oh, well.
R: "Number 2. Faculty members may not bring their lunch to school. They must purchase their lunch at the cafeteria every day."
A: Every day? / **L:** Oh, no!
R: Ha ha! **Just kidding!**
A and L: Oh, Richard!

Can you come?

Skit Aでは、まだそれほど親しくないジョーがミユキにWould you like to come?といってホームパーティーに誘っていたが、ここではアナが同僚のリチャードとレナを誘っている。このように親しい人を誘う場面では、Can you come?のほうが自然。

I'm there!

直訳は「僕はそこにいるよ！」だが、「もちろん参加するよ」「絶対行くよ！」「早く参加したいよ！」という意味の、楽しみにしている気持ちが伝わるインフォーマルな返事。

ages ago

「とっくに……」というレナのイギリス英語らしいフレーズ。

Just kidding.

I'm just joking.など「冗談だよ」は日常会話でよく使われる。

訳

Lena: Hmm… this pasta's a bit overcooked, isn't it? It's like one solid noodle.
Anna: I got stir-fried… something. I'm not sure what.
L: I heard there's a new cook. Let's hope it's a temporary situation.
A: Hey, Richard. Why don't you join us?
Richard: Sure—thanks. Let's hope what's a temporary situation?
L: That tie you're wearing.
R: Hey! This was a gift from my girlfriend—well, my ex-girlfriend. We broke up last week.
L: Because of the tie?
A: I'm sorry to hear that. How long were you together?
R: Almost five weeks.
Kobayashi: Hello, everyone.
A: Hi, Mr. Kobayashi!
R: How're you doing, Kobayashi-*san*?
K: Fine, thanks. Sorry to disturb you. I'm distributing these notices about the new school regulations.
L: New regulations? I don't like the sound of that.
K: Don't worry—just some small changes. By the way, how do you like the food?
A: Oh… very good. / **L:** Yummy!
K: Great! I'll tell the new cook! Well, goodbye! Enjoy your lunch.
L: Oh, we will.
A: Have you heard about the new cook, Richard?
R: Uh-huh. I can't wait to try this… curry? Oh, wow… this is… good!
A and L: You're kidding!
R: Yes. It's terrible.
A: Oh, Richard, we're having an open house party on June 8th—a Sunday. Can you come?
R: Party?! Hey, I'm there! But… isn't it rude to talk about the party in front of Lena?
L: Oh, very funny. I was invited ages ago. Well… ten minutes ago.
A: So what does that notice say?
R: Let's see… "New school regulations. Number 1. Faculty and staff must wear name tags at all times."
A and L: Name tags? … Oh, well.
R: "Number 2. Faculty members may not bring their lunch to school. They must purchase their lunch at the cafeteria every day."
A: Every day? / **L:** Oh, no!
R: Ha ha! Just kidding!
A and L: Oh, Richard!

レナ: うーん、このパスタはちょっとゆで過ぎじゃない？　なんだか麺のかたまりみたい。
アナ: 私のは炒めものよ……。何かのね。何だかよくわからないけど。
レナ: 新しいコックさんがいるって聞いたわ。当面の間だけならいいけど。
アナ: あら、リチャード！　いっしょに食べない？
リチャード: もちろん、ありがとう。当面の間ならいいって何の話？
レナ: あなたのそのネクタイ。
リチャード: おいおい！　彼女からのプレゼントなんだぜ、まあ、元彼女だけどね。先週別れたんだ。
レナ: そのネクタイのせいで？
アナ: それは残念ね。どのくらい付き合っていたの？
リチャード: ほぼ5週間。
コバヤシ: こんにちは、みなさん。
アナ: こんにちは、コバヤシ先生！
リチャード: コバヤシさん、お元気ですか？
コバヤシ: おかげさまで、ありがとう。おじゃまして悪いね。学校の新しい規則についてのお知らせを配ってるんだ。
レナ: 新しい規則ですか？　何だか嫌な感じですね。
コバヤシ: ご心配なく、小さな変更があるだけだから。ところで、食事のほうはどう？
アナ: ああ……とてもおいしいです。／**レナ:** おいしいです！
コバヤシ: それはよかった！　新しいコックに伝えるよ！　では、さようなら。よいランチを。
レナ: ええ、そうします。
アナ: リチャード、新しいコックさんのこと聞いた？
リチャード: うん。食べるのが待ちきれないよ、この……カレーかな？　おお、これは……おいしい！
アナとレナ: 冗談でしょ！
リチャード: ああ。これはひどい。
アナ: そうだ、リチャード、6月8日の日曜日にオープンハウス・パーティーをするの。来られる？
リチャード: パーティー？　行くよ！　でも……レナの前でそのパーティーのことを話すのは失礼じゃないか？
レナ: あら、つまらないこといって。私はもうとっくに招待されてるわ。まあ、10分前のことだけど。
アナ: それで、そのお知らせには何て書かれてるの？
リチャード: えーと……「新規定。その1：教員と職員は常に名札をつけること」
アナとレナ: 名札？　……あらそう。
リチャード: 「その2：教員は学校に昼食を持ってこないこと。毎日昼食はカフェテリアで買わなければならない」
アナ: 毎日？／**レナ:** うそでしょ！
リチャード: ハハハ！　冗談だよ！
アナとレナ: リチャードったら！

Chapter 2
May

Exercises

Part A Track 05

①リスニング、②パラレル・リーディング(音を聞きながらテキストを音読)、③プロソディ・シャドーイング（音の再現）④コンテンツ・シャドーイング（意味を意識）の順で会話を再現してみましょう。下記の Key Phrases を意識しながら、最低でも7回は会話を聞いてみましょう。

Key Phrases:
- Why don't you join us?
- I'm sorry to hear that.
- Sorry to disturb you.
- By the way,
- Can you come?
- I'm there!
- ages ago
- Just kidding.

Part B

相手の問いやコメントに対して、自分なりの答えを考えてみましょう。

1) **Waiter:** Enjoy your meal!
   You: _____
2) **Alison:** We're having a party on February 11th. Can you come?
   You: _____
3) **Alison:** How are you doing?
   You: _____

今度は相手に質問してみましょう。

4) 食事はどうですか、と聞いてみましょう。
   You: _____
   Alison: Oh, it's yummy.
5) 新しいシェフについて、何か聞いているのでしょうか。
   You: _____
   Alison: Yes, I heard he was the head chef at Maxim's in Paris!
6) Itはnotice「お知らせ」を指していると考えてみましょう。
   You: _____
   Alison: It says we have to wear our name tags at all times.

Exercises の解答例と訳

1) Thank you!
2) Yes, I'd love to. Thank you. / I'm sorry, I'm afraid I have another commitment that day.
3) Everything is going great. / Well, not that great.
4) How do you like the food?
5) Have you heard about the new cook?
6) What does the notice say?

問題と答えの訳

1) ウェイター：よい食事を！
 あなた：ありがとう！
2) アリソン：私たち2月11日にパーティーをするんだけど、来られる？
 あなた：喜んで。ありがとう。／ごめんなさい。申しわけないんだけどその日は別の約束があるんです。
3) アリソン：お元気ですか。
 あなた：絶好調です。／いえ、そんなによくないです。
4) あなた：料理の味はいかがですか。
 アリソン：とってもおいしいです。
5) あなた：新しいコックさんのことについて聞きましたか。
 アリソン：はい、彼はパリのマキシムというお店で料理長だったそうですよ。
6) あなた：お知らせには何て書いてあるんですか。
 アリソン：常に名札をつけること、と書いてあります。

コラム

ジョーク

　一般的にアメリカ人はジョークが好きです。親しい人同士でジョークを言い合ったり、からかい合ったりするのは、人間関係における潤滑油のようなものとされています。しかし、アメリカ人でも初対面同士ではそれほど冗談をいうことはありません。

　日本人には理解できないユーモアをアメリカン・ジョークなどということがありますが、アメリカ人なら誰しもジョークをいうというわけではなく、まったくいわない性格の人もいます。そういう人が柄にもなく無理して冗談をいう必要はありません。

　しかし、自分ではいわなくても、ジョークをいわれたときの受け方は非常に大切です。真顔でシリアスに受けるのは失礼と見なされ、場の雰囲気を悪くすることにもなります。うまい返しを思いつかなければ、素早く軽く笑うか、笑いながら、Uhhhと唸る (groan) のも自然なリアクションのひとつです。

　もし、あなたがジョークを理解できなくて、みんなが笑っているようなときには、近くにいる人に "Sorry, I didn't understand that—can you explain it?" (ごめんなさい。理解できなかったんですけど、説明していただけますか) などといってもよいでしょう。

Chapter 2 の 重要表現リスト

Skit A

- [ ] **Do you mind...-ing?** 〜してかまいませんか
- [ ] *No, I don't mind. かまいませんよ
- [ ] I mean つまり
- [ ] **It's a beautiful day today.** きょうはいい日ですね
- [ ] **Can I take your order?** ご注文をおうかがいしてよろしいですか
- [ ] **-Iced coffee, please.** アイスコーヒーをお願いします
- [ ] -I'll have a cappuccino. 私はカプチーノ
- [ ] So... tell me... さて本題に入ります
- [ ] -It's really interesting. とても興味があります
- [ ] -That's great. それはよかった
- [ ] How's everything going? どんな調子ですか
- [ ] Are there any problems? なにか問題がありますか
- [ ] I don't know how to say it. どういっていいかわからない
- [ ] That would be great. それはいいですね（それは助かります）
- [ ] **No problem.** 問題ありません
- [ ] Anything else? ほかに何かありますか
- [ ] **Actually** 実際
- [ ] *・Honestly speaking 正直にいって
- [ ] *・Frankly (speaking) 率直にいって
- [ ] Don't worry. 心配しないで
- [ ] **But I do want to mention something.** でもひとつだけいわせてください
- [ ] be nervous about... 〜に神経質になっている
- [ ] It's OK to... 〜しても大丈夫
- [ ] Anyway とにかく
- [ ] That's good to hear. それはいい知らせですね
- [ ] **Here you are.** どうぞ
- [ ] *Here you go. どうぞ
- [ ] Speaking of... 〜についていえば

- [ ] May I ask you a question? 質問をしてよいですか
- [ ] What brought you to...? どうして〜に来たのですか
- [ ] That reminds me. そういえば
- [ ] **-Would you like to come?** 来ませんか
- [ ] -I'd love to. ええ喜んで
- [ ] Please feel free to... 遠慮なく〜してください
- [ ] back at the salt mines 職場に戻る

Skit B

- [ ] a bit 少し
- [ ] ..., isn't it? 〜ですね
- [ ] **Why don't you join us?** こちらにいらっしゃいよ
- [ ] Sure—thanks. もちろん、ありがとう
- [ ] *I would like to..., but... 〜したいのですが、でも……
- [ ] Let's hope... 〜であることを願おう
- [ ] break up 別れる
- [ ] **I'm sorry to hear that.** それは残念ですね
- [ ] **Sorry to disturb you.** おじゃましてすいません
- [ ] I don't like the sound of that. あまりいい話ではなさそう
- [ ] **By the way,** ところで
- [ ] How do you like...? 〜についてどう思う?
- [ ] Have you heard about...? 〜のことは聞いた?
- [ ] I can't wait to... 〜をするのが楽しみだ
- [ ] It's terrible. まずい
- [ ] **Can you come?** 来ない?
- [ ] **I'm there!** 絶対行くよ
- [ ] **ages ago** とっくに
- [ ] at all times いつも
- [ ] **Just kidding.** 冗談だよ
- [ ] *I'm just joking. 冗談だよ

Chapter 3
June

Skit A	
場面・状況	**ジョーとアナの家でホームパーティー**
表現の テーマ	**パーティーにおける定番のやりとり**
Skit B	
場面・状況	**ミユキの家にジョーの家族を招く**
表現の テーマ	**お客を迎える／訪問する**

Chapter 3 June

Skit A

ストーリーについて

　天気のいい6月の午後、ジョーとアナの家のホームパーティーが始まりました。マンションの部屋とバルコニーはにぎやかになり始め、次々にゲストがやってきます。ミユキは少々遅れてやってきました。ここでも新しい出会いが待ち受けているようです。

ここで扱う表現について

　パーティーに招待されると、訪問の際のホストとのあいさつ、初対面の人たちとあいさつして、会話の中に入っていくときの表現など定番の表現がいくつかあります。

　例えばここではドアを開けたホストが Glad you could make it! と歓迎のあいさつをしています。「あなたが来てくれてうれしい」が直訳ですが、「来てくれてありがとう」という意味のほうがしっくりときます。あいさつの後は冬場なら Can I get your coat? (上着をお預かりしましょうか)と聞かれることもあるでしょう。

　遅れた場合は、ミユキのように Sorry I'm late. (遅れてごめんなさい)といいますが、早めもしくは時間ぴったりに到着すると、ホスト側がまだ準備に追われている可能性があるので、欧米では約束の時間よりも少し遅れて行くのはむしろ礼儀とされています。

　今回、ミユキは手土産を持参しました。そのような心遣いは喜ばれると同時に、You shouldn't have! と返されることもあります。直訳ですと「そんなことすることなかったのに！」ですが、決して相手は責めている訳ではありません。そんなに気をつかわせて悪かった、というようなニュアンスとしてとらえましょう。また、カジュアルなパーティーでは、Just bring yourself. (どうぞ手ぶらでお越しください)といわれることもあります。

　また、このスキットには実にさまざまなあいづちや応答の表現が見られます。応答のみに注意してスキットを聞いても、会話をスムーズに流していくコツがつかめるかもしれませんね。

Chapter 3 June

Skit A

Track 06

オープンハウスに招かれて

Joe: Hi, Miyuki! Glad you could make it! **Come on in.**
Miyuki: Thank you! Sorry I'm late.
J: You're not! It's an open house, remember? Miyuki, this is Anna.
M: I'm so happy to meet you.
Anna: Happy to meet you, too, Miyuki!
M: Your apartment is beautiful.
A: Thanks! We really like it here.
M: Oh—I brought you cookies… and this is for your daughter.
A: How nice of you! Emily, this is Miyuki. She brought you a present.
Emily: Thank you! … Oh, origami! It's so pretty! I'm gonna show this to Mai!
J: It's a hit. I'll go get the door.
A: Miyuki, **what can I get you to drink?** There's beer, wine, soft drinks…
M: Um… **some white wine, please.**
A: Sure. Oh—Richard. This is Miyuki. Could you get her a glass of white wine?

(I'm) Glad you…:
〜でうれしい、よかった
make it:
（make it には、何とか調整する、うまくいく、などいろいろな意味があるがここでは）来る

This is for…:
これは〜へ

It's a hit.:
とても気に入っている
get the door:
ドアを開ける

Could you…?:
〜してくれますか

Richard: Of course! Right this way, Miyuki! Let's see… This is Italian white wine… this is Australian white wine…
Lena: Why, Richard, I didn't know you were a wine expert.
R: Funny, Lena. Miyuki, Lena.
L: Hello. / **Miyuki:** Hi.
R: So, Miyuki… **how do you know Anna and Joe?**
M: I work with Joe. Actually, he's my boss. How about you?
R: I work with Anna—oh, and with Lena here.
L: Well… I should go and, um… help Anna.
R: Oh, going so soon?
M: Nice meeting you. So you're a teacher, Richard?
R: That's right. I teach second grade. A tough job, but an important one.
M: It sounds like a challenge.
L: Anna, look at those two. Have you been matchmaking?
A: Who, me?
J: What's going on? What are you whispering about?
A: Richard and Miyuki. They seem to like each other.
J: Hey, you may be right.
Dave: Great party, kids! I think I'll stay here all night.
Jennifer: Don't you have a presentation in the morning, Dave?
D: Thanks for reminding me, Jen. I'll write it on the train.
Je: Say, who's that guy Miyuki's talking to?
J: Anna's co-worker. This could be the start of a romance.
D: You don't say. Way to go, Miyuki!
The others: Shhh!

Right this way.: こちらです

funny: （皮肉に逆の意味で）おもしろい
How do you know…?: どうやって知り合ったの？

That's right.: そのとおり
tough: 大変な
It sounds like…: 〜のようだ
challenge: 大変なこと
matchmake: （恋仲を）取りもつ
What's going on?: 何ごとだ？
whisper about…: 〜についてコソコソ話す
You may be right.: そうかもしれない
kids: 君たち

remind: 思い出させる

co-worker: 同僚
This could be…: 〜かもしれない
You don't say.: まさか
Way to go!: よくやった、その調子

ポイント解説

Chapter 3 June — Skit A

ジョーとアナの家でホームパーティーが開かれます。ここでは家に迎えるときや飲み物をすすめるときなどのもてなしの表現や、それに対する答えかた、感想を述べるひとことなどをみていきましょう。

＊下線部の応答の仕方にも注意を向けて練習しましょう。

Sorry I'm late.
遅れたときの定番表現。I'm sorry that I'm late.（ごめんなさい。遅れました）より自然な表現。

Your apartment is beautiful.
相手の居住スペースをほめることで自然な会話が始めることができる。相手の良いところをほめる、というのはお互い会話を楽しむために効果的。

Thanks! We really like it here.
ほめられると日本人なら「とんでもありません」と消極的になりがち。でも英語の会話では、せっかくほめてくれたことに対し素直に感謝するのが普通。

What can I get you to drink?
あいさつの直後は、Can I get you something to drink? などと飲み物を聞かれる。What do you have?（何がありますか？）と聞いてから頼んでもいい。

Come on in.
Come in.（どうぞ）よりも Come on in. のほうが「どうぞ入って」というような、より相手を積極的に招き入れるニュアンスがある。

Joe: Hi, Miyuki! Glad you could make it! **Come on in.**
Miyuki: Thank you! **Sorry I'm late.**
J: You're not! It's an open house, remember? Miyuki, this is Anna.
M: I'm so happy to meet you.
Anna: Happy to meet you, too, Miyuki!
M: **Your apartment is beautiful.**
A: **Thanks! We really like it here.**
M: Oh—I brought you cookies… and this is for your daughter.
A: How nice of you! Emily, this is Miyuki. She brought you a present.
Emily: Thank you! … Oh, origami! It's so pretty! I'm gonna show this to Mai!
J: It's a hit. I'll go get the door.
A: Miyuki, **what can I get you to drink?** There's beer, wine, soft drinks…
M: Um… **some white wine, please.**
A: Sure. Oh—Richard. This is Miyuki. Could you get her a glass of white wine?
Richard: Of course! Right this way, Miyuki! Let's see… This is Italian white wine… this is Australian white wine…

Lena: Why, Richard, I didn't know you were a wine expert.
R: Funny, Lena. Miyuki, Lena.
L: Hello. / **Miyuki:** Hi.
R: So, Miyuki… **how do you know Anna and Joe?**
M: I work with Joe. Actually, he's my boss. How about you?
R: I work with Anna—oh, and with Lena here.
L: Well… I should go and, um… help Anna.
R: Oh, going so soon?
M: Nice meeting you. So you're a teacher, Richard?
R: That's right. I teach second grade. A tough job, but an important one.
M: It sounds like a challenge.
L: Anna, look at those two. Have you been matchmaking?
A: Who, me?
J: What's going on? What are you whispering about?
A: Richard and Miyuki. They seem to like each other.
J: Hey, you may be right.
Dave: Great party, kids! I think I'll stay here all night.
Jennifer: Don't you have a presentation in the morning, Dave?
D: Thanks for reminding me, Jen. I'll write it on the train.
Je: Say, who's that guy Miyuki's talking to?
J: Anna's co-worker. This could be the start of a romance.
D: You don't say. Way to go, Miyuki!
The others: Shhh!

How do you know…?

初対面で、ホストや共通の友人との関係や、知り合った経緯をたずねるときよく使われる質問。How did you get to know each other?（お互いどうやって知り合ったの？）も同じ意味。

You don't say.

「まさか！」「本当？」「どうだかね」というあいづち。

Way to go!

「でかした！」日本語同様、くだけた言い方。

Some white wine, please.

飲み物を頼むときは、最後に please をつけるのを忘れずに。I'll have… Thank you. でも OK。

Joe: Hi, Miyuki! Glad you could make it! Come on in.
Miyuki: Thank you! Sorry I'm late.
J: You're not! It's an open house, remember? Miyuki, this is Anna.
M: I'm so happy to meet you.
Anna: Happy to meet you, too, Miyuki!
M: Your apartment is beautiful.
A: Thanks! We really like it here.
M: Oh—I brought you cookies… and this is for your daughter.
A: How nice of you! Emily, this is Miyuki. She brought you a present.
Emily: Thank you! … Oh, origami! It's so pretty! I'm gonna show this to Mai!
J: It's a hit. I'll go get the door.
A: Miyuki, what can I get you to drink? There's beer, wine, soft drinks…
M: Um… some white wine, please.
A: Sure. Oh—Richard. This is Miyuki. Could you get her a glass of white wine?
Richard: Of course! Right this way, Miyuki! Let's see… This is Italian white wine… this is Australian white wine…
Lena: Why, Richard, I didn't know you were a wine expert.
R: Funny, Lena. Miyuki, Lena.
L: Hello. / **Miyuki:** Hi.
R: So, Miyuki… how do you know Anna and Joe?
M: I work with Joe. Actually, he's my boss. How about you?
R: I work with Anna—oh, and with Lena here.
L: Well… I should go and, um… help Anna.
R: Oh, going so soon?
M: Nice meeting you. So you're a teacher, Richard?
R: That's right. I teach second grade. A tough job, but an important one.
M: It sounds like a challenge.
L: Anna, look at those two. Have you been matchmaking?
A: Who, me?
J: What's going on? What are you whispering about?
A: Richard and Miyuki. They seem to like each other.
J: Hey, you may be right.
Dave: Great party, kids! I think I'll stay here all night.
Jennifer: Don't you have a presentation in the morning, Dave?
D: Thanks for reminding me, Jen. I'll write it on the train.
Je: Say, who's that guy Miyuki's talking to?
J: Anna's co-worker. This could be the start of a romance.
D: You don't say. Way to go, Miyuki!
The others: Shhh!

ジョー： やあ、ミユキ。来てくれてうれしいよ。入って。
ミユキ： ありがとうございます。遅くなってすいません。
ジョー： そんなことないよ。きょうはオープンハウスなんだから。ミユキ、アナだよ。
ミユキ： はじめまして。
アナ： こちらこそはじめまして、ミユキさん。
ミユキ： すてきなお宅ですね。
アナ： ありがとう。私たちはとても気に入っているのよ。
ミユキ： そうだ、クッキーを持ってきたんです……それと、これはお嬢様に。
アナ： ご親切に。エミリー、ミユキさんよ。あなたにプレゼントを持ってきてくださったの。
エミリー： ありがとう。わあ、オリガミ！ かわいい。マイに見せよう。
ジョー： 気に入ったみたいだね。僕がドアを開けにいくよ。
アナ： ミユキ、飲み物は何がいいかしら。ビール、ワイン、ジュースがあるわ。
ミユキ： えーと……白ワインをお願いします。
アナ： もちろん。あら、リチャード。こちらはミユキさん。彼女に白ワインを持ってきてくれない？
リチャード： もちろん！ ミユキ、こっちだよ。さて……これがイタリアの白ワイン、これはオーストラリアの白ワイン……
レナ： あらやだ、リチャード、あなたがワインのエキスパートだったなんて知らなかったわ。
リチャード： おもしろいね、レナ。ミユキ、レナだよ。
レナ： こんにちは。
ミユキ： ハイ。
リチャード： それでミユキ……アナとジョーのことはどうして知ってるの？
ミユキ： ジョーと働いているんです。ジョーは私の上司なんです。あなたは？
リチャード： 僕はアナと働いているんだ、あ、レナも同じ。
レナ： さて、私はアナを手伝いにいくわ。
リチャード： え、もう行くの？
ミユキ： お会いできてよかったです。それでリチャード、あなたは先生なの？
リチャード： そうだよ。僕は2年生を教えているんだ。大変だけど、大事な仕事だよ。
ミユキ： 大変そうね。
レナ： アナ、あのふたりを見て。あなた、お見合いをアレンジしてるの？
アナ： 私が？
ジョー： なになに？ 何をコソコソ話しているんだ？
アナ： リチャードとミユキのことよ。お互い気に入ってるみたい。
ジョー： おお、そうかもしれない。
デーブ： 楽しいパーティーじゃないか。ひと晩中おじゃましようかな。
ジェニファー： デーブ、あなたは明日の朝にプレゼンテーションがあるんじゃないの。
デーブ： ジェン、思い出させてくれてありがとう。電車の中で書くよ。
ジェニファー： ねえ、ミユキが話している男性は誰？
ジョー： アナの同僚だよ。これはロマンスの始まりかもしれない。
デーブ： 本当？ いいぞ、ミユキ！
皆： しーっ！

Chapter 3
June

Exercises

Part A Track 06

①リスニング、②パラレル・リーディング(音を聞きながらテキストを音読)、③プロソディ・シャドーイング（音の再現）④コンテンツ・シャドーイング（意味を意識）の順で会話を再現してみましょう。下記の Key Phrases を意識しながら、最低でも7回は会話を聞いてみましょう。

Key Phrases:

- Come on in.
- Your apartment is beautiful.
- Thanks! We really like it here.
- What can I get you to drink?
- Some white wine, please.
- How do you know…?
- You don't say.
- Way to go!

Part B

相手の問いやコメントに対して、自分なりの答えを考えてみましょう。

1) **Sean:** Your apartment is beautiful!
   You: _____
2) **Sean:** I brought you a gift.
   You: _____
3) **Sean:** What can I get you to drink?
   You: _____

今度は相手に質問してみましょう。

4) 飲み物は何がいいか、聞いています。
   You: _____
   Sean: Oh, I would love a beer.
5) Angelaをなぜ知っているのかたずねてみましょう。
   You: _____
   Sean: Angela is my boss.
6) Angelaと話している人は誰でしょう。
   You: _____
   Sean: That's Trevor. He's Angela's husband.

Exercises の解答例と訳

1) Oh, thank you.
2) How nice of you! / Thank you. You shouldn't have.
3) I would like (a cup of cappuccino), please.
4) What can I get you to drink?
5) How do you know Angela?
6) Who is that man talking to Angela?

問題と答えの訳

1) ショーン：あなたのアパートはとてもキレイですね！
   あなた：ありがとう。
2) ショーン：おみやげを持ってきました。
   あなた：ありがとう。／ありがとう、そんな気をつかわなくてよかったのに。
3) ショーン：飲み物は何にしますか。
   あなた：……をお願いします。
4) あなた：飲み物は何にしますか。
   ショーン：ええと、ビールをください。
5) あなた：アンジェラとはどうやって知り合ったのですか。
   ショーン：アンジェラは私の上司なんです。
6) あなた：アンジェラと話しているのは誰ですか。
   ショーン：あちらはトレバーです。彼はアンジェラのだんなさんです。

コラム　ハウスパーティー

　欧米ではよく友人を招いて自宅でパーティーをします。各自が一品ずつ料理を持ち寄る potluck が人気です。ホストが食事を用意し、ゲストが飲み物（ワインが多い）を持ち寄ることもあります。カジュアルなパーティーだと、six-pack と呼ばれる6本入りのビールやチップスなどを持ってきます。

　北米における大きめのカジュアルなパーティーでは、ゲストがリビングやダイニング、テラスなど家中いたるところに散らばっていることが多いので、正式なパーティーのスタート時間よりも30分～1時間半くらい遅れるのは珍しくなく、fashionably late（かっこよく遅れている）ということばがあるくらいです。ただ、カッコよく見せようと思って非常に遅れてくる人を、"There's Debbie—fashionably late as usual." （ほら、デビーよ。いつものように遅れてきたわ）などと皮肉って用いられることもあります。

　いくら遅れることがあるとはいえ、ピークの時間を過ぎて、ゲストがそろそろ帰りかけるころにやってくるなどということは好ましくありません。

　ゲストの数が少ない場合には、いくら遅れても30分くらいが限度でしょう。ただ、席について食事をするような場合には、遅れてもおそらく15分から20分が限度です。

　いずれにしても、指定された時刻にピタリと行かないように。ホストのほうがまだ準備中であせってドタバタしているかもしれませんから。

Chapter 3 June

Skit B

ストーリーについて

　パーティーから2週間ほどたったある雨の日の午後、ジョーとアナ、エミリーの一家はミユキの家にやってきました。ミユキの両親がアメリカ人の家族に会うのはこれが初めて。ジョーたちは伝統的な日本の家を訪れることを楽しみにしています。

ここで扱う表現について

　前回は外国人のお宅に訪問するシーンでしたが、ここでは逆に外国人を自宅に招いたときの会話の一例を紹介します。

　来客にミユキの父ヒロシがThank you for coming.（ようこそいらっしゃいました）といっています。これはよく使われる表現です。それに対しアナがThank you for inviting us!（お招きくださって、ありがとうございます）と返していますね。

　会話の運び方ですが、ジョー一家とミユキ一家、お互い自分のことばかり話すのではなく、相手のことについて質問やコメントをすることで、相手の話を聞くという謙虚さがうかがえます。ジョーはミユキの両親の英語力についてYou both speak English very well!とほめたり、ヒロシはジョーが上手に正座していることにI am surprised.と感心しています。アナはミユキの両親のオーストラリア旅行についてコメントしています。ひとりよがりの会話ではなく、お互いを思いやれるような会話が理想的ですね。

　また、ミユキの発言I hope you all like tempura.（みなさん天ぷらがお好きだといいのですが）からは、ゲストに対する配慮が感じられます。

　食前の「いただきます」は英語にはない表現ですが、あえてフランス語のBon appétit!（おいしい食事を）ということもあります。

Chapter 3 **June**

Skit B

Track 07

ジョーの家族を家に招いて

Miyuki, Joe, Anna, Emily: Hi!
M: **Are you all right? I hope** you didn't get wet.
J: No, we have raincoats from the rainy season last year.
M: **Oh, good.** Well, please come in. **Here are slippers.**
E: My slippers are so cute! **I love Pretty Kitty!**
M: Me, too! Those were mine when I was little.
Miyuki's mother: Welcome! My name is Masako.
Miyuki's father: My name is Hiroshi. **Thank you for coming.**
A: **Thank you for inviting us! These are for you.**
Masako: For us? Thank you! Beautiful *ajisai*! **How do you say…?**
A: Hydrangea.

slippers:
スリッパ（複数形で）

Ma: Difficult word… but my favorite flowers!
J: You both speak English very well!
M: They're taking a class. In October they're going to Australia.
E: Oh, you can see koalas! I love koalas!
Ma: Me, too! So cute!
M: My mother was worried you would not like sitting at the low table.
A: It's very comfortable! Besides, we want to experience traditional Japanese life.
Hiroshi: Joe-*san*, why can you sit… *seiza*? I am… surprised.
J: Well, I study aikido, so…
H: Aikido? I do—I did—aikido… long time ago.
J: Really?! For how many years? And what style of aikido did you do?
E: Daddy, I'm hungry.
M: I hope you all like tempura.
E: I love tempura! *Itadakimasu!*
Everyone: *Itadakimasu!*
J: What kind of soup is this?
M: It's called *suimono*. We like to make it for special occasions.
A: It's delicious!

その後……

Ma: More ice cream, Emily-*chan*?
E: Yes, please! I love strawberry ice cream!
A: You must be excited about your trip to Australia.
H: Yes. But… ah… a little afraid.
M: They're worried about getting around and dealing with problems.
J: I have an idea. You can be their travel consultant, Miyuki.
M: Consultant? Oh… I don't feel ready for that!
J: No worries, as Dave says. Come to think of it, Dave can help you.
Ma and H: Please… speak more slowly!

---

hydrangea: アジサイ

be worried…: 〜を心配する

besides: それに

be surprised: 驚く

What kind of… is this?: これはどんな種類の〜ですか

You must be…: きっと〜でしょう
deal with problems: 問題に対処する
I have an idea.: そうだ、いい案がある
You can…: 〜をしてはどうですか
No worries.: 心配しないで（オーストラリア英語）
I don't feel ready for…: まだ〜には自信がない
Come to think of it…: そういえば

ポイント解説

Chapter 3 June Skit B

ジョーとアナ、エミリーの一家は、ミユキの実家にやってきます。Aで覚えた「人を招待したとき、されたとき」の表現が出てきます。英語で何というか尋ねたり、相手を気づかう表現にも注目してみましょう。

Are you all right?
「大丈夫ですか？」と相手を気づかってよく使われる表現。誰かが危険な目に合ったり、動揺していたりするときにも使う。

Oh, good.
「ああ、それならよかった」。Good. だけよりも Oh, をつけたほうが感情が伝わる。

Here are (some) slippers.
「スリッパをどうぞ」。「どうぞ」といっても、何かをすすめるときは、直訳の please ではなく、Here is/are... を使う。

I love...
love の直訳は「愛」。でも「……が大好きです」というときに動詞 love はよく使われる。I love playing tennis.（テニスをするのが大好きです）、I love strawberries.（イチゴが大好きです）など。

- Thank you for coming.
- Thank you for inviting us!
人を招待したとき、招待されたときに対になって使われる決まり文句。考えなくても自然に口をついて出てくるようにしておきたい。

Miyuki, Joe, Anna, Emily: Hi!
M: Are you all right? I hope you didn't get wet.
J: No, we have raincoats from the rainy season last year.
M: Oh, good. Well, please come in. **Here are slippers.**
E: My slippers are so cute! **I love Pretty Kitty!**
M: Me, too! Those were mine when I was little.
Miyuki's mother: Welcome! My name is Masako.
Miyuki's father: My name is Hiroshi. **Thank you for coming.**
A: Thank you for inviting us! These are for you.
Masako: For us? Thank you! Beautiful *ajisai*! **How do you say...?**
A: Hydrangea.
Ma: Difficult word... but my favorite flowers!
J: You both speak English very well!
M: They're taking a class. In October they're going to Australia.
E: Oh, you can see koalas! I love koalas!
Ma: Me, too! So cute!
M: My mother was worried you would not like sitting at the low table.
A: It's very comfortable! Besides,

we want to experience traditional Japanese life.
Hiroshi: Joe-*san*, why can you sit… *seiza*? I am… surprised.
J: Well, I study aikido, so…
H: Aikido? I do—I did—aikido… long time ago.
J: Really?! For how many years? And what style of aikido did you do?
E: Daddy, I'm hungry.
M: I hope you all like tempura.
E: I love tempura! *Itadakimasu!*
Everyone: *Itadakimasu!*
J: What kind of soup is this?
M: It's called *suimono*. We like to make it for special occasions.
A: It's delicious!

Ma: More ice cream, Emily-*chan*?
E: Yes, please! I love strawberry ice cream!
A: You must be excited about your trip to Australia.
H: Yes. But… ah… a little afraid.
M: They're worried about getting around and dealing with problems.
J: I have an idea. You can be their travel consultant, Miyuki.
M: Consultant? Oh… **I don't feel ready for that!**
J: No worries, as Dave says. **Come to think of it,** Dave can help you.
Ma and H: Please… speak more slowly!

I hope you all like…
「……だといいのですが」と、相手に対する気づかいをさりげなく表すことのできる便利な表現。「さあ食べましょう」と促すときは shall we eat now? といえる。

I don't feel ready for that.
何かすることを促され、「まだ……するには自信がない」という意味。

Come to think of it,…
「そういえば」とそれまでの話に触発されて、思いついたことを切り出すときに用いることば。

Please speak more slowly.
相手の英語が早すぎて聞き取れないときは、遠慮なくこういって、ゆっくり話してもらおう。

These are (This is) for you.
プレゼントやお土産を渡すときの表現。I've brought you a gift. も同様。I hope you like it. (気に入っていただけるといいのですが) と加えるとさらにいい。

How do you say… (in English)?
英語の単語がわからないときは How do you say… in English? (これは英語で何というのですか?) とたずねる。

訳

Miyuki, Joe, Anna, Emily: Hi!
M: Are you all right? I hope you didn't get wet.
J: No, we have raincoats from the rainy season last year.
M: Oh, good. Well, please come in. Here are slippers.
E: My slippers are so cute! I love Pretty Kitty!
M: Me, too! Those were mine when I was little.
Miyuki's mother: Welcome! My name is Masako.
Miyuki's father: My name is Hiroshi. Thank you for coming.
A: Thank you for inviting us! These are for you.
Masako: For us? Thank you! Beautiful *ajisai*! How do you say…?
A: Hydrangea.
Ma: Difficult word… but my favorite flowers!
J: You both speak English very well!
M: They're taking a class. In October they're going to Australia.
E: Oh, you can see koalas! I love koalas!
Ma: Me, too! So cute!
M: My mother was worried you would not like sitting at the low table.
A: It's very comfortable! Besides, we want to experience traditional Japanese life.
Hiroshi: Joe-*san*, why can you sit… *seiza*? I am… surprised.
J: Well, I study aikido, so…
H: Aikido? I do—I did—aikido…long time ago.
J: Really?! For how many years? And what style of aikido did you do?
E: Daddy, I'm hungry.
M: I hope you all like tempura.
E: I love tempura! *Itadakimasu!*
Everyone: *Itadakimasu!*
J: What kind of soup is this?
M: It's called *suimono*. We like to make it for special occasions.
A: It's delicious!

Ma: More ice cream, Emily-*chan*?
E: Yes, please! I love strawberry ice cream!
A: You must be excited about your trip to Australia.
H: Yes. But… ah… a little afraid.
M: They're worried about getting around and dealing with problems.
J: I have an idea. You can be their travel consultant, Miyuki.
M: Consultant? Oh… I don't feel ready for that!
J: No worries, as Dave says. Come to think of it, Dave can help you.
Ma and H: Please… speak more slowly!

ジョー、アナ、エミリー：ハイ！
ミユキ：大丈夫ですか。濡れませんでしたか。
ジョー：いや、去年の梅雨のときからレインコートを持っているんだ。
ミユキ：よかった。さあ、どうぞ入ってください。スリッパをどうぞ。
エミリー：私のスリッパ、すごくかわいい。ハロー・キティ大好き。
ミユキ：私も。それは私が子どものときのものなの。
ミユキの母：ようこそ。マサコです。
ミユキの父：ヒロシです。ようこそいらっしゃいました。
アナ：お招きくださってありがとうございます。これをどうぞ。
マサコ：私たちに？　ありがとう。きれいなアジサイ。何ていうのかしら……。
アナ：「ハイドレンジア」です。
マサコ：難しいことばね……でも私の大好きなお花よ。
ジョー：おふたりとも英語がとてもお上手ですね。
ミユキ：ふたりともレッスンに通っているんです。10月にはオーストラリアにいくんですよ。
エミリー：じゃあ、コアラに会えるのね。コアラって大好き！
マサコ：私も！　すごくかわいいもの。
ミユキ：低いテーブルはいやなんじゃないかって母は気になっていたんです。
アナ：とても楽よ。それに、私たちは伝統的な日本の生活を体験したいの。
ヒロシ：ジョーさん、あなたはどうして正座ができるんですか？　とても驚きました。
ジョー：それは、合気道を習っているので……
ヒロシ：合気道？　私も……ずいぶん昔に合気道をやっていました。
ジョー：本当ですか。何年間ですか。何式の合気道でしたか。
エミリー：パパ、私お腹すいた。
ミユキ：みなさん、てんぷらがお好きだといいんですが。
エミリー：てんぷら大好き。イタダキマース！
全員：イタダキマース！
ジョー：これは何のスープですか。
ミユキ：「スイモノ」といいます。特別なときに作るんです。
アナ：おいしい！
マサコ：エミリーちゃん、もっとアイスクリームはどう？
エミリー：はい、お願いします。イチゴのアイスクリーム大好き。
アナ：オーストラリア旅行はお楽しみでしょうね。
ヒロシ：はい。でも少々不安で……
ミユキ：いろんな所をまわって、問題が起きることを心配してるんです。
ジョー：そうだ。（いい案がある。）ミユキ、君が彼らの旅行コンサルタントになるといいよ。
ミユキ：コンサルタント？　それは……私にはまだ無理です。
ジョー：心配ご無用、ってデーブがいうだろ。そういえば、デーブが手伝ってくれるよ。
マサコとヒロシ：お願いします。もっとゆっくり話してください！

Chapter 3
June

Exercises

Part A `Track 07`

①リスニング、②パラレル・リーディング(音を聞きながらテキストを音読)、③プロソディ・シャドーイング（音の再現）④コンテンツ・シャドーイング（意味を意識）の順で会話を再現してみましょう。下記の Key Phrases を意識しながら、最低でも7回は会話を聞いてみましょう。

Key Phrases:
- Are you all right?
- Oh, good.
- Here are (some) slippers.
- I love…
- -Thank you for coming.
  -Thank you for inviting us!
- How do you say… (in English)?
- These are (This is) for you.
- I hope…
- I don't feel ready for that.
- Please speak more slowly.

Part B

相手の問いやコメントに対して、自分なりの答えを考えてみましょう。

1) **Diane:** Are you all right? I hope you didn't get wet.
   You: _____
2) **Diane:** Thank you for coming today.
   You: _____
3) **Diane:** I hope you like roast beef.
   You: _____

今度は相手の応答にふさわしい語りかけをしてみましょう。

4) 雨が降ったと聞いて……。
   You: _____
   Diane: Thank you, I'm fine. I brought a big umbrella with me.
5) ホームパーティーでゲストが来ました。
   You: _____
   Diane: Thank you for inviting us.
6) 相手がアメリカへ帰国すると聞いて……。
   You: _____
   Diane: Yes, I'm looking forward to seeing my parents.

Exercises の解答例と訳

1) I'm fine. I have an umbrella with me.
2) Thank you for the invitation.
3) Yes, I love roast beef.
4) Are you all right? I hope you didn't get wet.
5) Thank you for coming today.
6) You must be excited about going back to America.

問題と答えの訳

1) ダイアン：大丈夫ですか。濡れませんでしたか。
   あなた：大丈夫です。カサを持ってきましたから。
2) ダイアン：今日は来てくれてありがとう。
   あなた：誘ってくれてありがとう。
3) ダイアン：ローストビーフがお好きだといいんですが。
   あなた：はい、ローストビーフは大好物です。
4) あなた：大丈夫ですか。濡れませんでしたか。
   ダイアン：ありがとう、大丈夫です。大きなカサを持ってきましたから。
5) あなた：今日は来てくれてありがとう。
   ダイアン：私たちを招待してくれてありがとう。
6) あなた：アメリカに帰るのが楽しみでしょう。
   ダイアン：はい、両親と会うのを楽しみにしています。

コラム　座る位置

　長方形のテーブルのまわりに座るときに、日本では上座、下座の区別があり、ドアから離れた側の端（上座）に年長の男性が座るのが習慣となっていますが、欧米でも似たような感覚はあるものの、それほど厳密ではありません。年長の人やメインゲスト（guest of honor）にはしばしば座りたい席を先に決める（first choice）の権限がありますが、そのときにも上座に座らないこともあります。

　ディナー・パーティーなどでどこに座ればいいかわからないときは、ホストが "Please have a seat." といって指示してくれるのを待つか、"Where should I sit?" とか "Is it OK if I sit here?" とたずねるのが礼儀です。いきなりドスンと腰かけると失礼な印象を与えるかもしれないので気をつけましょう。

　欧米のパーティーでは、しばしば新しい人と出会うのが重要な目的でもあるので、特によりフォーマルなディナー・パーティーでは、カップルや夫婦はあえて席につくときに隣同士に座らずに、他のゲストたちとの交流を楽しむのが一般的です。そのため、知らない人同士を紹介してあげるのもホストの大切な役割なのです。

Chapter 3 の 重要表現リスト

Skit A

- [ ] *Just bring yourself.
  どうぞ手ぶらでお越しください
- [ ] make it うまくいく、やりとげる
- [ ] Come on in. どうぞ入って
- [ ] Sorry I'm late. 遅れてごめんなさい
- [ ] Your (apartment) is beautiful.
  とてもすてきなお宅ね
- [ ] Thanks! We really like it here.
  ありがとう。私たちはとても気に入っているの
- [ ] This is for (your daughter).
  (娘さん)へどうぞ
- [ ] What can I get you to drink?
  飲み物は何がいいかしら
- [ ] *-Can I get you something to drink? お飲み物を何かおもちしましょうか
  *-What do you have? 何がありますか？
- [ ] Some white wine, please.
  白ワインをいただけますか
- [ ] Could you…? ～してくれますか
- [ ] Right this way. こちらです
- [ ] How do you know…?
  どうやって知り合ったの
- [ ] *How did you get to know each other? どうやって知り合ったの
- [ ] That's right. そのとおり
- [ ] It sounds like… ～のようだ
- [ ] What's going on? 何ごとだ？
- [ ] You may be right. そうかもしれない
- [ ] This could be… ～かもしれない
- [ ] You don't say. まさか
- [ ] Way to go! その調子

Skit B

- [ ] Are you all right? 大丈夫ですか
- [ ] Oh, good. ああ、それならよかった
- [ ] Here are (slippers). ～をどうぞ
- [ ] I love… ～が大好きです
- [ ] -Thank you for coming.
  来てくださってありがとう
  -Thank you for inviting us!
  お招きくださってありがとう
- [ ] These are for you. これをどうぞ
- [ ] *I hope you like it.
  気に入っていただけるといいのですが
- [ ] How do you say… in English?
  英語では何というのですか
- [ ] be worried… ～を心配する
- [ ] Besides それに
- [ ] for how many years 何年間
- [ ] I hope you all like…
  みなさん～がお好きだといいのですが
- [ ] *Shall we eat now?
  さあ食べましょう
- [ ] What kind of (soup) is this?
  これはどんな種類の(スープ)ですか
- [ ] You must be… きっと～でしょう
- [ ] deal with… ～に対処する
- [ ] I have an idea. そうだ、いい案がある
- [ ] You can… ～してはどうですか
- [ ] I don't feel ready for (that).
  まだそうするには自信がない
- [ ] Come to think of it そういえば
- [ ] Please speak more slowly.
  もっとゆっくり話してください

Chapter 4

July

場面・状況	**レストランでミユキとリチャードが初デート**
表現のテーマ	**レストランでの定番のやりとり／感想・意見をいう**

Skit B

場面・状況	**居酒屋でジョーがタケシにアドバイス**
表現のテーマ	**アドバイスを求める／アドバイスをする**

Chapter 4 July

Skit A

ストーリーについて

　七夕が近づいた夏の日の夕方、ジョーの家のパーティーで出会ったミユキとリチャードは初めてのデートをすることになりました。彼らは映画を観た後、リチャードのおすすめのイタリアン・レストランにやってきました。早くもふたりの間には意見の相違が……

ここで扱う表現について

　Chapter 2 Skit A のカフェでのミユキとジョーの会話の応用としてレストランでの表現がたくさん含まれたこのスキット。フレンドリーなウェイターさんにあたれば、この章のような会話が交わされるでしょう。例えば注文したときのExcellent choice. (いい選択ですね) というコメント。男性の客は sir、女性は madam と呼ぶのが一般的です。ここでは、リチャードの注文に Certainly. (もちろんです) と返したり、食事を運んでくる際、Enjoy. (「ごゆっくり」というニュアンス) といったりして、接客を楽しんでいる感じがします。

　何かの感想を尋ねるときは What did you think of...? のほかに、How did you like...? と聞いても同じ意味です。ミユキは映画の感想を emotional「感情的」と伝えていますが、「感動的」といいたいのであれば、moving のほうが適切です。

　映画に関する感想が対立するふたりですが、北米の文化では異論を唱えるのは、決して悪いことではありません。感情的にまくし立てるようなのは論外ですが。お互いに理解を深めるには、率直に意見を交換するプロセスも必要です。

　相手に対して反論をしたいときにも、いきなり I don't agree. などと全面否定に入るのではなく、I see what you mean.、That's an interesting point.、I agree that... (……という点は同感します) などと相手の意見を尊重しつつ、but to me, ... but I (don't) think...、but I feel that... などを用いて自分の意見をスマートに述べられるようになれるといいですね。

Chapter 4 July

Skit A

Track 08

イタリアンレストランで初デート

Waiter: Here are your drinks. **Are you ready to order?**

Miyuki: Um… **I'd like** the… "linguine with basil and sun-dried tomatoes."

W: Excellent choice. And you, sir?

Richard: I'll have the ravioli. And **can we get the antipasto plate to start?**

W: Certainly. Anything else?

R: I think **that's all for now.**

W: Very good. I'll be back soon.

R: Well… *kampai*!

M: Cheers!

R: So… **what did you think of** the movie, Miyuki?

M: Oh, **I liked it a lot. It was funny** and… um… oh… like, emotional?

R: Do you mean moving?

M: Yes, moving! The actors were great. **How about you?** What did you think?

R: Well… **I agree that** the acting was good,

Here are(is)…:
〜をどうぞ

antipasto: 前菜
Certainly.:
もちろんです。
Anything else?:
他には？
That's all for now.:
とりあえず以上です
Cheers!: 乾杯！

funny:
おもしろい
emotional:
感情的な
moving: 感動的な

but the story was… sort of boring.
M: Oh, I don't agree! **Why do you think so?**
R: Well, this man and woman just walk around New York and talk, and meet their friends and talk… and argue and make up. Nothing… happens.
M: But to me, the talking was really interesting. For example, even if they were angry, they were so… um… logical. I don't think Japanese are so good at arguing… in general.
R: I think you're doing very well right now, Miyuki.
M: Oh—am I arguing? Sorry!
R: Just kidding! Besides, there's nothing wrong with disagreeing, right?
W: Here's the antipasto plate. Enjoy.
M: Thank you. **It looks delicious.** How did you find this restaurant?
R: My sister came to Japan for a visit, and this place was in her guidebook.
M: Oh, **how many brothers and sisters do you have?**
R: I have two sisters. One is three years older, and the other is two years younger. Do you have brothers and sisters, Miyuki?
M: I have a younger brother. He's a university student.
R: What's his major?
M: Baseball. Well, he plays baseball more than he studies. Next month his club will go to a baseball camp in California.
R: Great! By the way, how did you learn to speak English so well?
M: Oh, I don't speak very well.
R: Yes, you do!
M: No, I make a lot of mistakes.
R: Now you're arguing.
M: No, I'm just… um… disagreeing.

---

sort of…: ちょっと〜みたいな
boring: つまらない
I don't agree.: 直接的な否定の仕方。かなり強い調子の否定なので注意。
argue: 言い争う
make up: 仲直りをする
logical: 論理的な
in general: 一般に

disagree: 反論する

major: 専攻
Yes, you do!: don't speak を否定して「いや、うまいよ」とリチャードがミユキを励ましている。「話している」と肯定しているので、Noではなく Yes を使っていることに注意。

ポイント解説

Chapter 4 July — Skit A

6月にパーティーで出会ったミユキとリチャードが、レストランでデートをしています。ここでは、料理の注文のしかたから、見た映画の感想を述べたり、相手の家族について聞く表現が使われています。

- I'd like…
- I'll have…

I'll have… は直訳すると「……をもらいます」だが、I'd like… と同様「……にします」ということ。

Can we get… to start?

Can we have…?「……をいただけますか」でも同じ。to start は「はじめに」。

That's all for now.

注文をすませたときの「とりあえず以上で全部です」というフレーズ。for now は「今のところ、とりあえず」。注文や要望をリストしていうときなどに幅広く使える。

What did you think of…?

感想や意見を求めるときの表現。下にある What did you think? も同じ。このほか、How did / do you like…?、How did you feel about…? も使える。

-I liked it a lot. -It was funny…

とても気に入ったのであれば I loved it. でも OK。「おもしろかった」は funny や interesting、「ひどかった」は terrible や awful など。

Are you ready to order?

p.34 の Can I take your order? と同じ「ご注文は？」。

Waiter: Here are your drinks. **Are you ready to order?**
Miyuki: Um… **I'd like** the… "linguine with basil and sun-dried tomatoes."
W: Excellent choice. And you, sir?
Richard: **I'll have** the ravioli. And **can we get the antipasto plate to start?**
W: Certainly. Anything else?
R: I think **that's all for now.**
W: Very good. I'll be back soon.
R: Well… *kampai*!
M: Cheers!
R: So… **what did you think of** the movie, Miyuki?
M: Oh, **I liked it a lot. It was funny** and… um… oh… like, emotional?
R: Do you mean moving?

M: Yes, moving! The actors were great. **How about you?** What did you think?
R: Well… **I agree that** the acting was good, **but** the story was… sort of boring.
M: Oh, I don't agree! **Why do you think so?**
R: Well, this man and woman just walk around New York and talk, and meet their friends and talk… and argue and make up. Nothing… happens.
M: But to me, the talking was really interesting. For example, even if they were angry, they were so… um… logical. I don't think Japanese are so good at arguing… in general.
R: I think you're doing very well right now, Miyuki.
M: Oh—am I arguing? Sorry!
R: Just kidding! Besides, there's nothing wrong with disagreeing, right?
W: Here's the antipasto plate. Enjoy.
M: Thank you. **It looks delicious.** How did you find this restaurant?
R: My sister came to Japan for a visit, and this place was in her guidebook.
M: Oh, **how many brothers and sisters do you have?**
R: I have two sisters. One is three years older, and the other is two years younger. Do you have brothers and sisters, Miyuki?
M: I have a younger brother. He's a university student.
R: What's his major?
M: Baseball. Well, he plays baseball more than he studies. Next month his club will go to a baseball camp in California.
R: Great! By the way, how did you learn to speak English so well?
M: Oh, I don't speak very well.
R: Yes, you do!
M: No, I make a lot of mistakes.
R: Now you're arguing.
M: No, I'm just… um… disagreeing.

How about you?

自分の意見や感想を伝えたら、相手の意見も尋ねよう。会話はキャッチボールとして成立するのが理想的。

I agree that…, but…

「〜には賛成ですが…」。相手の意見に対して、「賛成する部分もあるけれど、賛成できない部分もある」という自分の意見を述べる言い方。相手の意見に反対する気持ちが強いときでも、I don't agree (that)… とか、I disagree (that)… という言い方をするよりも、いったん相手の意見で同意できる部分を探して、でも「この部分は賛成できない」ともっていったほうが、客観的に聞こえ、感情的にならずに話を進められる。

Why do you think so?

相手の意見や感想をさらに詳しく尋ねれば、さらに会話が発展する。

It looks delicious.

見た感想を述べるときは It looks…。beautiful（すてきな）、wonderful（すばらしい）、great（すごい）など。

How many brothers and sisters do you have?

知り合った人とは、差し支えがなければ兄弟構成の話題などが会話のきっかけとして役立つ。Do you have brothers and sisters? も同じ。

Waiter: Here are your drinks. Are you ready to order?
Miyuki: Um… I'd like the… "linguine with basil and sun-dried tomatoes."
W: Excellent choice. And you, sir?
Richard: I'll have the ravioli. And can we get the antipasto plate to start?
W: Certainly. Anything else?
R: I think that's all for now.
W: Very good. I'll be back soon.
R: Well… *kampai*!
M: Cheers!
R: So… what did you think of the movie, Miyuki?
M: Oh, I liked it a lot. It was funny and… um… oh… like, emotional?
R: Do you mean moving?
M: Yes, moving! The actors were great. How about you? What did you think?
R: Well… I agree that the acting was good, but the story was… sort of boring.
M: Oh, I don't agree! Why do you think so?
R: Well, this man and woman just walk around New York and talk, and meet their friends and talk… and argue and make up. Nothing… happens.
M: But to me, the talking was really interesting. For example, even if they were angry, they were so… um… logical. I don't think Japanese are so good at arguing… in general.
R: I think you're doing very well right now, Miyuki.
M: Oh—am I arguing? Sorry!
R: Just kidding! Besides, there's nothing wrong with disagreeing, right?
W: Here's the antipasto plate. Enjoy.
M: Thank you. It looks delicious. How did you find this restaurant?
R: My sister came to Japan for a visit, and this place was in her guidebook.
M: Oh, how many brothers and sisters do you have?
R: I have two sisters. One is three years older, and the other is two years younger. Do you have brothers and sisters, Miyuki?
M: I have a younger brother. He's a university student.
R: What's his major?
M: Baseball. Well, he plays baseball more than he studies. Next month his club will go to a baseball camp in California.
R: Great! By the way, how did you learn to speak English so well?
M: Oh, I don't speak very well.
R: Yes, you do!
M: No, I make a lot of mistakes.
R: Now you're arguing.
M: No, I'm just… um… disagreeing.

ウェイター: お飲物です。ご注文はよろしいですか。
ミユキ: えーと……私は……「バジルとサンドライ・トマトのリングイネ」にします。
ウェイター: いいチョイスですね。そちらは？
リチャード: 僕はラビオリにします。それと、はじめにアンティパストの皿をお願いします。
ウェイター: かしこまりました。他には？
リチャード: とりあえず以上です。
ウェイター: かしこまりました。すぐにお持ちします。
リチャード: それじゃあ……カンパイ！
ミユキ: チアーズ！
リチャード: それでミユキ、映画はどう思った？
ミユキ: すごくよかった。おもしろいし……えーと……エモーショナル（感情的）というか。
リチャード: ムーヴィング（感動的）ってこと？
ミユキ: そう、ムーヴィング！　俳優たちがよかった。あなたは？　どう思った？
リチャード: そうだな……演技がいいっていうのは同感だけど、話は……ちょっと退屈だったかな。
ミユキ: え、私は反対。どうしてそう思うの？
リチャード: つまり、男と女がただニューヨークを歩いて、話して、友だちに会って、それで話して……けんかして、よりが戻って。何が……起こるってわけでもなく。
ミユキ: でも私には、あの会話が本当におもしろかった。例えば、彼らは怒ってるときも、とても……えーと……論理的。日本人はあんな風にうまく言い合えないと思うし。
リチャード: ミユキ、君は今すごくうまくやってるよ。
ミユキ: え、私、口論してる？　ごめん。
リチャード: 冗談だよ。それに、反対するってことは悪くない。
ウェイター: アンティパストです。どうぞ、お召し上がりください。
ミユキ: ありがとう。おいしそう。どうやってこのレストランを見つけたの？
リチャード: 僕の姉が日本に訪ねてきて、彼女のガイドブックにここが載ってたんだ。
ミユキ: へぇ、兄弟は何人いるの？
リチャード: ふたり姉妹がいるよ。ひとりは僕より３歳上で、もうひとりは２歳下なんだ。ミユキは兄弟いるの？
ミユキ: 弟がひとりいるの。大学生よ。
リチャード: 彼の専攻は？
ミユキ: 野球。つまり、勉強よりも野球のほうが多いの。来月、彼のチームはカリフォルニアへ野球の合宿をしにいくのよ。
リチャード: いいね。ところでミユキ、君はどうやってそんなにうまく英語を話せるようになったの？
ミユキ: そんなにうまくないわ。
リチャード: いや、うまいよ。
ミユキ: いいえ、たくさん間違えるもの。
リチャード: ほら、口論してるよ。
ミユキ: いいえ、私はただ……反論してるだけよ。

Chapter 4
July

Exercises

Part A Track 08

①リスニング、②パラレル・リーディング(音を聞きながらテキストを音読)、③プロソディ・シャドーイング（音の再現）④コンテンツ・シャドーイング（意味を意識）の順で会話を再現してみましょう。下記の Key Phrases を意識しながら、最低でも7回は会話を聞いてみましょう。

Key Phrases:
- Are you ready to order?
- -I'd like… -I'll have…
- Can we get… to start?
- That's all for now.
- What did you think of…?
- -I liked it a lot. -It was funny…
- How about you?
- I agree that..., but...
- Why do you think so?
- It looks delicious.
- How many brothers and sisters do you have?

Part B

相手の問いかけに対して、自分なりの答えを考えてみましょう。

1) **Victor:** I loved the movie! Didn't you?
   You: _____

2) **Victor:** What do you think of America?
   You: _____

3) **Victor:** Do you have any siblings?
   You: _____

今度は相手の応答にふさわしい語りかけや問いかけをしてみましょう。

4) トム・ハンクスについて意見をいってみましょう。
   You: _____
   Victor: I agree. I think his acting is very realistic.

5) 兄弟または姉妹がいるのかたずねてみましょう。
   You: _____
   Victor: Yes, I have one sister. She's three years older.

6) 相手の妹が大学で何を専攻しているのかたずねてみましょう。
   You: _____
   Victor: She's majoring in anthropology.

Exercisesの解答例と訳

1) Yes, I thought it was great. / Actually, I prefer his last movie.
2) I like the weather. / I love the food. / I think people are very nice.
3) Yes, I have a younger brother. / No, I'm an only child.
4) I think Tom Hanks is a really good actor.
5) Do you have any brothers or sisters?
6) What is your sister's major? / What is your sister studying?

問題と答えの訳

1) ビクター：映画素晴らしかったね。君もそう思うでしょう。
   あなた：うん、よかったよ。／彼の前の映画のほうがよかったな。
2) ビクター：アメリカをどう思いますか。
   あなた：天気が好きです。／食べ物がおいしいですね。／人がとてもいいですね。
3) ビクター：兄弟はいますか。
   あなた：はい、弟がひとり。／いえ、ひとりっ子です。
4) あなた：トム・ハンクスは本当にいい俳優だと思うよ。
   ビクター：賛成。彼の演技はとてもリアルだよね。
5) あなた：兄弟はいますか。
   ビクター：はい、3歳年上の姉がひとりいます。
6) あなた：お姉さんの専攻は何ですか。／お姉さんは何を勉強していますか。
   ビクター：彼女は人類学を専攻しています。

コラム　デート

　日本では男女がお付き合いする前に、どちらかが「付き合ってください」とフォーマルな告白をすることがありますが、欧米ではそのような告白はあまりありません。何回かデートを重ねるうちに自然と恋人関係になっていくケースが多いようです。映画や食事、お茶などに誘うのは日本と同じですが、欧米ではディズニーランドなどの遊園地は、ティーンエイジャーをのぞけば、一般的なデートスポットではありません。デートで映画を見る場合は、特に付き合い始めた頃は、女性が好きなタイプの映画（スラングで chick flick）に行くことが多く、特にロマンティックコメディーが人気の date movie です。

　また、今日では欧米でラブレターを書くことは珍しいことです。まずは軽いノリで "Would you like to go see a movie?" などといって、カジュアルなデートに誘うことから始めるのが基本です。

Chapter 4 July

Skit B

ストーリーについて

ミユキの弟タケシは、この夏カリフォルニアでの野球合宿に参加します。ミユキがジョーに、タケシがカリフォルニアに行くことを心配していると話したところ、タケシに会って励ましてあげることになりました。そしてふたりは居酒屋にやってきました。

ここで扱う表現について

ここでは、相談ごとを持ちかける会話を取り上げました。タケシは自分の相談事で相手を呼び出したので、タケシの第一声は、Thank you for meeting (with) me.（会ってくださってありがとうございます）。自分のために時間を割いて会ってくれている訳ですから、当然のマナーですね。It's nice of you to see me. も同じように丁寧な表現として使われます。それに対して、ジョーも快く My pleasure. と返しています。「どういたしまして」は You're welcome. ですが、「お役に立ててうれしいですよ」といった気持ちを表すにはこの言い回しのほうがしっくりきます。カジュアルに「気にしないで」という意味で、Don't mention it. ともいいます。

アドバイスを求めるときの質問の表現 Can you give me some advice about...?、そして厳しすぎず、かつ説得力のあるアドバイスをするときの表現を学んでください。

この会話のジョーの発言からはユーモアのセンスも学べます。タケシの How about talking to young people? に対し、ジョーが「痛いところをつかれた」という意味で Ouch. といっていますね。これはなぜだかわかりましたか？ 「若い人と話すときはどうですか？」と聞くことで、暗にジョーは若くないということをほのめかしているからです。ユーモアいっぱいの彼は、この後もふざけて when I was a student... back in the Stone Age（自分が学生だった頃、つまり石器時代のことだけど）とタケシをからかっています。

Chapter 4 July

Skit B

Track 09

男同士が居酒屋で！

Takeshi: **Thank you for meeting with me**, Joe-*san*.
Joe: **My pleasure**, Takeshi. Are you excited about your trip?
T: Yes, **I can't wait.**
Server: *Biiru ni narimasu.*
T: *San-ban to hachi-ban to nijyu-ni-ban de.* Do you want something else, Joe-*san*?
J: **Let's see.** Do you have bagels?
S: Uh… **Excuse me?**
J: Just a joke. *Jodan desu.* That's all for now, thank you.
S: OK.
J: She didn't laugh.
T: Do most Americans… make jokes… all the time?
J: No, just some of us. And many of the jokes are bad.

My pleasure.:
どういたしまして

Excuse me?:
何ていいましたか？

That's all for now.:
いまのところそれで全部です

all the time:
いつも

T: Sometimes I don't understand. American jokes are…different.
J: That's a good point. Humor is different in every country.
T: Can you give me some advice about, uhh… communicating with Americans?
J: Well… **my advice is** to **be yourself**. After all, you're communicating very well right now.
T: But… how about talking to young people?
J: Ouch.
T: Oh—sorry! I mean other players… same age.
J: I understand. Well, when I was a student… back in the Stone Age… guys talked about school and hobbies… and girls, of course.
T: Oh, same in Japan!
J: And you can always talk about baseball, **right?**
S: *Omatase itashimashita.* Sorry, no bagel.
J: No problem! So, **what else would you like to ask me?**
T: Um, I'll do a homestay with a family. So… **please tell me about**, uh, manners and…?
J: Ah. Well, they'll probably be happy if you help them.
T: Uh… what kind of helping?
J: Oh, setting the table, taking out the trash, painting the house…
T: Painting the… ah! That's a joke!
J: Yes, it is. Also, **be sure to** say "thank you" when they do something for you. By the way, **you should** always thank people in stores and restaurants, too.
T: Oh, yes. My sister told me.
J: What else did she tell you about America?
T: That's all. I have not seen her for… two weeks. I think she is busy.
J: Oh, really? Hmm…

That's a good point.: それはいい点に気がついたね
humor: ユーモア、笑い
be yourself: 自分らしくいなさい
after all: つまり
Ouch.: いたい

back in…: 〜のころは
Stone Age: 石器時代

No problem!: かまいません

trash: ゴミ

be sure to…: 〜をすることを忘れないように

ポイント解説

Chapter 4 July Skit B

タケシが居酒屋でジョーに相談をするシーンで、人にアドバイスするときによく使う表現が出てきます。相手の意見や指摘に対する答え方や、相手に質問を促すための表現なども注意して見ておきましょう。

- Thank you for meeting with me.
- My pleasure.

自分の都合で相手を呼び出したときには、まず感謝の気持ちを表そう。My pleasure. は「お役に立ててうれしい」という積極的な気持ちが表現できる。

I can't wait.

待ち遠しいです、すごく楽しみです。「楽しみで待ちきれない」という少々興奮気味な感情を伝える表現。

Let's see.

メニューを見て何かを決めるときなどに「さて何にしようか」「どうしようかな」と、思案中、時間かせぎに使うといい。Let me see. も同様。

Excuse me?

聞き取れなかったことをもう一度いってもらうときの「失礼ですが」。ここの場合は冗談が理解しきれず「冗談でしょう」というニュアンスも含まれている。

That's a good point.

相手の意見や指摘したことに対して「それはいい点に気がついたな」と肯定的に対応している。相手のいったことを理解し、自分がどう思っているかを相手に伝えるのがいい会話のポイント。

Takeshi: Thank you for meeting with me, Joe-*san*.
Joe: My pleasure, Takeshi. Are you excited about your trip?
T: Yes, **I can't wait.**
Server: *Biiru ni narimasu.*
T: *San-ban to hachi-ban to nijuni-ban de.* Do you want something else, Joe-*san*?
J: Let's see. Do you have bagels?
S: Uh… **Excuse me?**
J: Just a joke. *Jodan desu.* That's all for now, thank you.
S: OK.
J: She didn't laugh.
T: Do most Americans… make jokes… all the time?
J: No, just some of us. And many of the jokes are bad.
T: Sometimes I don't understand. American jokes are… different.
J: That's a good point. Humor is different in every country.
T: Can you give me some advice about, uhh… communicating with Americans?
J: Well… **my advice is** to **be yourself**. After all, you're communicating very well right now.
T: But… how about talking to young people?
J: Ouch.
T: Oh—sorry! I mean other players… same age.

J: I understand. Well, when I was a student... back in the Stone Age... guys talked about school and hobbies... and girls, of course.
T: Oh, same in Japan!
J: And you can always talk about baseball, **right?**
S: *Omatase itashimashita.* Sorry, no bagel.
J: No problem! So, **what else would you like to ask me?**
T: Um, I'll do a homestay with a family. So... **please tell me about**, uh, manners and...?
J: Ah. Well, they'll probably be happy if you help them.
T: Uh... what kind of helping?
J: Oh, setting the table, taking out the trash, painting the house...
T: Painting the... ah! That's a joke!
J: Yes, it is. Also, **be sure to** say "thank you" when they do something for you. By the way, **you should** always thank people in stores and restaurants, too.
T: Oh, yes. My sister told me.
J: What else did she tell you about America?
T: That's all. I have not seen her for... two weeks. I think she is busy.
J: Oh, really? Hmm...

..., right?
「そうだろう?」と自分のいったことを相手に確認するときは、最後に right? をつける。

What else would you like to ask me?
「ほかに何か私にたずねておきたいことはないか」と相手から質問を引き出そうとする表現。

Please tell me about...
「……について話してください」と比較的カジュアルに相手に頼むときの表現。

- Be sure to...
- You should...
「必ず……しなさい」「……するべきだ」というアドバイスをするときの表現。Remember to... も同じ。

Can you give me some advice about...?
「……についてアドバイスをいただけませんか」とストレートにアドバイスを求める表現。

My advice is...
アドバイスをするときのフレーズ。If I were you, I would... というのも、アドバイスをする際によく使われる。

Be yourself.
「自分らしく(ありのままのあなたで)いなさい」というアドバイスの定番。

Takeshi: Thank you for meeting with me, Joe-*san*.
Joe: My pleasure, Takeshi. Are you excited about your trip?
T: Yes, I can't wait.
Server: *Biiru ni narimasu.*
T: *San-ban to hachi-ban to nijyu-ni-ban de.* Do you want something else, Joe-*san*?
J: Let's see. Do you have bagels?
S: Uh… Excuse me?
J: Just a joke. *Jodan desu.* That's all for now, thank you.
S: OK.
J: She didn't laugh.
T: Do most Americans… make jokes… all the time?
J: No, just some of us. And many of the jokes are bad.
T: Sometimes I don't understand. American jokes are…different.
J: That's a good point. Humor is different in every country.
T: Can you give me some advice about, uhh… communicating with Americans?
J: Well… my advice is to be yourself. After all, you're communicating very well right now.
T: But… how about talking to young people?
J: Ouch.
T: Oh—sorry! I mean other players… same age.
J: I understand. Well, when I was a student… back in the Stone Age… guys talked about school and hobbies… and girls, of course.
T: Oh, same in Japan!
J: And you can always talk about baseball, right?
S: *Omatase itashimashita.* Sorry, no bagel.
J: No problem! So, what else would you like to ask me?
T: Um, I'll do a homestay with a family. So… please tell me about, uh, manners and…?
J: Ah. Well, they'll probably be happy if you help them.
T: Uh… what kind of helping?
J: Oh, setting the table, taking out the trash, painting the house…
T: Painting the… ah! That's a joke!
J: Yes, it is. Also, be sure to say "thank you" when they do something for you. By the way, you should always thank people in stores and restaurants, too.
T: Oh, yes. My sister told me.
J: What else did she tell you about America?
T: That's all. I have not seen her for… two weeks. I think she is busy.
J: Oh, really? Hmm…

訳

タケシ：会ってくださってありがとうございます、ジョーさん。
ジョー：どういたしまして、タケシ。旅行は楽しみかい。
タケシ：はい、待ち遠しいです。
店員：ビールになります。
タケシ：3番と8番と22番で。ジョーさん、ほかに何かいりますか。
ジョー：そうだな。ベーグルはありますか。
店員：えーと……何ですか。
ジョー：ただの冗談です。とりあえず以上で、ありがとう。
店員：かしこまりました。
ジョー：彼女は笑わなかったね。
タケシ：たいていのアメリカ人は……いつも……ジョークをいうんですか。
ジョー：いや、そんなにいないよ。それに多くはつまらないジョークなんだ。
タケシ：ときどき僕にはわからないんですよ。アメリカンジョークは……ちがうから。
ジョー：いい点に気がついたね。笑いはそれぞれの国によってちがうんだ。
タケシ：アメリカ人とコミュニケーションを取ることについて……何かアドバイスをいただけませんか。
ジョー：そうだな、私のアドバイスは、自分らしく（自然に）していなさい、ということかな。それに、いま君はとても上手にコミュニケーションを取れているよ。
タケシ：でも……若いひとたちと話す場合はどうですか。
ジョー：痛っ。
タケシ：ああ、すみません。僕がいっているのは、ほかの選手のことです、僕と同じ年齢の。
ジョー：わかった。そうだな、私が学生のとき……石器時代にさかのぼると……男は学校や趣味のことを話してたな……それにもちろん女の子のこと。
タケシ：あ、日本と同じだ。
ジョー：それに、君はいつでも野球のことを話せる、だろう？
店員：お待たせいたしました。すみません、ベーグルはありません。
ジョー：かまいませんよ。それで、ほかに僕に聞きたいことは？
タケシ：えーと、ホームステイをするので……マナーとかについて教えてください。
ジョー：ああ、そうだな、手伝いをするとよろこんでもらえるだろうね。
タケシ：えーと……どういう手伝いですか。
ジョー：ああ、テーブルをセットしたり、ゴミを出したり、家のペンキを塗ったり……
タケシ：ペンキを……ああ！　ジョークですね！
ジョー：そうだよ。それと、何かしてもらったらお礼をいうことを忘れないように。そうだ、店やレストランでもいつもお礼をいったほうがいいよ。
タケシ：ああ、そうですね。姉がいってました。
ジョー：お姉さんはアメリカについてほかに何ていってた？
タケシ：それだけです。2週間……姉には会っていないので。忙しんでしょう。
ジョー：ああ、本当に？　ふーん……

Chapter 4
July

Exercises

Part A Track 09

①リスニング、②パラレル・リーディング(音を聞きながらテキストを音読)、③プロソディ・シャドーイング（音の再現）④コンテンツ・シャドーイング（意味を意識）の順で会話を再現してみましょう。下記の Key Phrases を意識しながら、最低でも7回は会話を聞いてみましょう。

Key Phrases:
- -Thank you for meeting with me.
  -My pleasure.
- I can't wait.
- Let's see.
- Excuse me?
- That's a good point.
- Can you give me some advice about…?
- My advice is…
- Be yourself.
- …, right?
- What else would you like to ask me?
- Please tell me about…
- Be sure to…
- You should…

Part B

相手の語りかけや問いかけに対して、自分なりの答えを考えてみましょう。

1) **Trish:** Thank you for your time today. I really appreciate it.
   You: _____
2) **Trish:** Are you excited about starting your new job?
   You: _____
3) **Trish:** I wonder if you could give me some advice about living in Japan.
   You: Let's see, … _____

今度は相手の応答にふさわしい質問や語りかけをしてみましょう。

4) 仕事でのミーティングなどを終えて別れるときに……。
   You: _____
   Trish: My pleasure! It's always nice to see you.
5) アメリカの習慣やマナーについてアドバイスを求めてみましょう。
   You: _____
   Trish: Well… at restaurants, people usually tip about 15%.
6) ほかに何か、とたずねてみましょう。
   You: _____
   Trish: Let's see… Always say "thank you" to people in stores.

Exercises の解答例と訳

1) My pleasure!
2) Yes, I can't wait!
3) Japanese people usually take a gift when they visit someone.
4) Thank you for meeting with me today.
5) Could you give me some advice about customs and manners in America?
6) Anything else?

問題と答えの訳

1) トリッシュ：今日は時間をありがとう。本当に感謝しています。
   あなた：喜んで。
2) トリッシュ：新しい仕事を始めるのに興奮していますか。
   あなた：はい、待ちきれません！
3) トリッシュ：日本で住むことについて何かアドバイスしてもらえますか。
   あなた：そうですね……日本人はふつう誰かの家を訪れるときはおみやげを持っていきます。
4) あなた：今日は私と会ってくれてありがとう。
   トリッシュ：喜んで。いつも会えるのを楽しみにしています。
5) あなた：アメリカでの習慣と作法についてアドバイスをいただけますか。
   トリッシュ：レストランでは通常 15％のチップを払います。
6) あなた：ほかには何かありますか。
   トリッシュ：お店では常にありがとうといってください。

コラム　お客さんと店員さんの関係

　日本ではお客さんと店員さんとの関係は概してよそよそしく、お客さんが終始無言でいることも珍しくありません。一方、アメリカではお店に入るとまず店員さんが "How are you doing today?" などとフレンドリーに話しかけてくることが多く、お客さんも "Pretty good, thanks. How about you?" などと気さくに答えるのが普通です。マニュアル的な応対にしか慣れていない日本人は、最初はちょっとびっくりするかもしれません。レジで買い物を終えると、店員さんが "Have a nice day." といってくれたりするので、その際には "You, too." と答えるのを忘れないようにしましょう。

　また、欧米ではウェイターやウェイトレスが料理を運んできてくれたときなどには、必ず "Thank you." とお礼をいうのが習慣となっているので、覚えておいてください。

Chapter 4 の 重要表現リスト

Skit A

- [ ] **Are you ready to order?** ご注文は?
- [ ] **・I'd like…** 〜にします
    ・I'll have… 〜をもらいます
- [ ] **Can we get… to start?** はじめに〜をいただけますか
- [ ] **Anything else?** 他には?
- [ ] **That's all for now.** とりあえず以上で全部です
- [ ] **What did you think of…?** 〜をどう思いましたか
- [ ] ***How did you like…?** 〜をどう思いましたか?
- [ ] ***How did you feel about…?** 〜をどう思いましたか?
- [ ] **I liked it a lot. It was funny.** とても気に入りました。おもしろかった
- [ ] **How about you?** あなたはどうですか
- [ ] **I agree that…, but…** 〜には賛成ですが……
- [ ] ***I see what you mean, but…** あなたのおっしゃりたいことはわかりましたが……
- [ ] ***That's an interesting point, but…** それはおもしろいポイントですが
- [ ] **sort of…** ちょっと〜みたいな
- [ ] **Why do you think so?** どうしてそう思うのですか
- [ ] **make up** 仲直りをする
- [ ] **It looks delicious.** おいしそうに見える
- [ ] **How many brothers and sisters do you have?** ご兄弟は何人いますか

Skit B

- [ ] **-Thank you for meeting with me.** 会ってくださってありがとうございます
    -My pleasure. どういたしまして
- [ ] ***It is nice of you to see me.** 会ってくださってありがとうございます
- [ ] ***You're welcome.** どういたしまして
- [ ] ***Don't mention.** 気にしないで
- [ ] **I can't wait.** (楽しみで)待ちきれない
- [ ] **Let's see.** さて、どうしようかな
- [ ] ***Let me see.** さて、どうしようかな
- [ ] **Excuse me?** 失礼ですが(何をおっしゃってるの、冗談でしょう、というニュアンスを含む)
- [ ] **all the time** いつも
- [ ] **That's a good point.** それはいい点に気がつきましたね
- [ ] **Can you give me some advice about…?** 〜についてアドバイスをいただけませんか
- [ ] **My advice is…** 私のアドバイスは〜
- [ ] ***If I were you, I would…** もしも私があなただったら〜
- [ ] **Be yourself.** ありのままのあなたでいなさい
- [ ] **after all** 結局
- [ ] **back in…** 〜のころは
- [ ] **No problem.** 問題ない
- [ ] **…, right?** そうでしょう?
- [ ] **What else would you like to ask me?** ほかに何か私にたずねておきたいことはありませんか
- [ ] **Please tell me about…** 〜について話してください
- [ ] **・Be sure to…** かならず〜しなさい
    ・You should… 〜するべきだ
- [ ] ***Remember to…** かならず〜しなさい

Chapter 5
August

Skit A	
場面・状況	ロサンゼルス空港に到着
表現の テーマ	入国審査でのやりとり／出迎える／ 出迎えを受ける
Skit B	
場面・状況	野球合宿の試合終了後の懇親会
表現の テーマ	ほめる／別れる

Chapter 5 August

Skit A

ストーリーについて

　タケシの所属する野球チームはロサンゼルス国際空港に到着しました。彼らはロサンゼルス郊外で3週間の野球合宿に参加し、それぞれ地元のホストファミリーの家に滞在することになっています。しかしその前に、彼らは空港の入国手続きを通過しなくてはなりません。最初に入国審査に入るのはキャプテンのユキオです。

ここで扱う表現について

　海外旅行で欠かせないのが空港の入国審査。正しく受け答えできるように準備しておきたいものですね。ここでは典型的なやりとりをご紹介します。審査官に会ったらまず Hello.、パスポート提示を求められたら、ひとこと Here you are. といって渡すだけでぐっと印象が変わります。最近アメリカでは、入国審査の段階で指紋を記録したり顔写真を撮影します。ひと通り手続きがすめば、Thank you. といって去るのがスマートです。

　空港にはサリバン一家が迎えにきていますね。ご主人の名前が Pete Sullivan。Pete は、Peter の略です。奥様は Melissa Myers。そう、ご夫婦で姓がちがいますね。北米では、旧姓をキープする人も増えています。夫婦別姓が法的に認められているので、このようなカップルもたくさんいるのです。息子さんの Matt は Matthew の略です。

　Melissa はさっそく We're glad you're here! You must be tired from the trip.（よく来たわね。長旅で疲れているでしょう）と歓迎し、Pete もはりきってタカシの荷物を持とうとします。タカシは遠慮しますが、Nope, no arguments.（ダメ、いうことを聞きなさい）と聞き入れません。Nope. は通常フォーマルな場では使いません。親しい間で使うのが一般的です。

Chapter 5 August

Skit A

Track 10

ロサンゼルス空港に到着

Immigration officer: Your passport, please.
Yukio: Here you are.
IO: Mr. Ikeda, **what is the purpose of your visit?**
Y: Our university baseball team is going to a baseball camp.
IO: Ah, I see. **How long will you be in the U.S.?**
Y: Three and a half weeks.
IO: And **where will you be staying?**
Y: Here is my homestay family's address.
IO: OK. Now, I need to take your fingerprint. Can you place your index finger here, please? Thank you. Have a nice stay! Next.

T: Hello.
IO: Hi, Mr. … Tsukazawa?
T: That's right. It's a little difficult.
IO: You're not kidding. So what's your position?
T: Position? Uh… I'm not working yet. I'm a student.

Here you are.:
どうぞ

Have a nice stay.:
楽しんで／よい滞在を
(stay の代わりに trip、weekend などを入れて、相手と別れるときに使える)

You're not kidding.:
その通り。

IO: Huh? No, I mean your position on the field. I hear you're baseball players.
T: Oh! Yes. Center field.

Customs officer: Anything to declare?
T: Um… I have some gifts. （申告書を見せる）
CO: No problem. Go ahead through those doors.
T: Thank you.

到着ロビーで、タケシは自分の名前が書かれた標示を持っている人たちを見つける。

T: Um… I'm Takeshi Tsukazawa. Mr. and Mrs. Sullivan?
Pete: Yes, I'm Pete Sullivan! Hello, Takeshi!
Melissa: I'm Melissa Myers. And this is our son, Matt.
Matt: Hi, Takeshi!
T: Hi. I'm happy to meet you all.
Me: We're glad you're here! **You must be tired from the trip.**
T: A little bit… but I'm excited to be here.
P: Here, let me take your suitcase.
T: Oh… thank you, but—
P: Nope, no arguments. Are you ready to go?
T: Oh… yes. But I would like to say goodbye to my friends.
Me: Of course! **Take your time.**
P: We're in no hurry. But our daughter Rachel is eager to meet you.
Ma: Yeah. She saw your photo and she thinks you're cute. But don't tell her I told you.
T: Cute? Me? By the way, **what grade are you in, Matt?**
Ma: I'm a high school **freshman.** And Rachel is going into her second year of college.
T: College? Really?

---

position: 守備位置

center field: センター

declare: （税関で）申告する、宣言する

No problem.: 結構です、大丈夫です

Go ahead.: さあどうぞ、前に進んでください

You must be tired from the trip.: 長旅でお疲れでしょう

Let me…: （私に〜）させてください (…には動詞の原形)

No arguments.: 言う通りにしなさい

say goodbye (to…): （〜に）さよならという

Take your time.: ごゆっくり

in no hurry: 急いでいない

be eager to…: 〜したがっている

cute: かっこいい

grade: 学年

freshman: 1年生

ポイント解説

Chapter 5 August Skit A

タケシは野球合宿のためロサンゼルス空港に到着しました。渡航目的をはじめ、入国審査での表現は海外旅行などの際に空港で必ず聞かれる質問なので、正しい受け答えを流れに沿って覚えておきましょう。

- What is the purpose of your visit?
- How long will you be in the U.S.?
- Where will you be staying?

「訪問の目的」「滞在期間」「滞在予定地」は入国審査のときにかならず聞かれる質問。だからSightseeing.とか、For five days.とか、At the ○○ Hotel in Manhattan.などと簡潔に答えられるようにしておこう。

Anything to declare?

入国審査の後は税関。申告するものがあれば、北米の場合、機内で配布される指定書類に前もって記入する。

Immigration officer: Your passport, please.
Yukio: Here you are.
IO: Mr. Ikeda, **what is the purpose of your visit?**
Y: Our university baseball team is going to a baseball camp.
IO: Ah, I see. **How long will you be in the U.S.?**
Y: Three and a half weeks.
IO: And **where will you be staying?**
Y: Here is my homestay family's address.
IO: OK. Now, I need to take your fingerprint. Can you place your index finger here, please? Thank you. Have a nice stay! Next.

T: Hello.
IO: Hi, Mr. …Tsukazawa?
T: That's right. It's a little difficult.
IO: You're not kidding. So what's your position?
T: Position? Uh… I'm not working yet. I'm a student.
IO: Huh? No, I mean your position on the field. I hear you're baseball players.
T: Oh! Yes. Center field.

Customs officer: **Anything to declare?**

T: Um… I have some gifts.
CO: No problem. Go ahead through those doors.
T: Thank you.

T: Um… I'm Takeshi Tsukazawa. Mr. and Mrs. Sullivan?
Pete: Yes, I'm Pete Sullivan! Hello, Takeshi!
Melissa: I'm Melissa Myers. And this is our son, Matt.
Matt: Hi, Takeshi!
T: Hi. I'm happy to meet you all.
Me: We're glad you're here! **You must be tired from the trip.**
T: A little bit… but I'm excited to be here.
P: Here, let me take your suitcase.
T: Oh… thank you, but—
P: Nope, no arguments. Are you ready to go?
T: Oh… yes. But I would like to say goodbye to my friends.
Me: Of course! **Take your time.**
P: We're in no hurry. But our daughter Rachel is eager to meet you.
Ma: Yeah. She saw your photo and she thinks you're cute. But don't tell her I told you.
T: Cute? Me? By the way, **what grade are you in, Matt?**
Ma: I'm a high school **freshman**. And Rachel is going into her second year of college.
T: College? Really?

You must be tired from the trip.

「長旅でお疲れでしょう」。飛行機などで海外から来た人を出迎えるときの定番表現。翌日、会ったときに、Do you have jet lag?「時差ぼけはありますか」もよく問いかけることばだ。

- Take your time.
- We're in no hurry.

「急がなくていいよ、時間をかけて」といった意味の表現。

- What grade are you in?
- freshman

アメリカには学年を表すときにいろいろな言い方がある。高校では grade の代わりに year が使われることもあるが、大学では year を用いる場合が多い。学年ごとの言い方は、高校（3年制の場合）1年が freshman、2年が junior、3年が senior といい、大学1年生が freshman、2年生が sophomore、3年生が junior、4年生が senior という場合もある。

Immigration officer: Your passport, please.
Yukio: Here you are.
IO: Mr. Ikeda, what is the purpose of your visit?
Y: Our university baseball team is going to a baseball camp.
IO: Ah, I see. How long will you be in the U.S.?
Y: Three and a half weeks.
IO: And where will you be staying?
Y: Here is my homestay family's address.
IO: OK. Now, I need to take your fingerprint. Can you place your index finger here, please? Thank you. Have a nice stay! Next.

T: Hello.
IO: Hi, Mr. … Tsukazawa?
T: That's right. It's a little difficult.
IO: You're not kidding. So what's your position?
T: Position? Uh… I'm not working yet. I'm a student.
IO: Huh? No, I mean your position on the field. I hear you're baseball players.
T: Oh! Yes. Center field.

Customs officer: Anything to declare?
T: Um… I have some gifts.
CO: No problem. Go ahead through those doors.
T: Thank you.

T: Um… I'm Takeshi Tsukazawa. Mr. and Mrs. Sullivan?
Pete: Yes, I'm Pete Sullivan! Hello, Takeshi!
Melissa: I'm Melissa Myers. And this is our son, Matt.
Matt: Hi, Takeshi!
T: Hi. I'm happy to meet you all.
Me: We're glad you're here! You must be tired from the trip.
T: A little bit… but I'm excited to be here.
P: Here, let me take your suitcase.
T: Oh… thank you, but—
P: Nope, no arguments. Are you ready to go?
T: Oh… yes. But I would like to say goodbye to my friends.
Me: Of course! Take your time.
P: We're in no hurry. But our daughter Rachel is eager to meet you.
Ma: Yeah. She saw your photo and she thinks you're cute. But don't tell her I told you.
T: Cute? Me? By the way, what grade are you in, Matt?
Ma: I'm a high school freshman. And Rachel is going into her second year of college.
T: College? Really?

入国審査官：パスポートをお願いします。
ユキオ：どうぞ。
審査官：イケダさん、訪問の目的は何ですか？
ユキオ：大学の野球チームが野球合宿に行くんです。
審査官：そうですか。アメリカにはどのくらい滞在しますか。
ユキオ：３週間半です。
審査官：どこに滞在しますか。
ユキオ：これが私のホームステイ先の住所です。
審査官：結構です。では指紋を採取します。人差し指をここに置いてもらえますか。どうも。よい滞在を。次どうぞ。

タケシ：こんにちは。
審査官：ハーイ、えーと、ツカザワさん？
タケシ：そうです。ちょっと難しいんです。
審査官：本当ですね。それで、君のポジションは。
タケシ：ポジション？ えーと……僕はまだ働いていません。学生なんです。
審査官：え？ ちがうよ、フィールドでのポジション（守備）のことだよ。君たちは野球の選手だって聞いたから。
タケシ：ああ！ はい。センターです。

税関検査官：何か申告するものは。
タケシ：えーと……贈物がいくつかあります。（申告書を見せる）
検査官：結構です。このドアを通っていってください。
タケシ：ありがとう。

タケシ：えーと、タケシ・ツカザワです。サリバンさんご夫妻ですか？
ピート：そう、ピート・サリバンです！ こんにちは、タケシ！
メリッサ：メリッサ・マイヤーズです。そしてこれが息子のマット。
マット：ハーイ、タケシ！
タケシ：ハーイ。みなさん、はじめまして。
メリッサ：よく来たわね。長旅で疲れているでしょう。
タケシ：少し……でもここに来ることができてわくわくしています。
ピート：ほら、スーツケースを持つよ。
タケシ：あ、ありがとうございます、でも……。
ピート：だめだよ、いうことを聞きなさい。もう行ける？
タケシ：あ……はい。でも友だちにさよならをいわせてください。
メリッサ：もちろん！ ゆっくりでいいわよ。
ピート：私たちは急いでいないからね。でも娘のレイチェルが君に会うのを楽しみにしてるんだ。
マット：そう。彼女は君の写真を見て、君のことをかっこいいと思ってるんだ。でもこのことを僕がいったって彼女にはいわないで。
タケシ：かっこいい？ 僕が？ ところで君は何年生、マット？
マット：高校１年生だよ。レイチェルは大学２年生になるんだ。
タケシ：大学？ 本当に？

Chapter 5
August

Exercises

Part A `Track 10`

①リスニング、②パラレル・リーディング(音を聞きながらテキストを音読)、③プロソディ・シャドーイング (音の再現) ④コンテンツ・シャドーイング (意味を意識) の順で会話を再現してみましょう。下記の Key Phrases を意識しながら、最低でも7回は会話を聞いてみましょう。

Key Phrases:
- -What is the purpose of yourvisit?
- -How long will you be in the U.S.?
- Where will you be staying?
- Anything to declare?
- You must be tired from the trip.
- Take your time.
- We're in no hurry.
- -What grade are you in?
  -I'm a freshman.

Part B
相手の問いかけやコメントに対して、自分なりの答えを考えてみましょう。

1) **Immigration officer:** What is the purpose of your visit to Canada?
   You: _____
2) **Michael:** We're so glad you're here!
   You: _____
3) **Michael:** Is it OK if I stay on the computer a bit longer?
   You: _____

今度は相手の応答にふさわしい語りかけをしてみましょう。

4) 何年生かをたずねています。
   You: _____
   Michael: I'm a senior.
5) お仕事が大変なのでお疲れでしょう、と相手をねぎらいましょう。
   You: _____
   Michael: A little bit…but I'm almost finished.
6) 招待されて相手のうちを訪問したMari。まず、名前をいって……。
   You: _____
   Michael: I'm Michael. Thank you for coming.

Exercises の解答例と訳

1) I'm here on business for three days. / I'm here as a tourist.
2) Thank you. I'm happy to be here.
3) No problem. Take your time.
4) What year are you in?
5) You must be tired from working so hard.
6) I'm Mari. Thank you for inviting me today.

問題と答えの訳
1) 入国審査官：カナダ滞在の目的は何ですか。
   あなた：仕事で3日間滞在します。／観光です。
2) マイケル：あなたとお会いできてうれしいです。
   あなた：ありがとう。私もここにいられてうれしいです。
3) マイケル：もう少しパソコンをつけていてもいいですか。
   あなた：いいですよ。ごゆっくり。
4) あなた：今何年生ですか。
   マイケル：3年生です。
5) あなた：一生懸命働いてお疲れでしょう。
   マイケル：少しだけ……でもほとんど終わりましたよ。
6) あなた：マリです。今日は誘ってくれてありがとう。
   マイケル：マイケルです。来てくれてありがとう。

コラム　夫婦別姓

　アメリカやカナダなど北米の国では結婚後もそれぞれの名字をキープする「夫婦別姓」が法律によって認められており、個人主義や男女平等の精神を色濃く反映しています。最近は日本でも仕事上では旧姓を使い続ける女性が増えていますが、日本では習慣的に戸籍上は98%の夫婦が夫の姓に統一しているのが現状です。

　夫婦別姓が認められている国でも、個人差、地域差（たとえば都市か田舎か）などがあり、伝統的な価値観を重視する人々は夫の姓に統一する場合が多いということもあります。また、キャリア志向の強い女性は結婚後も旧姓をキープすることが多く、専業主婦 (stay-at-home moms) は夫の名字に変える傾向があるようです。名字をハイフンで連結する (hyphenate) 中間策もありますが（例：Jones-Smith）、女性の名字にだけ適用されることが多いので、フェアではないという意見もあります。

Chapter 5 August

Skit B

ストーリーについて

　カリフォルニアでの野球キャンプは、あっという間に3週間がたち、最終日は日本とアメリカ、両チームによる親善試合で幕を閉じました。試合結果は6対5で日本チームの勝利。でも、思い出深いときを共にし、すばらしい友情を築いたのですから、選手全員が勝者です。打ち上げに彼らはピザ・レストランにやってきました。

ここで扱う表現について

　親善試合終了後は、対戦相手とほめ合いですね。Great game!（いい試合だった）、Congratulations!（おめでとう!）、awesome（すごくいい）、Way to go.（その調子）、great（すごい）、impressive（印象的な）などポジティブな言葉が目白押し。そのほかにも Good job!（job といっても仕事に限らず、一般的に「よくやった!」の意味）や You did it!（やったね!）など、英語にはほめたり励ましたりする表現が実に豊富です。特にスポーツ観戦などをするとさまざまなフレーズを耳にします。スポーツマンシップは北米でも大切にされているもの。負けて悔しがっていると、sore loser（負け惜しみが強い人）といって揶揄されます。勝っても負けても気持ちのよい終わり方をしたいものです。

　会話の中にはありませんが、英語独特の、相手が何か立派なことしたり、何かをやり遂げたときにほめる表現のひとつに I'm proud of you. があります。謙虚さが美徳とされるお国柄の日本では、まず自分のことを I'm proud of myself.「自分を誇りに思っている」とか相手のことを「誇りに思う」とはいいませんが、北米では母親が子どものことを I'm proud of my son.（息子のことを誇りに思う）などと使うのは至極普通です。相手のよいところを見つけて、それを常にストレートに表現するアメリカ人と、謙虚さを美徳とする日本人。それぞれのよいところを身につけられたらいいですね。

Chapter 5 August

Skit B

Track 11

素晴らしき友情に乾杯！

All players: Great game, everyone! / Congratulations! / *Banzai*, Japan!
Kevin: You guys played an awesome game!
Takeshi: Thanks! **So did you!**
Derek: I think we did pretty well… but you guys did better.
Kazu: Actually, we were terrible at first. We made a lot of errors.
T: Your team's batting was great.
Ka: In the first three innings, we didn't even get a hit!
D: But Yukio's triple in the fourth turned the tide.
Ke: Kazu, your pitching was impressive.
Ka: The coaches really helped me with my curveball.
D: And then Takeshi got that home run with two men on base! What timing!
All: Way to go, Takeshi!

---

awesome: 最高の
So did you!: 君たちも（そうだった）！
pretty: かなり
Actually: 実際のところ
terrible: ひどい
error: エラー
batting: バッティング
inning:（野球の）回
even: 〜さえ
triple: 三塁打
turn the tide: 流れを変える
pitching: ピッチング
impressive: すばらしい
curveball: カーブ
on base: 出塁して
What timing!: 絶妙のタイミングだ！
Way to go!: よくやった！

T: Thanks, but… it was just luck.
Ke: Don't be so modest, Tak. You could be the next Ichiro.
T: Then I could live in America!
D: Too bad you guys have to leave so soon. Hey, can we get your e-mail addresses?
Ka: Of course! We want your addresses, too.
T: Hey, you guys should come to Japan! You can stay at our house!
D: Really?
T: Sure! We have a lot of room since my sister moved out. And my parents love to meet people from overseas.
Ke: Well, we might just show up at your door one day!
T: Uh… maybe you should e-mail first.

タケシのホストファミリーは見送りに空港にやってきました。

Rachel: I wish you could stay here longer, Takeshi. I'll miss you.
T: You will? I'll miss you, too. But… maybe you can come to Japan sometime.
R: You know, I've been thinking the same thing! How about cherry blossom time?
T: Uh… Yes, that's a good idea!
Matt: Come on, Rachel, we want to say good-bye, too!
R: OK, OK.
Ma: Bye, Takeshi! It's been really fun!
Melissa: It's been wonderful having you here, Takeshi.
Pete: We'll see you back here when you get into the Major Leagues, OK?
T: Yes! The Dodgers, I hope! Thank you so much for everything!
R, Ma, Me, P: Take care, Takeshi! / Keep in touch! / Bye!

---

modest: 謙虚な
Too bad…: 〜なのは残念だ

Sure!: もちろん！

show up: 現れる

I wish you could…: あなたが〜できればいいのに
I'll miss you.: さみしくなるわ。
You know: 実はね

having you here: ここで一緒に時間を過ごせて

We'll see you back here when…: 〜するときにまた会いましょう
Keep in touch!: 連絡を取り合おうね

ポイント解説

Chapter 5 August Skit B

前半は懇親会でのやりとりで、ほめことばのオンパレードです。相手の称賛に対する感謝、謙遜の表現が出てきます。後半のホストファミリーとの別れのシーンでは、定番のやりとりはもちろんですが、寂しさを表す表現にも注目してみましょう。

So did you!

ほめられたら「君こそ!」と返して相手もほめよう。「……もね／……もそうだね」と応答するときには、まず So がきて、前に使われた動詞が be 動詞や do、have などに置きかわり、主語も代名詞になってそのあとに倒置される。この場合は、前の You guys played... を受けて、You guys が you、played が did となり、So did you. と倒置されている。

- It was just luck.
- Don't be so modest.

ほめられて照れ隠しや謙遜するときは I was just lucky. や、「いや、もっとがんばれたでしょう」というときは I could have done better. ともいう。Don't be so modest. は相手が謙遜しているときの「ご謙遜を」という表現。

You could be the next...

「君は次の……になれるかも」。……に大物の名前が入ると、やや大げさにほめる表現になる。

Too bad you (guys) have to leave so soon.

「もう行っちゃうのか……」と別れを惜しむ表現。Come back soon, OK?（すぐ戻ってこいよ！）と加えるとその場の雰囲気も希望的になる。

All players: Great game, everyone! / Congratulations! / *Banzai*, Japan!
Kevin: You guys played an awesome game!
Takeshi: Thanks! **So did you!**
Derek: I think we did pretty well… but you guys did better.
Kazu: Actually, we were terrible at first. We made a lot of errors.
T: Your team's batting was great.
Ka: In the first three innings, we didn't even get a hit!
D: But Yukio's triple in the fourth turned the tide.
Ke: Kazu, your pitching was impressive.
Ka: The coaches really helped me with my curveball.
D: And then Takeshi got that home run with two men on base! What timing!
All: Way to go, Takeshi!
T: Thanks, but… **it was just luck.**
Ke: **Don't be so modest**, Tak. **You could be the next** Ichiro.
T: Then I could live in America!
D: **Too bad you guys have to leave so soon.** Hey, can we get your e-mail addresses?
Ka: Of course! We want your addresses, too.
T: Hey, **you guys should come**

to Japan! You can stay at our house!
D: Really?
T: Sure! We have a lot of room since my sister moved out. And my parents love to meet people from overseas.
Ke: Well, **we might just show up at your door one day!**
T: Uh… maybe you should e-mail first.

Rachel: I wish you could stay here longer, Takeshi. **I'll miss you.**
T: You will? I'll miss you, too. But… maybe you can come to Japan sometime.
R: You know, I've been thinking the same thing! How about cherry blossom time?
T: Uh… Yes, that's a good idea!
Matt: Come on, Rachel, we want to say goodbye, too!
R: OK, OK.
Ma: Bye, Takeshi! **It's been really fun!**
Melissa: It's been wonderful having you here, Takeshi.
Pete: We'll see you back here when you get into the Major Leagues, OK?
T: Yes! The Dodgers, I hope! **Thank you so much for everything!**
R, Ma, Me, P: Take care, Takeshi! / **Keep in touch!** / Bye!

We might just show up at your door one day.

招待を受けて「ある日突然玄関に現れるよ」とからかっているが、相手によっては社交辞令ではなく素直に招待をよろこび、再会を果たす可能性も大いにある。

-I wish you could stay here longer. -I'll miss you.

これもよく交される別れの際の表現。I'll miss you. は特に長期的に相手に会うことがない場合に使う。

- It's been (really) fun!
- It's been wonderful having you here.
- We'll see you back here when…

ホスト側からいわれるとうれしい別れ際のひとこと。Come back and stay with us anytime! ともいえる。逆の立場でも使える。

Thank you (so much) for everything!

「いろいろとお世話になりました」という心からの感謝の表現。

- Take care.
- Keep in touch!

こちらは会話だけでなく、手紙やメールなどに応用しても自然な表現。

-You (guys) should come to Japan!
-You can stay at our house!

いいときを過ごさせてもらった感謝と、「またぜひ会いたいね」という気持ちが込められている。海外や外国人宅でお世話になったら、気持ちだけでも「次回はぜひ日本へ」と相手を招待しよう。

訳

All players: Great game, everyone! / Congratulations! / *Banzai*, Japan!
Kevin: You guys played an awesome game!
Takeshi: Thanks! So did you!
Derek: I think we did pretty well... but you guys did better.
Kazu: Actually, we were terrible at first. We made a lot of errors.
T: Your team's batting was great.
Ka: In the first three innings, we didn't even get a hit!
D: But Yukio's triple in the fourth turned the tide.
Ke: Kazu, your pitching was impressive.
Ka: The coaches really helped me with my curveball.
D: And then Takeshi got that home run with two men on base! What timing!
All: Way to go, Takeshi!
T: Thanks, but... it was just luck.
Ke: Don't be so modest, Tak. You could be the next Ichiro.
T: Then I could live in America!
D: Too bad you guys have to leave so soon. Hey, can we get your e-mail addresses?
Ka Of course! We want your addresses, too.
T: Hey, you guys should come to Japan! You can stay at our house!
D: Really?
T: Sure! We have a lot of room since my sister moved out. And my parents love to meet people from overseas.
Ke: Well, we might just show up at your door one day!
T: Uh... maybe you should e-mail first.

Rachel: I wish you could stay here longer, Takeshi. I'll miss you.
T: You will? I'll miss you, too. But... maybe you can come to Japan sometime.
R: You know, I've been thinking the same thing! How about cherry blossom time?
T: Uh... Yes, that's a good idea.
Matt: Come on, Rachel, we want to say goodbye, too!
R: OK, OK.
Ma: Bye, Takeshi! It's been really fun!
Melissa: It's been wonderful having you here, Takeshi.
Pete: We'll see you back here when you get into the Major Leagues, OK?
T: Yes! The Dodgers, I hope! Thank you so much for everything!
R, Ma, Me, P: Take care, Takeshi! / Keep in touch! / Bye!

選手たち：みんな、いい試合だったね。／おめでとう。／バンザイ、日本！
ケヴィン：君たちは最高の試合をしたよ。
タケシ：ありがとう。君たちもね。
デレック：俺たちはかなりよくやったと思うけど……君たちのほうがもっとよかった。
カズ：実際、僕たちは最初はひどかったよ。たくさんエラーを出したし。
タケシ：そっちのバッティングはすばらしかったよ。
カズ：最初の3回は、僕たちヒットさえ出なかったからね。
デレック：でも、4回のユキオの三塁打で一変したね。
ケヴィン：カズ、君のピッチングはすばらしかったよ。
カズ：コーチたちがカーブ球の指導を本当にしっかりやってくれたんだ。
デレック：それでタケシがランナーふたりのところで、ホームラン！　絶妙のタイミングだった。
皆：よくやったな、タケシ。
タケシ：ありがとう、でも……あれは運がよかっただけだよ。
ケヴィン：そう謙虚になるなって、タック。君は次のイチローになれるかもしれない。
タケシ：そしたらアメリカに住めるね。
デレック：君たちがもういかなきゃならないなんて残念だな。そうだ、Eメールアドレス教えてくれよ。
カズ：もちろん。君たちのも教えてほしいな。
タケシ：そうだ、君たち日本にくるべきだよ。僕たちの家に泊まればいいよ。
デレック：本当に？
タケシ：もちろん。姉貴が出てから、うちにはスペースがいっぱいあるんだ。それに僕の両親も外国人と会うのが大好きなんだ。
ケヴィン：そうだな、俺たちはある日突然玄関に現れるかもしれないよ。
タケシ：うーん……まずはEメールしてくれよ。

レイチェル：タケシ、もっと長くいてくれたらいいのに。さみしくなるわ。
タケシ：本当に？　僕もだよ。でも、いつか日本に来て。
レイチェル：実はね、私も同じこと考えてたの。桜の時期はどう？
タケシ：えーと……うん、いいアイディアだね。
マット：もういいだろう、レイチェル、僕たちもさよならをいいたいんだ。
レイチェル：はいはい。
マット：じゃあな、タケシ。すごく楽しかったよ。
メリッサ：あなたがきてくれて、本当によかったわ、タケシ。
ピート：メジャーリーグに入団したときに、ここでまた会おう、いいな？
タケシ：はい。できればドジャースがいいですね。本当にいろいろとありがとうございました。
皆：元気でね、タケシ。／連絡を取り合おうね。／じゃあね。

Chapter 5
August

Exercises

Part A Track 11

①リスニング、②パラレル・リーディング(音を聞きながらテキストを音読)、③プロソディ・シャドーイング（音の再現）④コンテンツ・シャドーイング（意味を意識）の順で会話を再現してみましょう。下記の Key Phrases を意識しながら、最低でも7回は会話を聞いてみましょう。

Key Phrases:
- So did you!
- -It was just luck.
  -Don't be so modest.
- You could be the next…
- Too bad you have to leave so soon.
- You should come to Japan.
- You can stay at our house.
- We might just show up at your door one day.
- I wish you could stay here longer. I miss you.
- It's been (really) fun!
- It's been wonderful having you here.
- We'll see you back here when…
- Thank you (so much) for everything!
- Take care.
- Keep in touch!

Part B

相手のことばに自分なりの応答を考えてみましょう。

1) **Elaine:** Thank you for letting me stay with you.
   You: _____
2) **Elaine:** Let's go see a movie.
   You: _____
3) **Elaine:** Keep in touch!
   You: _____

今度は相手に質問してみましょう。

4) ホームステイ先の人々に別れるとき、お礼をいいましょう。
   You: _____
   Elaine: It's been wonderful having you stay with us.
5) 別れるとき「連絡を取り合おうね」といってみましょう。
   You: _____
   Elaine: Yes, I'll write you for sure.
6) 相手のプレゼンテーションをほめてみましょう。
   You: _____
   Elaine: Thank you. I thought your presentation was great, too.

Exercisesの解答例と訳

1) It's been wonderful having you here. / Do you have to leave so soon? / We'll miss you.
2) That's a good idea!
3) I will.
4) Thank you for all your hospitality. I really enjoyed my stay.
5) Please keep in touch.
6) Your presentation was so impressive.

問題と答えの訳

1) エレーヌ：泊めてくれてありがとう。
   あなた：あなたがいて素晴らしかったです。もうすぐに発たないといけないの？ / さみしくなるわ。
2) エレーヌ：映画を見に行きましょう。
   あなた：いいね。
3) エレーヌ：連絡してね。
   あなた：必ずするよ。
4) あなた：いろいろもてなしてくれてありがとう。滞在は本当に楽しかったです。
   エレーヌ：あなたがいて素晴らしかったです。
5) あなた：連絡してくださいね。
   エレーヌ：ええ、必ず手紙を書くわ。
6) あなた：あなたのプレゼンテーションにはとても感銘を受けました。
   エレーヌ：ありがとう。あなたのプレゼンテーションも良かったわよ。

コラム

ほめる

　北米では相手の外見や服装、持ち物などをほめることが多く、ほとんどあいさつのような意味合いで "You look really nice today." などといいます。

　日本人は謙遜してほめられたことを否定するようなコメントをついいってしまいがちですが、"You look really nice today." といわれて、"No, I don't." などと真っ向から否定してしまうと、失礼な印象を与えるので気をつけましょう。ほめられたら、"Oh, thanks!" などと素直にお礼をいうのが普通です。

　また、自分の子どものことをほめられたときに、日本人は「でも、家では本当にきかん坊で」などとネガティブなことをいって、あえてけなす傾向がありますが、欧米では "I'm really proud of him (my son)." と他人の前で自分の子どもの成功などを称えるのは微笑ましいことだとされています。

　"Your wife is nice." といわれたら、"Isn't she?" (でしょう?)と肯定するのが欧米的な発想なので、ぜひ覚えておきましょう。

Chapter 5 の 重要表現リスト

Skit A

- [ ] **What is the purpose of your visit to the U.S.?** アメリカ訪問の目的は?
- [ ] **How long will you be in the U.S.?** アメリカにはどのくらい滞在する予定ですか
- [ ] **Where will you be staying?** どこに滞在する予定ですか
- [ ] **Have a nice stay.** 楽しんで
- [ ] ***Have a nice trip.** よい旅行を
- [ ] ***Have a nice weekend.** よい週末を
- [ ] **Anything to declare?** 申告するものはありますか
- [ ] **Go ahead.** さあどうぞ、前に進んでください
- [ ] **You must be tired from the trip.** 長旅でお疲れでしょう
- [ ] ***Do you have jet lag?** 時差ぼけはありますか
- [ ] **No arguments.** 言う通りにしなさい
- [ ] **Take your time.** ごゆっくり
- [ ] **We're in no hurry.** 急いでいませんから
- [ ] **be eager to...** 〜したがっている
- [ ] **-What grade are you in?** 何年生ですか
  -I'm a freshman. 1年生です

Skit B

- [ ] **So did you!** あなたも
- [ ] **turn the tide** 流れを変える
- [ ] **Way to go!** よくやった!(その調子!)
- [ ] ***You did it!** やったね!
- [ ] ***Good job!** よくやった!
- [ ] ***sore loser** 負け惜しみの強い人
- [ ] ***I'm proud of...** 〜を誇りに思う
- [ ] ***What timing!** 絶妙のタイミングだ!
- [ ] **-It was just luck.** 運がよかったんですよ
  -Don't be so modest. ご謙遜を
- [ ] ***I could have done better.** もっとうまくやれたでしょう
- [ ] **You could be the next...** 君は次の〜になれるかも
- [ ] **Too bad you have to leave so soon.** もう行っちゃうなんて残念
- [ ] ***Come back soon, OK?** すぐに戻ってこいよ
- [ ] **You should come to Japan!** 君たち、ぜひ日本へ来るべきだよ
- [ ] **You can stay at our house!** 僕らの家に泊まればいいよ
- [ ] **Sure.** もちろん
- [ ] **We might just show up at your door one day.** ある日突然玄関に現れるかもしれない
- [ ] **I wish you could stay here longer.** もっと長くいてくれたらいいのに
- [ ] **I'll miss you.** さみしくなるわ
- [ ] **You know,** 実はね
- [ ] **It's been really fun!** 本当に楽しかった
- [ ] **It's been wonderful having you here.** あなたが来てくれて楽しかった
- [ ] **We'll see you back here when...** 〜のときにここに戻ってきてね
- [ ] **Thank you so much for everything!** 本当にいろいろとありがとうございました
- [ ] **Take care.** 元気で
- [ ] **Keep in touch!** また連絡してね

Chapter 6

September

場面・状況	タケシが小学生を前に教室で簡単なスピーチをする
表現のテーマ	インフォーマルなスピーチのスタートから終了まで

Skit A

場面・状況	陶芸教室で作品を作る
表現のテーマ	ほめる／励ます／いらだつ

Skit B

Chapter 6 September

Skit A

ストーリーについて

夏休みが終わり、アナ、レナ、リチャードが働くインターナショナルスクールも新しい学年がスタートしました。リチャードが担任を務めるのは2年生。生徒には新学期を迎えて、リチャードのクラスになったアナの娘のエミリーもいます。きょう、リチャードはクラスにお楽しみを用意してきました。2年生のクラスにやってきた人とは……

ここで扱う表現について

日本人にとって慣れない人前でのスピーチ、それを英語で、となると気後れしますね。ここでは、インフォーマルなスピーチの始め方などをご紹介します。

まずリチャードがゲストスピーカーを紹介するにあたって、This morning we have a special guest speaker.(今朝は特別なゲストをお迎えしています)という表現で始めています。他にも、講演会などで司会はよく It is my great honor to present...(……さんをご紹介できることを光栄に思います)や、This morning we are very fortunate to have with us...(今朝は大変幸いなことに……さんをお迎えしています)などの表現を使います。

そしてスピーカーも It is a great honor to be here today.(本日こちらにうかがうことができて光栄です)や Thank you for having me today.(本日はお招きいただきありがとうございます)など、その場に招待されたことに対しての感謝の意を表現します。

タケシのスピーチは無事終了。「話を終わらせる」は英語で wrap up a talk といいます。スピーカーが話の終わりに差しかかると、よくまとめとして To wrap up my talk, ...(まとめると……)と話の結論を語ります。覚えておくと便利な表現です。そして最後に Thank you for listening. ということで、スピーチが終わったことを合図しています。スピーチの後は質疑応答。リチャードが Are there any questions? と質問を促しています。日本では遠慮して誰も手をあげないこともよくありますが、質問をすることによって相手の話した内容に興味が持てた、という合図になりますので、ささいなことでも積極的に質問しましょう。

Chapter 6 **S**eptember

Skit A

Track 12

小学生にアメリカでの異文化体験を語る

Richard: Morning, Emily!
Emily: Good morning! Richard—I mean Mr. Levinson—who's that baseball player in the hallway?
R: **Good question.** OK, everyone, **settle down**. This morning we have a special guest speaker. He plays baseball at his university. Please come in, Takeshi-*san*.
Takeshi: **Hi, everyone.** My name is Takeshi Tsukazawa.
Students: Your uniform is cool! / You look like Yuki Saitoh! / You look like Ichiro!
T: Um… **I'm sorry, I'm a little nervous speaking in English.**
Student: *Gambatte!*
T: Thanks! Um, I'd like to—
S: What's your position?

hallway: 廊下

Good question.:
いい質問だ、いいところに気がついた
settle down: 静かに

be nervous:
緊張する

T: Center field… like Ichiro!
R: You have them now, Takeshi. Go for it.
T: Well, **I'd like to tell you about** my experience in America this summer. I went to a baseball camp near Los Angeles with my team, and I stayed with an American family. **This may surprise you, but** it was the first time I ever went to another country. As you know, American and Japanese customs are different. **Can anyone tell me** one difference?
S: Wearing shoes in the house!
T: Right! The first time I went to my host family's house, I took off my shoes—but there was no place to put them. So I put them back on my feet! And sometimes I misunderstood what people said. **For example, one day** a baseball coach said, "Throw to home, Takeshi!" But I thought he said "Go home, Takeshi!" So I started to walk off the field.

スピーチも終わりに近づき……

T: **Here is a photo of** me with my host family. This is Pete, Melissa, Matt… and Rachel. They showed me that even if the language and customs are different, people are the same everywhere. **Thank you for listening.**
R: Thank you, Takeshi-*san*! **Are there any questions?**
E: Yes!
R: Emily?
E: Takeshi-*san*, is Rachel your girlfriend?
T: Girlfriend? Oh, no—we're just friends!
S: Takeshi has a girlfriend!
R: Kids understand everything, Takeshi.
T: Yes. So do younger brothers.
R: Uh… Oh.

---

put them back on my feet: 靴を履きなおした

show: 教える

So do/does…: 〜も同じだ

ポイント解説

Chapter 6 September Skit A

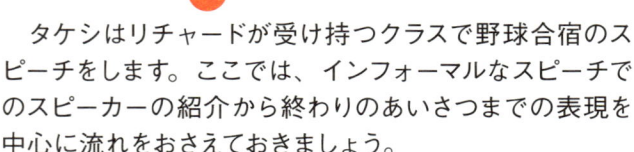

タケシはリチャードが受け持つクラスで野球合宿のスピーチをします。ここでは、インフォーマルなスピーチでのスピーカーの紹介から終わりのあいさつまでの表現を中心に流れをおさえておきましょう。

Richard: Morning, Emily!
Emily: Good morning! Richard—I mean Mr. Levinson—who's that baseball player in the hallway?
R: Good question. OK, everyone, **settle down**. This morning we have a special guest speaker. He plays baseball at his university. Please come in, Takeshi-*san*.
Takeshi: Hi, everyone. My name is Takeshi Tsukazawa.
Students: Your uniform is cool! / You look like Yuki Saitoh! / You look like Ichiro!
T: Um… **I'm sorry, I'm a little nervous speaking in English.**
Student: *Gambatte!*
T: Thanks! Um, I'd like to—
S: What's your position?
T: Center field… like Ichiro!
R: You have them now, Takeshi. Go for it.
T: Well, **I'd like to tell you about** my experience in America this summer. I went to a baseball camp near Los Angeles with my team, and I stayed with an American family. **This may surprise you, but** it was the first time I ever went to another country. As you know, American and Japanese customs

---

Good question.

Who's that baseball player...? の質問に、Good question.（いいことに気がついたね。）といって、はっきりとした答えをせず、相手をじらしている。

Settle down.

直訳は「落ち着いて」だがここでは「静かにと」生徒たちに注意している。また、何かを話し始める前は、May I have your attention, please? といって観衆の注意を引くといい。

Hi, everyone.

紹介をされて、話を始めるとき、フォーマルな場では Hello. や Good morning / afternoon / evening, ladies and gentlemen.（観衆が女性だけの場合は ladies、男性だけの場合は gentlemen だけで OK）と変えたほうが無難。

I'm sorry, I'm a little nervous speaking in English.

英語で話すのが不安だ、または人前で話すのは緊張するというときは I'm nervous speaking in front of people. とあらかじめ断っておくこともひとつのコツ。

are different. **Can anyone tell me** one difference?
S: Wearing shoes in the house!
T: Right! The first time I went to my host family's house, I took off my shoes—but there was no place to put them. So I put them back on my feet! And sometimes I misunderstood what people said. **For example, one day** a baseball coach said, "Throw to home, Takeshi!" But I thought he said "Go home, Takeshi!" So I started to walk off the field.

T: **Here is a photo of** me with my host family. This is Pete, Melissa, Matt… and Rachel. They showed me that even if the language and customs are different, people are the same everywhere. **Thank you for listening.**
R: Thank you, Takeshi-*san*! **Are there any questions?**
E: Yes!
R: Emily?
E: Takeshi-*san*, is Rachel your girlfriend?
T: Girlfriend? Oh, no—we're just friends!
S: Takeshi has a girlfriend!
R: Kids understand everything, Takeshi.
T: Yes. So do younger brothers.
R: Uh… Oh.

Can anyone tell me…?
この表現を用いれば、スピーカーが一方的に話すだけではなく、スピーチの途中で「誰か私に……をいえますか」と聞き手に問いかけて、双方向性を出しながら聞き手に能動的に参加するきっかけを作ることができる。

For example, one day…
その前に述べたことの具体的な例を挙げる際に使う表現。one day と続けることで、過去の自分の体験や出来事が具体的に語りやすくなる。

Here is a photo of…
「ここに……の写真があります」。こういいながら写真を取り出して聞き手に示す。具体的なものを見せて説明すると聞き手も具体的なイメージを持ちやすい。写真のかわりに絵でも本でもハガキでもなんでも使える。

Thank you for listening.
「聞いてくださってありがとうございました」。予定のスピーチを終えた後に、スピーカーが聞き手に対して聞いてくれたことに対して謝意を表すことば。

Are there any questions?
「質問はありませんか」。スピーチがひととおり終わった後などに、司会者などが聞き手に向かってこうたずねて質疑応答を引き出す。

I'd like to tell you about…
スピーチや説明を始めるときに、「……について話したい」と切り出すことば。

This may surprise you, but…
「これを聞くと驚かれるかもしれませんが……」と相手の興味を引いて、自分の話に引き込むときに使う表現。

Richard: Morning, Emily!
Emily: Good morning! Richard—I mean Mr. Levinson—who's that baseball player in the hallway?
R: Good question. OK, everyone, settle down. This morning we have a special guest speaker. He plays baseball at his university. Please come in, Takeshi-*san*.
Takeshi: Hi, everyone. My name is Takeshi Tsukazawa.
Students: Your uniform is cool! / You look like Yuki Saitoh! / You look like Ichiro!
T: Um… I'm sorry, I'm a little nervous speaking in English.
Student: *Gambatte!*
T: Thanks! Um, I'd like to—
S: What's your position?
T: Center field… like Ichiro!
R: You have them now, Takeshi. Go for it.
T: Well, I'd like to tell you about my experience in America this summer. I went to a baseball camp near Los Angeles with my team, and I stayed with an American family. This may surprise you, but it was the first time I ever went to another country. As you know, American and Japanese customs are different. Can anyone tell me one difference?
S: Wearing shoes in the house!
T: Right! The first time I went to my host family's house, I took off my shoes—but there was no place to put them. So I put them back on my feet! And sometimes I misunderstood what people said. For example, one day a baseball coach said, "Throw to home, Takeshi!" But I thought he said "Go home, Takeshi!" So I started to walk off the field.

T: Here is a photo of me with my host family. This is Pete, Melissa, Matt… and Rachel. They showed me that even if the language and customs are different, people are the same everywhere. Thank you for listening.
R: Thank you, Takeshi-*san*! Are there any questions?
E: Yes!
R: Emily?
E: Takeshi-*san*, is Rachel your girlfriend?
T: Girlfriend? Oh, no—we're just friends!
S: Takeshi has a girlfriend!
R: Kids understand everything, Takeshi.
T: Yes. So do younger brothers.
R: Uh… Oh.

リチャード：おはよう、エミリー。
エミリー：おはようございます、リチャード、じゃなくてレビンソン先生。廊下にいるあの野球選手は誰ですか。
リチャード：いいところに気がついたね。さてみんな、席に座って。今朝はみんなに特別なお客さまがいます。彼は大学で野球をやっています。タケシさん、どうぞ入ってください。
タケシ：みなさん、こんにちは。僕の名前はタケシ・ツカザワです。
生徒たち：そのユニフォーム、かっこいい。／ユウキ・サイトウに似てる。／イチローみたい。
タケシ：えー……ごめんなさい、英語で話すのに少し緊張しています。
生徒：ガンバッテ。
タケシ：ありがとう。えー、僕は‥‥
生徒：守備は？
タケシ：センターです……イチローみたいにね。
リチャード：みんな聞いてますよ。タケシさん。さあどうぞ。
タケシ：今年の夏にアメリカに行った経験についてお話ししたいと思います。大学のチームのみんなで、ロサンゼルスの近くに野球の合宿に行ってきました。泊めてもらったのはアメリカ人の家です。こういうと驚くかもしれないけど、これが初めての海外でした。みんなも知っているように、日本とアメリカでは習慣がちがいます。誰かそのちがいをいってくれる人はいますか。
生徒：家の中でも靴を履いてるんだよ。
タケシ：正解。ホストファミリーの家に初めて行ったとき、靴を脱いでしまったけど、置いておくところがありませんでした。それでまた履き直したんです。それから、人の話を誤解してしまうこともありました。例えばある日、野球のコーチにThrow to home, Takeshi!（ホームに投げろ）といわれました。でも僕は Go home, Takeshi!（家に帰れ）だと思ってしまい、グラウンドから歩き去ろうとしてしまったんです。

タケシ：ここにホストファミリーといっしょの僕の写真があります。これがピート、メリッサ、マットとレイチェルです。彼らは、ことばや習慣はちがっても、人間はどこでも同じだということを教えてくれました。聞いてくれてありがとうございます。
リチャード：ありがとうございました、タケシさん。質問はありますか。
エミリー：はい！
リチャード：エミリー。
エミリー：タケシさん、レイチェルはあなたのガールフレンドですか。
タケシ：ガールフレンド？　ああ、いや、僕たちはただの友だちです。
生徒：タケシにはガールフレンドがいる〜！
リチャード：子どもはすべてわかってるね、タケシ。
タケシ：そう。弟もね。
リチャード：ああ……

Chapter 6
September

Exercises

Part A `Track 12`

①リスニング、②パラレル・リーディング(音を聞きながらテキストを音読)、③プロソディ・シャドーイング（音の再現）④コンテンツ・シャドーイング（意味を意識）の順で会話を再現してみましょう。下記の Key Phrases を意識しながら、最低でも７回は会話を聞いてみましょう。

Key Phrases:
- Good question.
- Settle down.
- Hi, everyone.
- I'm sorry, I'm a little nervous speaking in English.
- I'd like to tell you about…
- This may surprise you, but…
- Can anyone tell me…?
- For example, one day…
- Here is a photo of…
- Thank you for listening.
- Are there any questions?

Part B

相手の問いかけに自分なりの答えを考えてみましょう。

1) **Phil:** Who's that in Joe's office?
   You: _____
2) **Phil:** Please give a warm welcome to Mrs. Tsukazawa.
   You: _____
3) **Phil:** Can anyone tell me a difference between television and the Internet?
   You: _____

今度は相手の応答にふさわしい質問や語りかけをしてみましょう。

4) 質問があるか確認してみましょう。
   You: _____
   Phil: Actually, I was wondering about this figure here. Could you please explain it to me?
5) 見覚えのない人を見かけたら？
   You: _____
   Phil: Oh, that's Mr. Walker, one of Joe's clients.
6) プレゼンを前に緊張している時に使う表現は？
   You: _____
   Phil: Don't worry. You'll be fine.

Exercises の解答例と訳

1) Oh, that's his wife.
2) Thank you very much. Today, I'd like to tell you about my family.
3) Yes. Television is not interactive, and the Internet is.
4) Are there any questions? / Do you have any questions?
5) Who is that man sitting in the lobby?
6) I'm a bit nervous about giving a presentation.

問題と答えの訳

1) フィル：ジョーのオフィスにいるのは誰ですか。
   あなた：ああ、あれは彼の奥さんです。
2) フィル：ツカザワさんを温かい拍手でお迎えください。
   あなた：ありがとうございます。今日は私の家族についてお話ししたいと思います。
3) フィル：誰かテレビとインターネットのちがいを教えてくれる人はいませんか。
   あなた：はい。テレビは双方向性がありませんが、インターネットはあります。
4) あなた：質問はありますか。
   フィル：実のところ、数値について疑問だったんです。説明していただけますか。
5) あなた：ロビーに座っているのは誰ですか。
   フィル：ああ、ウォーカーさんですね、ジョーの顧客のひとりですよ。
6) あなた：プレゼンテーションするのに少し緊張しています。
   フィル：心配しないで。大丈夫だから。

コラム　小学校のスクールランチ

　日本の小学校ではお昼になると生徒が白い割烹着を着て、給食室から教室に食べ物を運んできます。そして他の生徒の分を器に盛ってあげて、教室の中で担任の先生と一緒に食べますが、北米ではそのような光景は見られません。そもそも給食というシステムがないので、北米では生徒たちは家からお弁当 (box lunch / bag lunch) を持ってきて屋外などで食べるか、学校のカフェテリアで用意される食事を購入して食べます。

　「教室は勉強するところ」という意識が強く、食事をするのに教室は使われないのが普通です。先生は生徒とは別にカフェテリアや食事室などで食べますが、当番で昼休み中に生徒を監視することもあります。また、歩いて帰れる距離に家がある生徒は、一度帰宅してお昼を食べてくることもあります。

　お弁当の中身はいたって質素で、サンドイッチ（中身はピーナツバターとジャム、ツナ、ハムとレタスなど）と果物（バナナやリンゴ）、チップス、クッキーなどが一般的です。日本のようにお弁当の中身を母親が競い合うというようなことはまずありません。

Chapter 6 September

Skit B

ストーリーについて

　今年はミユキには様々な新しいことが訪れる年のようです。4月に新しい仕事が始まり、7月にリチャードと付き合い始め、そして今月彼女はアナの通う陶芸教室で陶芸を始めました。先輩のアナはいろいろとアドバイスをしてくれます。しかし、彼女たちの話題は、陶芸のことだけではなさそうです。

ここで扱う表現について

　陶芸教室に通うようになったミユキ。まずは基礎を身につけたい、と希望する彼女にアナは That's a good idea. There's no hurry.(いい考えね。急ぐことないわ)と彼女を励まします。Am I doing this coil pot right? (これで大丈夫かしら)と不安げなミユキに対しても、アナはあくまでもポジティブな姿勢を崩さず、Yes, that's great! (いいじゃない!)とほめていますね。日本人はほめられたり、励まされたりすることに慣れていませんが、ほめられたり励まされるとうれしいですし、やる気が出てきますよね。これまでにもいくつかのスキットでほめる場面が出てきました。復習、応用してください。

　一方、ボウルの使い道が定まらないアナに対し、先生は、That is the reason the shape is not clear. (だから形がはっきりしないのよ)となかなか手厳しい指摘をします。自分の作品にそこそこ満足していたアナは、She makes me crazy sometimes. (彼女にはときどきイライラさせられるわ)と苛立ちを隠しきれない様子。そんな彼女の気持ちを察してミユキが I think your bowl is nice. (あなたのボウルはいいと思うわ)とフォローしています。

　会話の最後には再度先生が登場。ミユキの作品をまたほめています。それに対してアナの反応は Teacher's pet.。「先生のお気に入り」という意味ですね。ちょっと大人気ないかもしれませんが、この表現は英語独特のおもしろい表現。覚えておくと便利でしょう。

Chapter 6 September

Skit B

Track 13

器作りもラクじゃない

Anna: … Then you pull up the clay like this.
Miyuki: The potter's wheel looks difficult. I think I should learn the basic techniques first.
A: That's a good idea. There's no hurry.
M: Am I doing this coil pot right?
A: Let's see… Yes, **that's great!**
Teacher: Miyuki-*san*, **very good!** Anna-*san*, what are you making?
A: Well, I think it's a bowl.
T: I think so, too. But what will you put in this bowl? Do you have an image in mind?
A: Sort of.
T: Only sort of? **That is the reason** the shape is not clear.

---

pull up: 引き上げる
clay: 粘土
potter's wheel: ロクロ
coil pot: 手びねりのつぼ
Let's see…: どれどれ

bowl: ボウル、器

Sort of.: まあなんとなく

A: But… I like the shape, *sensei*.

T: The shape and the purpose of the bowl must be united. Then the bowl will be beautiful.

A: Do you mean it won't be beautiful if I don't know what I'm going to put in it?

T: That is not exactly what I mean. Please think about it. I'll come back.

A: Oh! **She makes me crazy sometimes.**

M: I think your bowl is nice, Anna.

A: Thanks, Miyuki. **So tell me**… how are things going with Richard?

M: Richard? Um… **maybe you should concentrate on** your bowl.

A: I won't be able to concentrate unless you tell me.

M: Well… it isn't so interesting.

A: Miyuki, American women tell their friends everything, even the boring stuff.

M: But… I feel strange. Richard is your friend.

A: Don't worry! Richard always tells me and Lena about—um…

M: It's OK. I know he's dated other people. So… has he told you about… us?

A: Actually, no. Wait a minute. Richard isn't talking—you're not talking—**now I get it!**

M: What?

A: You two are really in love, aren't you?

M: Oh… well… I don't know… I mean… I suppose we… well, yes.

A: Miyuki, that's wonderful! And just think—I introduced you.

M: Yes! Thank you!

T: Anna, have you decided about your bowl?

A: Uh… not yet, *sensei*. It's a tough decision.

T: Miyuki-*san*, your coil pot is excellent.

M: Thank you, *sensei*.

A: Teacher's pet.

Do you mean…?:
〜ということですか？

make … crazy:
〜を腹立たせる、〜をイライラさせる

So tell me…:
ところで

How are things going with…?:
〜に関してはどうなってるの？

concentrate on…:
〜に集中する

unless…:
〜でない限り

boring:
つまらない

stuff: こと、もの

date: 付き合う

Wait a minute.:
ちょっと待って。

get it: わかる

be in love:
恋愛中で

just think:
考えてもみて

tough:
困難な

Teacher's pet.:
先生のお気に入り（強烈な皮肉）

ポイント解説

Chapter 6 September Skit B

ミユキはアナとともに陶芸教室に通い始めました。ここではほめたり励ますときに使う表現や、誤解されたり言い訳をするときに使う表現、さらに苛立ったときに感情を表す表現が使われています。

That's a good idea. There's no hurry.
相手がいったことを受けて、「いい考えね。急ぐことはないわ」とたたみかけ、相手のいったことを認めて励ましている。

- That's great!
- Very good!
Wonderful!、You're doing great!、Excellent!、Brilliant! など、さすが英語にはほめたり励ましたりする表現がたくさん。

Sort of.
「まあなんとなく」というあまり自信がない、関心がない返事。Kind of. ともいう。いわれたほうはあまり感じのいい印象を受けないので、使うときは相手や状況を考えて。

That's the reason...
「それが……である理由です」。前にいわれたことを That が受けるかたちで、「それが理由です」というように That を強く発音する。

That's not exactly what I mean.
誤解されたとき、または痛いところをつかれて「そういうわけではありません！」と言い訳をするときにいうフレーズ。

Anna: … Then you pull up the clay like this.
Miyuki: The potter's wheel looks difficult. I think I should learn the basic techniques first.
A: **That's a good idea. There's no hurry.**
M: Am I doing this coil pot right?
A: Let's see… Yes, **that's great!**
Teacher: Miyuki-*san*, **very good!** Anna-*san*, what are you making?
A: Well, I think it's a bowl.
T: I think so, too. But what will you put in this bowl? Do you have an image in mind?
A: **Sort of.**
T: Only sort of? **That is the reason** the shape is not clear.
A: But… I like the shape, *sensei*.
T: The shape and the purpose of the bowl must be united. Then the bowl will be beautiful.
A: Do you mean it won't be beautiful if I don't know what I'm going to put in it?
T: **That is not exactly what I mean.** Please think about it. I'll come back.
A: Oh! **She makes me crazy sometimes.**
M: I think your bowl is nice, Anna.
A: Thanks, Miyuki. **So tell me…** how are things going with Rich-

ard?
M: Richard? Um... **maybe you should concentrate on** your bowl.
A: I won't be able to concentrate unless you tell me.
M: Well... it isn't so interesting.
A: Miyuki, American women tell their friends everything, even the boring stuff.
M: But... I feel strange. Richard is your friend.
A: Don't worry! Richard always tells me and Lena about—um...
M: It's OK. I know he's dated other people. So... has he told you about... us?
A: Actually, no. Wait a minute. Richard isn't talking—you're not talking—**now I get it!**
M: What?
A: You two are really in love, aren't you?
M: Oh... well... I don't know... I mean... I suppose we... well, yes.
A: Miyuki, that's wonderful! And just think—I introduced you.
M: Yes! Thank you!
T: Anna, have you decided about your bowl?
A: Uh... not yet, *sensei*. It's a tough decision.
T: Miyuki-*san*, your coil pot is excellent.
M: Thank you, *sensei*.
A: Teacher's pet.

- Maybe you should concentrate on...
- Well, it isn't so interesting.

しつこく聞きたがろうとする相手に、「……に集中したほうがいい」「そんなにおもしろい話ではない」とにごすのもいいが、本当に話題に触れたくないときは I (really) don't want to talk about it. や I'd rather not talk about it. Sorry. とはっきり断ってもかまわない。親しい相手や、「しつこい！」と苛立ちを伝えたいときの Mind your own business. (放っといて) も使われる言い回しだが、かなりきつい言い方なので、使う際には注意が必要。

Now I get it!

「そういうことか」。ここでの get は「理解する」。「わかった！」という表現。

Oh... well... I don't know... I mean... I suppose we... well, yes.

何といおうかためらったときには、無言でいるのではなく、このように Oh とか well などをつなぎながら話し続けていくとよい。

She makes me crazy sometimes.

「彼女にはときどきイラつくのよね」。She を主語にして「彼女が私をいらつかせる」といっているが、要するに「……に腹が立つ」ということ。drive... crazy ともいう。

So tell me...

「ところで」と話題を変えるときの言い回し。

訳

Anna: … Then you pull up the clay like this.
Miyuki: The potter's wheel looks difficult. I think I should learn the basic techniques first.
A: That's a good idea. There's no hurry.
M: Am I doing this coil pot right?
A: Let's see… Yes, that's great!
Teacher: Miyuki-*san*, very good! Anna-*san*, what are you making?
A: Well, I think it's a bowl.
T: I think so, too. But what will you put in this bowl? Do you have an image in mind?
A: Sort of.
T: Only sort of? That is the reason the shape is not clear.
A: But… I like the shape, *sensei*.
T: The shape and the purpose of the bowl must be united. Then the bowl will be beautiful.
A: Do you mean it won't be beautiful if I don't know what I'm going to put in it?
T: That is not exactly what I mean. Please think about it. I'll come back.
A: Oh! She makes me crazy sometimes.
M: I think your bowl is nice, Anna.
A: Thanks, Miyuki. So tell me… how are things going with Richard?
M: Richard? Um… maybe you should concentrate on your bowl.
A: I won't be able to concentrate unless you tell me.
M: Well… it isn't so interesting.
A: Miyuki, American women tell their friends everything, even the boring stuff.
M: But… I feel strange. Richard is your friend.
A: Don't worry! Richard always tells me and Lena about—um…
M: It's OK. I know he's dated other people. So… has he told you about… us?
A: Actually, no. Wait a minute. Richard isn't talking—you're not talking—now I get it!
M: What?
A: You two are really in love, aren't you?
M: Oh… well… I don't know… I mean… I suppose we… well, yes.
A: Miyuki, that's wonderful! And just think—I introduced you.
M: Yes! Thank you!
T: Anna, have you decided about your bowl?
A: Uh… not yet, *sensei*. It's a tough decision.
T: Miyuki-*san*, your coil pot is excellent.
M: Thank you, *sensei*.
A: Teacher's pet.

アナ：……そしてこういう風に粘土を上に引き上げるの。
ミユキ：ロクロは難しそう。私はまず基本的なテクニックから習ったほうがいいみたい。
アナ：そうね。急ぐことはないわ。
ミユキ：この手びねりのつぼ、これでいいのかしら。
アナ：どれどれ……そう、うまいわ。
先生：ミユキさん、とてもいいわよ。アナさん、あなたは何を作ってるの。
アナ：えっと、ボウルだと思うんですけど。
先生：私もそうだと思うわ。でもあなたはこのボウルに何を入れるつもり？　イメージはある？
アナ：なんとなく。
先生：「なんとなく」だけ？　だから形がはっきりしないのよ。
アナ：でも……形は気に入っているんです、先生。
先生：器の形と目的は一体でなければいけないの。そうすれば美しいボウルになるわよ。
アナ：つまり何を入れるかわからなければ、美しくならないということですか。
先生：必ずしもそういう意味ではないわ。考えてみて。後で戻ります。
アナ：もーっ！　彼女にはときどきイラつくのよね。
ミユキ：アナ、私はそのボウルいいと思うけど。
アナ：ありがとう、ミユキ。それで……リチャードとはどうなってるの。
ミユキ：リチャード？　えーと……あなたは自分のボウルのほうに集中したほうがいいわよ。
アナ：教えてくれないと、集中できないわよ。
ミユキ：でも……そんなにおもしろいことじゃないわよ。
アナ：ミユキ、アメリカの女性は友だちには何でも話すのよ、どうでもいいことも。
ミユキ：でも……なんだか変な感じ。リチャードはあなたの友だちだし。
アナ：心配しないで。リチャードはいつも私やレナに……
ミユキ：大丈夫、彼がほかの人たちと付き合ってたのは知ってるから。それで、彼は私たちのことをあなたに話したの？
アナ：いいえ。ちょっと待って。リチャードも話してない……あなたも話してない……これでわかった。
ミユキ：何を？
アナ：あなたたちふたりって真剣に付き合ってるのね。
ミユキ：えっと、まあ、わからない、つまり、そうだと思う、そうね。
アナ：ミユキ、よかったじゃない。考えてみて、私があなたを紹介したのよ。
ミユキ：そうよ。ありがとう。
先生：アナ、ボウルのことは考えた？
アナ：あ、まだです、先生。むずかしい決断です。
先生：ミユキさん、あなたの手びねりのつぼはすばらしいわ。
ミユキ：ありがとうございます、先生。
アナ：先生のお気に入りね。

Chapter 6
September

Exercises

Part A Track 13

①リスニング、②パラレル・リーディング(音を聞きながらテキストを音読)、③プロソディ・シャドーイング (音の再現) ④コンテンツ・シャドーイング (意味を意識)の順で会話を再現してみましょう。下記の Key Phrases を意識しながら、最低でも7回は会話を聞いてみましょう。

Key Phrases:
- That's a good idea.
- There's no hurry.
- -That's great! -Very good!
- Sort of.
- That's the reason…
- That's not exactly what I mean.
- She makes me crazy sometimes.
- So tell me…
- Maybe you should concentrate on…
- Well, it isn't so interesting.
- Now I get it!

Part B

相手の問いかけに自分なりの答えを考えてみましょう。

1) **Heather:** How are things going in your new job?
   You: _____

2) **Heather:** Have you decided about your trip to England?
   You: _____

3) **Heather:** I think I should go back to school. What do you think?
   You: _____

今度は相手の応答にふさわしい質問や語りかけをしてみましょう。

4) 「調子はどう？」という一般的な言い方は？
   You: _____
   Heather: Oh, things could be better.

5) 相手にもう決めたかどうかをたずねてみましょう。
   You: _____
   Heather: Not yet. It's a tough decision.

6) 「ちょっと考えてみたい」といってみましょう。
   You: _____
   Heather: That's a good idea. There's no hurry.

Exercises の解答例と訳

1) Everything's going well, thank you. / I find it interesting. / I like my boss.
2) Yes, I'm leaving next month. / No, not yet.
3) I think that's a great idea!
4) How are things going?
5) Have you decided yet?
6) I think I'd like some time to think. / I'd like to take my time.

問題と答えの訳

1) ヘザー：新しい仕事はどうですか。
   あなた：何もかも順調ですよ、ありがとう。／面白いです。／上司が好きです。
2) ヘザー：イギリス旅行については決まりましたか。
   あなた：はい、来月に出発します。／いいえ、まだです。
3) ヘザー：私は学校に戻ったほうがいいと思います。あなたはどう思いますか。
   あなた：いいアイデアですね！
4) あなた：調子はどうですか。
   ヘザー：ああ、イマイチです。
5) あなた：もう決めましたか。
   ヘザー：まだです。難しい決断ですので。
6) あなた：もう少し考える時間が必要だと思います。／時間をかけたいです。
   ヘザー：いいですね。急ぎませんよ。

コラム　先生の呼び方

日本では先生を呼ぶときに、「先生」あるいは「○○先生」というのが普通ですが、英語では "Teacher" とか "Teacher Smith" などということはありません。逆にこのような呼び方をすると失礼になります。英語の teacher には、日本語の「先生」のように敬称としての意味がないからです。

しかし、「○○教授」という場合には、professor ということばが、日本の「教授」と同じような感覚で使われ、"Professor Smith" または "Doctor Smith" といいます。むろ教授クラスの人に "Mr. Smith" というと失礼に聞こえてしまいます。

小学校から高校までは、Mr. / Ms. Smith のように名前の前に Mr. か Ms. をつけて先生を呼ぶのが普通です。また、欧米では一般的に大学生以上の大人の場合には、先生と生徒が対等な立場であるという認識が強く、趣味や習い事の先生など年がそれほど離れていない場合には、first name で呼ぶことも珍しくありません。

Chapter 6 の 重要表現リスト

Skit A

- [ ] **This morning we have a special guest speaker.** 今朝私たちは特別ゲストスピーカーをお迎えしています
- [ ] ***It is my great honor to present...** ～さんをご紹介できることを光栄に思います
- [ ] ***This morning we are very fortunate to have... with us.** 今朝大変幸いなことに～さんをお迎えしています
- [ ] ***It is a great honor to be here today.** 本日こちらにうかがうことできて光栄です
- [ ] ***Thank you for having me here today.** 本日はお招きいただきありがとうございます
- [ ] ***How did you like...?** ～をどう思いましたか?
- [ ] **Good question.** いいことに気づいたね
- [ ] **Settle down.** 静かに
- [ ] ***May I have your attention, please?** みなさん、ご注目をお願いいたします
- [ ] **Hi, everyone.** みなさん、こんにちは
- [ ] **I'm sorry, I'm a little nervous speaking in English.** 英語で話すのに少し緊張しています
- [ ] ***I'm nervous speaking in front of people.** 人の前で話すのに緊張しています
- [ ] **I'd like to tell you about...** ～について話したい
- [ ] **This may surprise you, but...** これを聞くと驚くかもしれませんが
- [ ] **Can anyone tell me...?** 誰か～をいってくれる人はいますか
- [ ] **For example, one day...** たとえばある日～
- [ ] **Here is a photo of...** ここに～の写真があります
- [ ] **Thank you for listening.** 聞いてくださってありがとうございました
- [ ] ***wrap up a talk** 話を終わらせる
- [ ] ***To wrap up my talk...** まとめると～
- [ ] **Are there any questions?** 質問はありませんか

Skit B

- [ ] **That's a good idea.** いい考えね
- [ ] **There's no hurry.** 急ぐことはないわ
- [ ] **・That's great!** うまいわ
      ・Very good! とてもいい
- [ ] ***・Wonderful! ・You are doing ・Great! ・Excellent! ・Brilliant!** すばらしい
- [ ] **in mind** 心の中に
- [ ] **Sort of.** まあなんとなく
- [ ] ***Kind of.** まあなんとなく
- [ ] **That is the reason...** それが～である理由です
- [ ] **Do you mean...?** ～ということですか
- [ ] **That's not exactly what I mean.** そういうわけではありません
- [ ] **She makes me crazy sometimes.** 彼女にはときどきイライラする
- [ ] ***She drives me crazy.** 私は彼女に夢中だ
- [ ] **So tell me...** ところで (それで)
- [ ] **How are things going with...?** ～に関してはどうなっているの?
- [ ] **Maybe you should concentrate on...** ～に集中したほうがよい
- [ ] **Well, it isn't so interesting.** そんなに面白い話ではない
- [ ] ***I really don't want to talk about it.** それについては本当に話したくないの
- [ ] ***I'd rather not talk about it. Sorry.** それについては話したくないの。ごめんなさい
- [ ] ***Mind your own business.** 放っておいて
- [ ] **boring stuff** つまらないこと
- [ ] **Now I get it!** そういうことか
- [ ] **Just think...** 考えてもみて
- [ ] **It's a tough decision.** 難しい判断だ
- [ ] **teacher's pet** 先生のお気に入り

Chapter 7
October

Skit A	
場面・状況	ミユキの両親がオーストラリアを旅行する
表現のテーマ	旅行などで使える、覚えておくと便利なことば
Skit B	
場面・状況	ふた組のペアが箱根の温泉に行く
表現のテーマ	感動を表す／意見を述べる

Chapter 7 October

Skit A

ストーリーについて

　10月、春の訪れを感じます……というのは南半球のお話。ミユキの両親ヒロシとマサコは、オーストラリア旅行の最初の滞在先であるシドニーに到着しました。彼らのために飛行機、ホテル、ツアーを手配したのはミユキです。様々な役立つ情報も事前に伝えました。でも旅というのは予期せぬことが起こるもの。ツカザワ夫婦の日本での英語の先生はアメリカ人でした。そのため、この旅で彼らはオーストラリア英語の壁に直面します。

ここで扱う表現について

　イギリス英語、アメリカ英語、オーストラリア英語、それぞれに独特な発音や表現があります。今回は、ミユキの両親がオーストラリアで、それまで知っていた発音とのちがいに戸惑っていますね。

　チェックインの際に、May I have your name, please?(お名前をいただけますか) と聞かれ、name が nine に聞こえてしまっています。ヒロシは Pardon me? と聞き返していますが、r の発音が難しかったら、Excuse me? としても差し支えありません。また、Can you repeat that, please? (もう一度いっていただけますか) といえばていねいです。

　wildlife reserve (自然保護地域) を訪問するふたり。コアラを見て How exciting! や They are big! と感想をいったり、Are they sleeping? What was that? とガイドに質問したりしていますね。黙って見ているよりも、思っていることを口に出したほうが周りと交流が生まれていいでしょう。感動したときには、This is such a beautiful place! (ここはなんて美しいところでしょう)、I'll never forget this day. (私はこの日を決して忘れないわ) などといえます。ホテルやツアー、レストランなどで予約を確認する We have a reservation. はフレーズとして覚えておきましょう。例えば2泊の宿泊の場合は、We have a reservation for two nights.、レストランにて7時に2名の予約の場合は We have a reservation for two people at seven o'clock. と、応用がききます。予約をしたい場合には、I'd like to make a reservation... といいます。

Chapter 7 October

Skit A

Track 14

熟年夫婦、オーストラリアを旅する

Hiroshi: Uh… hello. **We want to… check in.**
Front desk clerk: Certainly. May I have your name, please?
H: Sorry… nine what?
FDC: Uh… may I see your passport?
H: Oh, yes. Here you are.
FDC: Thank you. Yes, I have your reservation. Three nights?
H: Pardon me?
Masako: Yes, we will stay three nights. **Sorry… it's our first trip outside Japan.**
FDC: **No worries!** Uh… *O-namae to go-jusho o kaite kudasai.*
H: Pardon? Ah! Name and address! OK!

2日後、シドニー近くの野生動物保護公園で……

Guide: Take a look in that tree, everyone.
M: Oh! Koalas! **How exciting!**

May I have your name, please?: お名前をいただけますか
Certainly.: 承知しました
Here you are.: どうぞ
reservation: 予約
Pardon me?: 何ていいましたか？
No worries.: （オーストラリア英語）心配しないで
Pardon?: 何ですか？
take a look: 見る
How exciting!: わくわくする！

H: They are big! Are they sleeping?
G: Yes, koalas sleep about 16 hours a day.
H: What was that?
G: Kangaroos, I reckon. Let's go and see.
M: Oh! Please wait! A koala woke up!

2日後、アデレードのホテルで……

M: Hello. We have a reservation on the… two-day wine country tour. The name is Tsukazawa—T-S-U—
Receptionist: Yes, I have your name here. The tour bus leaves Wednesday morning at nine o'clock.
H: Uh… we will take a train to Melbourne Friday morning. **Will it be… all right?**
R: Well… **I cannot promise** you'll be back here by Thursday.
M: Um… **what do you mean?**
R: The scenery is beautiful and the wines are delicious. You may not want to come back.

夫妻はメルボルンに到着、駅の近くで夕食をとることにしました。この時点で、もうオーストラリア人の親しみやすい雰囲気に慣れ、オーストラリア特有の表現も少し使えるようになってきました。

Server: Can I get you dessert, or coffee or tea?
M: Not for me, thank you.
H: I would like a… short black, please.
S: Certainly. **Here's your coffee… and your bill.** Take your time.
H: I'll give you my credit card. Oh… I reckon I left my wallet on the train.
S: Oh, no!
H: Well… I will call the train company—and the credit card company.
M: Yes. No worries.
S: Are you sure you're not Australian?

---

reckon: 推測する、思う（オーストラリアでよく使われる表現）

Can I get you...?: 〜をお持ちしましょうか？
short black: エスプレッソ（espressoのオーストラリア的表現）

wallet: 財布

Chapter 7 October Skit A

ポイント解説

ミユキの両親が旅行でオーストラリアを訪れます。ホテルでチェックインするときの決まり文句のほか、「海外ははじめて」「どういう意味ですか?」などの表現は覚えておくといざ困ったときに役立ちます。

We want to check in.
もちろんこれでも十分伝わるが、もっと丁寧な表現 We would like to check in. でもいい。最後に please をつければさらにきちんとした印象に。

Sorry... it's our first trip outside Japan.
言語や文化のちがいに戸惑ったら、素直に「海外ははじめてなので」と断っておくとたいていは親切に対応してもらえる。It's our first trip to Australia. (オーストラリアは初めてなので)といってもよい。

No worries!
No worries! はオーストラリア特有の言い方。「心配しないで」は、Don't worry (about it). や No problem. もよく使われる。

How exciting!
How sweet!(何てすてきなの!)、How wonderful!(すばらしい!)など、How...! は感情表現にとても便利。

Hiroshi: Uh... hello. **We want to... check in.**
Front desk clerk: Certainly. May I have your name, please?
H: Sorry... nine what?
FDC: Uh... may I see your passport?
H: Oh, yes. Here you are.
FDC: Thank you. Yes, I have your reservation. Three nights?
H: Pardon me?
Masako: Yes, we will stay three nights. **Sorry... it's our first trip outside Japan.**
FDC: No worries! Uh... *O-namae to go-jusho o kaite kudasai.*
H: Pardon? Ah! Name and address! OK!

Guide: Take a look in that tree, everyone.
M: Oh! Koalas! **How exciting!**
H: They are big! Are they sleeping?
G: Yes, koalas sleep about 16 hours a day.
H: What was that?
G: Kangaroos, I reckon. Let's go and see.
M: Oh! Please wait! A koala woke up!

M: Hello. We have a reservation on the... two-day wine country

tour. The name is Tsukazawa—T-S-U—
Receptionist: Yes, I have your name here. The tour bus leaves Wednesday morning at nine o'clock.
H: Uh… we will take a train to Melbourne Friday morning. **Will it be… all right?**
R: Well… **I cannot promise** you'll be back here by Thursday.
M: Um… **what do you mean?**
R: The scenery is beautiful and the wines are delicious. You may not want to come back.

Server: Can I get you dessert, or coffee or tea?
M: Not for me, thank you.
H: I would like a… short black, please.
S: Certainly. **Here's your coffee… and your bill.** Take your time.
H: I'll give you my credit card. Oh… I reckon I left my wallet on the train.
S: Oh, no!
H: Well… I will call the train company—and the credit card company.
M: Yes. No worries.
S: Are you sure you're not Australian?

Will it be all right?
「(このような条件でも)大丈夫ですか?」という言い回し。

I cannot promise…
「……のお約束はできません」。I can't guarantee….(……の保証はできません)も同じ。

What do you mean?
わからないこと、はっきりしないことはこのようにとしっかり説明を求めるべき。大切なことは文書に残してもらうといい。

Not for me, thank you.
スマートで失礼のない断り方。他に No, I'm okay, thank you. や No, I'm fine, thank you. など。

Here's your coffee… and your bill.
欧米のレストランではテーブルでの支払いが主。こちらがいわないと請求書がこない場合も多いため、会計を頼むには、Could we have the bill, please? という。The bill, please. / (The) Check, please. (おもにアメリカで使われる)でも大丈夫。

Hiroshi: Uh… hello. We want to… check in.
Front desk clerk: Certainly. May I have your name, please?
H: Sorry… nine what?
FDC: Uh… may I see your passport?
H: Oh, yes. Here you are.
FDC: Thank you. Yes, I have your reservation. Three nights?
H: Pardon me?
Masako: Yes, we will stay three nights. Sorry…it's our first trip outside Japan.
FDC: No worries! Uh… *O-namae to go-jusho o kaite kudasai.*
H: Pardon? Ah! Name and address! OK!

Guide: Take a look in that tree, everyone.
M: Oh! Koalas! How exciting!
H: They are big! Are they sleeping?
G: Yes, koalas sleep about 16 hours a day.
H: What was that?
G: Kangaroos, I reckon. Let's go and see.
M: Oh! Please wait! A koala woke up!

M: Hello. We have a reservation on the… two-day wine country tour. The name is Tsukazawa—T-S-U—
Receptionist: Yes, I have your name here. The tour bus leaves Wednesday morning at nine o'clock.
H: Uh… we will take a train to Melbourne Friday morning. Will it be… all right?
R: Well… I cannot promise you'll be back here by Thursday.
M: Um… what do you mean?
R: The scenery is beautiful and the wines are delicious. You may not want to come back.

Server: Can I get you dessert, or coffee or tea?
M: Not for me, thank you.
H: I would like a… short black, please.
S: Certainly. Here's your coffee… and your bill. Take your time.
H: I'll give you my credit card. Oh… I reckon I left my wallet on the train.
S: Oh, no!
H: Well… I will call the train company—and the credit card company.
M: Yes. No worries.
S: Are you sure you're not Australian?

訳

ヒロシ：えー……ハロー。チェックイン……したいのですが。
フロント：もちろんです。「ネーム（お名前）」をいただけますか。
ヒロシ：すいません……「ナイン（9）」何ですか。
フロント：えーと……パスポートを拝見させていただけますか。
ヒロシ：ああ、はい。どうぞ。
フロント：ありがとうございます。はい、ご予約いただいております。3泊ですね。
ヒロシ：何ですか？
マサコ：はい、私たちは3泊します。ごめんなさい……国外の旅は初めてなので。
フロント：ご心配なく！　えー……オナマエトゴジュウショヲカイテクダサイ。
ヒロシ：何ですか。ああ。名前と住所だね。OK！

ガイド：みなさん、あの木の中を見てください。
マサコ：まあ。コアラだわ。わくわくするわね。
ヒロシ：大きいねえ。寝てるのかな。
ガイド：はい、コアラは1日16時間ほど睡眠をとります。
ヒロシ：いまのは何でしたか。
ガイド：カンガルー、だと思います。行って見てみましょう。
マサコ：あ。待って。コアラが起きたわ。

マサコ：ハロー。2日間ワイン地方の旅……に予約をしているのですが。名前はツカザワ、T、S、U……
受付係：はい、こちらにお名前をいただいております。ツアーのバスは水曜日の朝9時に出発します。
ヒロシ：えーと……金曜日の朝にメルボルン行きの電車に乗らなくてはならないのですが、それは……大丈夫ですか。
受付係：そうですね……木曜日までにお戻りになれるかどうかはお約束できません。
マサコ：えーと……それはどういうことです？
受付係：景色は美しいですし、ワインはおいしいです。お戻りになりたくなくなるかもしれません。

ウェイトレス：デザート、コーヒーまたはお紅茶をお持ちしましょうか。
マサコ：私は結構です、ありがとう。
ヒロシ：私は……エスプレッソをお願いします。
ウェイトレス：かしこまりました。コーヒーと……請求書になります。ごゆっくり。
ヒロシ：クレジットカードでお願いします。あ……電車に財布を忘れてきてしまったみたいだ。
ウェイトレス：ああ、それはお気の毒に。
ヒロシ：まぁ、電車会社とクレジットカード会社に電話すればいいですから。
マサコ：そうね。心配ないわね。
ウェイトレス：あなた方は本当にオーストラリア人ではないのですか？

Chapter 7
October

Exercises

Part A Track 14

①リスニング、②パラレル・リーディング(音を聞きながらテキストを音読)、③プロソディ・シャドーイング（音の再現）④コンテンツ・シャドーイング（意味を意識）の順で会話を再現してみましょう。下記の Key Phrases を意識しながら、最低でも7回は会話を聞いてみましょう。

Key Phrases:
- We want to check in.
- Sorry… it's our first trip outside Japan.
- No worries! (=Don't worry.)
- How exciting!
- Will it be all right?
- I can't promise…
- What do you mean?
- Not for me, thank you.
- Here's your coffee… and your bill.

Part B
相手の問いかけや語りかけに対して自分なりの答えを考えてみましょう。

1) **Restaurant employee:** May I have your name, please?
   You: _____

2) **Immigration officer:** May I see your passport?
   You: _____

3) **George:** I just learned that my wife is pregnant. The baby is due next June.
   You: _____

今度は相手に質問してみましょう。

4) 相手の名前を聞いてみましょう。
   You: _____
   George: My name is George Cunningham.

5) 相手の意向をていねいにたずねてみましょう。
   You: _____ if I stayed a bit longer?
   George: No problem. Stay as long as you like.

6) 相手に「コーヒーのおかわりを持ってきましょうか」とたずねてみましょう。
   You: _____
   George: Not for me, thank you. I'm cutting down on caffeine.

Exercisesの解答例と訳

1) Yes, my last name is Tanaka.
2) Yes. Here you are.
3) How exciting! Congratulations!
4) May I ask your name, please?
5) Would it be all right
6) Can I get you more coffee?

問題と答えの訳

1) レストランの店員：お名前を伺ってもよろしいですか。
   あなた：はい、名字は田中です。
2) 入国審査官：パスポートを拝見してもよろしいですか。
   あなた：はい。どうぞ。
3) ジョージ：妻が妊娠したって聞いたところなんです。出産予定日は6月です。
   あなた：それはすごいですね！　おめでとうございます！
4) あなた：お名前を伺ってもよろしいですか。
   ジョージ：私の名前はジョージ・カニングハムです。
5) あなた：もう少しいてもいいですか。
   ジョージ：いいですよ。好きなだけいてください。
6) あなた：コーヒーのおかわりはいかがですか。
   ジョージ：私はいいです、ありがとう。カフェインを控えているので。

コラム　さまざまな英語

ネイティブスピーカーが話す英語にも、国によってちがいがあります。例えば、アメリカ英語とイギリス英語では、訛りだけでなくスペリングも微妙にちがいます。代表的なものには単語の語尾のちがい、erとre (center [米] /centre [英])、orとour (color [米] / colour [英])、zとs (realize [米] / realise [英]) などがあります。

カナダ英語はアメリカ英語に似ており、アメリカ人でもいわれなければ相手がカナダ人だとわからないこともよくありますが、スペリングのほうはイギリス英語の綴りが混じっています。

イギリス英語とオーストラリア英語の訛りは似ているといわれていますが、オーストラリア訛りの最大の特徴は二重母音のa [エィ] を [アィ] と発音するところでしょう。例えば、nameは [ナィム] と発音されるので、スキットでもあったように、nineと似たような音に聞こえますし、payの発音は [パィ] なので、pieのように聞こえます。しかし、ちがいは発音だけではありません。たとえばオーストラリア英語の "No worries." (かまわないよ) のように、それぞれの国に独特の単語やイディオムがあります。

Chapter 7 October

Skit B

ストーリーについて

　北半球では秋の到来です。ミユキとリチャード、ジョーとアナは箱根の温泉に行くことになりました。ちょうどエミリーはこの週末、友だちの家にお泊まりすることになったので、大人だけの会話を楽しむいいチャンスとなりそうです。温泉につかって開放的になると、会話の内容も深まるものです。

ここで扱う表現について

　箱根に温泉旅行に行くアナとジョー、ミユキとリチャードのふた組のカップル。「ロマンスカー」という名称を疑問に思うアナに対し、ミユキが I think it's because…（……という理由だと思う）と説明を始めます。提供する情報に確たる自信があるのであれば、It's because… と始めてもいいのですが、そうでない場合は私的な意見として、ということで I think などを加えたほうがいいでしょう。I think のほかにも、I guess… や I suppose… も使えます。

　リチャードが Any train Miyuki and I are on is a romance car.（ミユキと僕が乗っていれば、どんな列車でもロマンス・カーさ）といっていますね。日本人だったら照れてしまってまずいわないようなセリフですが、きっと場を和ませるためのひとことでしょう。

　それぞれ温泉につかって、Ah, this is great.（ああ、こりゃあいい）、Fantastic!（すばらしい！）、Ah, this water is wonderful.（ああ、このお湯は最高だわ）と感想を述べていますね。This is so relaxing.（ここはとてもくつろげる）、I feel really refreshed.（気分がさっぱりした）などともいえそうですね。このほか、The temperature is perfect.（湯加減は完璧）、逆に熱すぎるときには、The water is too hot for me. などといいます。ジョーとリチャードの男同士の会話で、リチャードが There's just one thing.（ひとつだけ気になることがある）と少し戸惑いを隠せない様子。ミユキが気持ちをオープンに話してくれない、というのです。それに対しジョーは、I thought…, Maybe it's… と自分の見解を述べています。日本人女性の奥ゆかしさは、ちょっとわかりづらいのでしょうか。

Chapter 7 October

Skit B

Track 15

温泉、サイコー！

朝の新宿駅

Anna: **Why is it called** a Romance Car?
Miyuki: **I think it's because** Hakone is a romantic place.
Richard: Any train Miyuki and I are on is a romance car.
A: Aww… how romantic!
Joe: Hey, we're romantic, too… aren't we?
A: **Well… I suppose…in a way… sometimes.** Oh! Joe!
M and R: Aww… how romantic!

午後、箱根の旅館の男湯

R: Ah, this is great—the outdoor bath, the leaves changing color… fantastic! Miyuki found a good place.
J: You two seem to be getting along pretty well.
R: **There's just one thing.** She doesn't really like to talk about her feelings.
J: I thought all women liked to talk about their

How romantic!:
何てロマンチックなんだろう！
in a way:
ある意味では

outdoor bath
露天風呂
fantastic:
すばらしい
get along:
うまくいく、ウマが合う
pretty well:
かなりよく

feelings. Maybe it's hard to explain in English.
R: Hmm… Know any good Japanese teachers?

一方女湯では

M: Anna, you know the system, don't you? **First** you wash yourself**, then** you go in the bath.
A: Right. Um… are there many people out there?
M: Just a few. I didn't know you were shy about *onsen*s.
A: Well… a little. But once I'm in the water, I'm OK.

そして……

M: Ah, this water is wonderful.
A: Yes. So… you and Richard seem happy.
M: Mm-hm. **But… one thing bothers me.** Richard always asks me about my feelings.
A: Is that bad? I wish Joe would ask me more often.
M: Well, sometimes I want to keep my feelings… in the water. **Do you know what I mean?**
A: I'm not sure. Can you explain?
M: I want him to… understand how I feel… even if I don't tell him. **I mean**… people can see under the water if they try.
A: Uh… where's my towel?
M: Anna, don't worry—nobody is trying!

その夜の夕食で……

J, A, M, R: *Kampai*! Cheers!
A: Everything looks so delicious. By the way, how was the *onsen*, you two?
J: Great! The water was perfect, the view was superb, and the conversation was fascinating.
A: Really? So was ours.
J: Oh, yeah? What did you talk about?
M: You know, I'm starving!
R: Yeah, let's eat!

---

out there:
ここでは内風呂ではなく露天風呂をイメージしている

Once…, I'm OK.:
一度〜してしまえば大丈夫

bother: 悩ます

I wish… would…
〜だったらいいのに

Cheers!: 乾杯！

The water was perfect.:
湯加減は完璧
The view was superb.:
景色はすばらしい
fascinating:
興味をそそる
So was ours.:
私たちもよ
You know: ねえ
starving: 空腹だ

ポイント解説

Chapter 7 October Skit B

ミユキとリチャード、ジョーとアナの4人が箱根にやってきました。ここでは順序立てて説明するとき、別の言葉でいうとき、自分の気持ちが相手に伝わっているか確認するときなどの表現が出てきます。

Why is it called…?
「なぜこれは……と呼ばれているのですか？」と名称の由来をたずねる質問。

I think it's because…
「それは……だからだと思う」。提供する情報に確信がなければ、このように I think、I guess、I suppose などを付け加えればよい。

Well… I suppose… in a way… sometimes
「まあ、っていうか、ある意味、たまには」などと、返答に困っている様子を表すフレーズのオンパレード。

There's just one thing.
たいていのことは大丈夫だが「ただひとつだけ問題がある」というときのフレーズ。

First…, then…
何かの使い方、やり方を説明するとき、段階が多いときは First（まず）…, second（第2に）…と続き、最後に finally…となる。

Anna: **Why is it called** a Romance Car?

Miyuki: **I think it's because** Hakone is a romantic place.

Richard: Any train Miyuki and I are on is a romance car.

A: Aww… how romantic!

Joe: Hey, we're romantic, too… aren't we?

A: **Well… I suppose…in a way… sometimes.** Oh! Joe!

M and R: Aww… how romantic!

R: Ah, this is great—the outdoor bath, the leaves changing color… fantastic! Miyuki found a good place.

J: You two seem to be getting along pretty well.

R: **There's just one thing.** She doesn't really like to talk about her feelings.

J: I thought all women liked to talk about their feelings. Maybe it's hard to explain in English.

R: Hmm… Know any good Japanese teachers?

M: Anna, you know the system, don't you? **First** you wash yourself**, then** you go in the bath.

A: Right. Um… are there many people out there?

M: Just a few. I didn't know you

were shy about *onsen*s.
A: Well… a little. But once I'm in the water, I'm OK.

M: Ah, this water is wonderful.
A: Yes. So… you and Richard seem happy.
M: Mm-hm. **But… one thing bothers me.** Richard always asks me about my feelings.
A: Is that bad? I wish Joe would ask me more often.
M: Well, sometimes I want to keep my feelings… in the water. **Do you know what I mean?**
A: I'm not sure. Can you explain?
M: I want him to… understand how I feel… even if I don't tell him. **I mean**… people can see under the water if they try.
A: Uh… where's my towel?
M: Anna, don't worry—nobody is trying!

J, A, M, R: *Kampai*! Cheers!
A: Everything looks so delicious. By the way, how was the *onsen*, you two?
J: Great! The water was perfect, the view was superb, and the conversation was fascinating.
A: Really? So was ours.
J: Oh, yeah? What did you talk about?
M: You know, I'm starving!
R: Yeah, let's eat!

But one thing bothers me.

bother は「気にする」という意味。Don't bother me.（放っておいて）などよく使われる動詞。One thing bothers me. は There is just one thing. のように「ひとつ気になることがある」ということ。

Do you know what I mean?

くだけた You know what I mean?（いってる意味、わかるでしょう?）同様、会話中のあいづちでとてもよく使われる。

I'm not sure. Can you explain?

Do you know what I mean? といわれても、よく理解できないときは、No, I don't.（いいえ）とストレートに返すよりも、I'm not sure. といったほうがやわらかい印象になる。理解しきれないときは、そのままにせず、Do you mean…?（……ということですか?）などといって、言い方を変えて説明してもらおう。

I mean…

「っていうか」、「つまり」というニュアンス。自分がいいたいことを言い換えたり、まとめたりするときの前置きになることばで、これも会話でよく使われる。

Anna: Why is it called a Romance Car?
Miyuki: I think it's because Hakone is a romantic place.
Richard: Any train Miyuki and I are on is a romance car.
A: Aww… how romantic!
Joe: Hey, we're romantic, too… aren't we?
A: Well… I suppose…in a way… sometimes. Oh! Joe!
M and R: Aww… how romantic!

R: Ah, this is great—the outdoor bath, the leaves changing color… fantastic! Miyuki found a good place.
J: You two seem to be getting along pretty well.
R: There's just one thing. She doesn't really like to talk about her feelings.
J: I thought all women liked to talk about their feelings. Maybe it's hard to explain in English.
R: Hmm… Know any good Japanese teachers?

M: Anna, you know the system, don't you? First you wash yourself, then you go in the bath.
A: Right. Um… are there many people out there?
M: Just a few. I didn't know you were shy about *onsen*s.
A: Well… a little. But once I'm in the water, I'm OK.

M: Ah, this water is wonderful.
A: Yes. So… you and Richard seem happy.
M: Mm-hm. But… one thing bothers me. Richard always asks me about my feelings.
A: Is that bad? I wish Joe would ask me more often.
M: Well, sometimes I want to keep my feelings… in the water. Do you know what I mean?
A: I'm not sure. Can you explain?
M: I want him to… understand how I feel… even if I don't tell him. I mean… people can see under the water if they try.
A: Uh… where's my towel?
M: Anna, don't worry—nobody is trying!

J, A, M, R: *Kampai*! Cheers!
A: Everything looks so delicious. By the way, how was the *onsen*, you two?
J: Great! The water was perfect, the view was superb, and the conversation was fascinating.
A: Really? So was ours.
J: Oh, yeah? What did you talk about?
M: You know, I'm starving!
R: Yeah, let's eat!

訳

アナ: なんでロマンスカーっていうのかしら。
ミユキ: 箱根がロマンチックな場所だからだと思うけど。
リチャード: ミユキと僕が乗っていれば、どんな電車だってロマンスカーだよ。
アナ: あらー……なんてロマンチック。
ジョー: おい、俺たちだってロマンチック、だろ？
アナ: まあ……ある意味……たまには……だと思うけど。もう！　ジョーったら。
ミユキとリチャード: オー……なんてロマンチック。

リチャード: ああ、こりゃあいい、露天風呂に紅葉に……すばらしい。ミユキはいい所を見つけたな。
ジョー: 君たちふたりはなかなかうまくやってるみたいじゃないか。
リチャード: でも一点だけ。彼女は自分の気持ちをあまり話したがらないんだ。
ジョー: 女性はみんな自分の気持ちを話したがるものだと思ってたけどな。英語で説明するのが難しいのかもしれない。
リチャード: んー……誰かいい日本語の先生を知らない？

ミユキ: アナ、お風呂の入り方はわかってるわよね。まず体を洗って、それから湯船に入る。
アナ: わかったわ。えーと……人はいっぱいいるかしら？
ミユキ: 少しだけ。あなたが温泉で恥ずかしがるなんて知らなかったわ。
アナ: まあ……少しだけ。でも一度お湯に入っちゃえば大丈夫。

ミユキ: ああ、このお湯はサイコー。
アナ: そうね。それで……あなたとリチャードは幸せそうね。
ミユキ: まあね。でも……ひとつ気になることが。リチャードはいつも私の気持ちを聞いてくるの。
アナ: それって悪いの？　私はジョーはもっと聞いてくれればいいと思ってるけど。
ミユキ: というか、自分の思いはしまっておきたいときもあるの……お湯の中にでも。いっている意味わかる？
アナ: よくわからないわ。説明してくれる？
ミユキ: 私がどう感じているか……彼にわかってほしいの……口に出さなくても。やろうと思えば、水の中も見れるものでしょ。
アナ: えーと……私のタオルはどこ？
ミユキ: アナ、心配しないで、誰も実際にやろうとしてないから。

全員: カンパイ！　チアーズ！
アナ: どれもおいしそう。ところで、そちらのおふたりは、温泉はどうだったの？
ジョー: すごくよかった。お湯は完璧、眺めは最高、それにおもしろい話題。
アナ: そう。私たちもよ。
ジョー: ああ、そう。何を話したの？
ミユキ: ねえ、お腹減った！
リチャード: そうだ、さあ食べよう。

Chapter 7
October

Exercises

Part A Track 15

①リスニング、②パラレル・リーディング(音を聞きながらテキストを音読)、③プロソディ・シャドーイング（音の再現）④コンテンツ・シャドーイング（意味を意識）の順で会話を再現してみましょう。下記の Key Phrases を意識しながら、最低でも７回は会話を聞いてみましょう。

Key Phrases:
- Why is it called…?
- I think it's because…
- Well… I suppose… in a way… sometimes.
- There's just one thing.
- First…, then…
- But one thing bothers me.
- Do you know what I mean?
- I'm not sure.
- Can you explain?
- I mean…

Part B

相手の質問や語りかけに対して自分なりの答えを考えてみましょう。

1) **Helen:** Why is it called "karaoke"?
   You: Well, _____

2) **Helen:** I made roast turkey and all the fixings. I hope you like it.
   You: _____

3) **Helen:** How did you like the book?
   You: _____

今度は相手に質問してみましょう。

4) 「サンドイッチ」という語の由来をたずねてみましょう。
   You: _____
   Helen: I think it's because the Earl of Sandwich invented it.

5) ディナーはどうだったか、たずねてみましょう。
   You: _____
   Helen: It was great! Everything was delicious. Thank you.

6) 温泉はどうだったか、たずねてみましょう。
   You: _____
   Helen: I thought the water was just right. I would love to go again.

Exercises の解答例と訳

1) "*kara*" means "empty" and "*oke*" means "orchestra."
2) Wow! Everything looks delicious!
3) It was great! The story was fascinating.
4) Why is it called a sandwich?
5) How did you like your dinner?
6) How did you like the *onsen*?

問題と答えの訳

1) ヘレン：なぜ「カラオケ」と呼ぶのですか。
   あなた：ええと、「カラ」が「空っぽ」で、「オケ」が「オーケストラ」を意味しているからですよ。
2) ヘレン：ローストターキーとサイドメニューも全部私が作ったんですよ。お口にあうといいんだけど。
   あなた：わあ。みんなおいしそう！
3) ヘレン：本はどうでしたか。
   あなた：すごくよかった！　話がおもしろかったよ。
4) あなた：なぜサンドウィッチと呼ぶのですか。
   ヘレン：サンドウィッチ伯爵が発明したからだと思います。
5) あなた：ディナーはどうでしたか。
   ヘレン：最高です。全部おいしかったです。ありがとう。
6) あなた：温泉はどうでしたか。
   ヘレン：湯加減がちょうど良かったと思います。ぜひもう一度行きたいです。

コラム

愛情の表し方

日本人には hug（抱擁）する習慣がありませんが、欧米の人はあらゆる場面で hug をします。しばらく会ってなかった人と再会したときや、別れるとき、泣いている人を慰めるときや、うれしいニュースがあったときなど、hug をするのが生活の一部のようになっています。

英語ではよく Give me a hug. といいますが、日本語で「抱擁して」とか「抱きしめて」などということはほとんどないでしょう。日本でも、まだ抱っこが必要な小さい子どもには hug をしたりしますが、子どもが成長すると親が子を hug するなどということはほとんど見られません。しかし、欧米では何歳になっても親子で hug をするのは当たり前で、決して照れくさいことではありません。

加えて、親戚と会ったときなどには、cheek kiss（頬にする軽いキス）もよくします（とはいえ、北米では男女間、女性同士では一般的ですが、男同士の cheek kiss は一般的ではありません）。また、日本では老夫婦が手をつないで歩いているのを見ることは滅多にありませんが、欧米では至って普通の光景であり、いつまでもカップル気分を忘れないようにしています。

Chapter 7 の **重要表現リスト**

Skit A

- [ ] **We want to check in.**
  チェックインしたい
- [ ] **Certainly.**　承知しました
- [ ] **May I have your name, please?**
  お名前をいただけますか
- [ ] **Pardon me?**　何ていいましたか
- [ ] ***Can you repeat that, please?**
  もう一度いっていただけますか
- [ ] **Sorry… it's our first trip outside Japan.**
  すいません。日本国外へ旅行するのははじめてなんです
- [ ] **No worries!(=Don't worry.)**
  心配しないで
- [ ] **take a look (at…)**　(〜を)見る
- [ ] **How exciting!**　わくわくするなあ
- [ ] ***We have a reservation.**
  予約しています
- [ ] ***We have a reservation for two nights.**　私たちは2日予約しています
- [ ] ***We have a reservation for two people at seven o'clock.**
  7時にふたりで予約しています
- [ ] ***I'd like to make a reservation.**
  予約をしたいのですが
- [ ] **Will it be all right?**　大丈夫ですか
- [ ] **I cannot promise…**
  〜のお約束はできません
- [ ] **What do you mean?**
  どういう意味ですか
- [ ] **Can I get you…?**　〜へお持ちしましょうか
- [ ] **Not for me, thank you.**
   ***No, I'm OK, thank you.**
   ***No, I'm fine, thank you.**
  私は結構です。ありがとう
- [ ] **Here's your coffee… and your bill.**　コーヒーをどうぞ。それからお勘定です

Skit B

- [ ] ***This is so relaxing.**
  ここはとてもくつろげる
- [ ] ***I feel really refreshed.**
  気分がさっぱりした
- [ ] ***The tempreture is perfect.**
  湯加減は最高
- [ ] ***The water is hot for me.**
  お湯が私には熱すぎる
- [ ] **Why is it called…?**
  なぜこれは〜と呼ばれているのですか
- [ ] **I think it's because…**
  それは〜だからだと思う
- [ ] **Well… I suppose… in a way**
  まあ、っていうか、ある意味、たまには
- [ ] **get along**　うまくいく
- [ ] **There's just one thing.**
  ただひとつだけ問題がある
- [ ] **First…, then…**　最初は〜、それから〜
- [ ] **Once…, I'm OK.**
  一度〜してしまえば大丈夫
- [ ] **But one thing bothers me.**
  ただひとつ気になることがある
- [ ] **Do you know what I mean?**
  いっている意味、わかるでしょう?
- [ ] **I'm not sure.**　よくわかりません
- [ ] **Can you explain?**
  説明していただけますか
- [ ] **I mean…**　つまり

November

Chapter 8

Skit A

場面・状況	顧客からの電話にうまく応対できない
表現の テーマ	電話での基本応答

Skit B

場面・状況	リチャードの誕生日をミユキが 祝うが……
表現の テーマ	自分の気持ちを表す

Chapter 8 November

Skit A

ストーリーについて

　ミユキがヒット・ザ・ロード・トラベルで働き始めて約7カ月がたちました。仕事の手際もだいぶよくなり、英語にも自信がついてきました。でも電話での対応はいまだに緊張します。そんなところへ手強そうなクライアントから電話がかかってきました。

ここで扱う表現について

　ここでは、基本となる電話の受け答えを練習してみましょう。

　電話がかかってきたのが午後なので、まずミユキは Good afternoon. といって会話を始めていますね。次に会社名 Hit the Road Travel を名乗っています。会社などにかけると、「あいさつ (Good morning. など)」+「会社名」+「Miyuki (名前) speaking.」と応対されます。さらに How may I help you? (どのようなご用件ですか) が加わることもあります。

　あいにくデーブは不在、ミユキは I'm sorry と切り出してから彼がいないことを相手に伝えますが、デーブからの電話を待っていた相手はおかんむり。そこに I'll take the phone. といってジョーが助けに入ります。

　ここでクライアントに対し、ジョーが使う表現が Can I help you? と I'm afraid...。この場合、I'm afraid... は、日本語に訳すと「申し訳ありませんが」、「恐れ入りますが」。相手に対して恐縮している気持ちを伝えます。クライアントの気持ちを損なわないよう、続いてジョーが使う表現が May I ask what this is in regard to? 「何のご用件かうかがってもよろしいでしょうか」。May I がつくことで、あくまでも相手の機嫌を損ねない、丁寧な表現を使い続けます。

　またジョーの Can you hold a moment? (少々お待ちいただけますか) も電話を保留にするとき、ほかの人に電話を替わるときに必要な表現なので、覚えておきましょう。待たせた後は、Thank you for holding, Mr. Moloney. と続きます。「お待たせいたしました」ということですね。

Chapter 8 November

Skit A

Track 16

一筋縄ではいかない電話の応対

Miyuki: **Good afternoon.** Hit the Road Travel.
Moloney: Hello. Is Dave there?
M: **I'm sorry, he's out of the office now.**
Mo: He's out? He said he'd call me by three today. It's almost three now.
M: Oh. I'm sorry, but… **would you like to leave a message?** I think he'll be back soon.
Mo: You think? You mean you don't know?
M: I'm… very sorry, sir, but…
Joe: Miyuki, I'll take the phone. Hello. Can I

help you?

Mo: I hope so. Dave promised he'd call me by three o'clock.

J: **I'm afraid** Dave had an outside emergency. **May I ask what this is in regard to?**

Mo: He was going to give me some flight information.

J: I see. Can I have your name, sir?

Mo: It's Andrew Moloney.

J: OK, Mr. Moloney. **Can you hold a moment?**

Mo: Well, all right.

J: Thanks. Moloney, Moloney… Ah, here. **Thank you for holding**, Mr. Moloney.

Dave: Moloney? I'll take that, Joe.

J: Wait a sec—

D: Mr. Moloney, Dave Collier here. **Sorry to keep you waiting.** I was out having a smoke.

J: Oops. Oh, well.

M: Joe, I'm sorry about—

J: Miyuki… when someone is upset, **it doesn't help to** apologize over and over. **The important thing is to** keep your cool and try to solve the problem logically. If you can't solve it, **you need to** ask someone.

M: I know. I'm sor—um… never mind.

J: That's OK. Oh, **one more thing. Never** try to cover up for Dave, like I did. **It could backfire.**

D: Cover up for me? What did I do?

J: You should tell us where you're going and when you'll be back.

D: Every time I go out for a smoke?

M: Maybe you should stop smoking.

J: Excellent problem-solving!

D: Miyuki… **what's got into you?**

I hope so.:
そう願いたいけど、そうだといいけど。
I'm afraid…:
残念ながら〜なのですが
Oh, well.:
まあ、いいか
be upset:
機嫌が悪い、がっかりしている
apologize: 謝る
over and over:
何回も
keep one's cool:
冷静さを保つ
logically:
論理的に
Never mind.:
気にするな、どうでもいい（あきらめのニュアンスが含まれる。ここでは「何回謝ってもどうにもならない」と助言されたことに対して、また、謝ろうとしてしまったことについていっている）
cover up for…:
〜をかばう
like I did:
私がしたように
backfire:
逆効果になる
What's got into you?:
どうしたの

ポイント解説

Chapter 8 November Skit A

　ここではビジネスシーンでの電話の受け答えがメインとなります。電話をとったときのあいさつ、不在を伝える、相手の名前をたずねる、アドバイスをするといったときによく使われる表現が出てきます。

I'm sorry, he's out of the office now.
「外出しております」。社用の電話なら必ず I'm sorry をつけて。

Would you like to leave a message?
不在の場合は「メッセージを残されますか？」と尋ねるのがマナー。または、Would you like him/her to call you back?（かけ直すように伝えましょうか？）と伝えてもいい。その際は May I take your phone number?（お電話番号をいただけますか？）と聞くのを忘れずに。

I'm afraid…
あまりよくないことを相手に告げるときに、いいたいことの前に置いて使う便利な表現。

May I ask what this is in regard to?
「何のご用件かうかがってもよろしいでしょうか」。May I ask…? は相手に質問するときのていねいな尋ね方。

Good afternoon.
午前中なら Good morning.、夜なら Good evening.。ふだんの電話なら Hello. と応答してもよい。Good night.（おやすみなさい）は夕方以降での電話を切る際の表現として使える。

Miyuki: Good afternoon. Hit the Road Travel.
Moloney: Hello. Is Dave there?
M: I'm sorry, he's out of the office now.
Mo: He's out? He said he'd call me by three today. It's almost three now.
M: Oh. I'm sorry, but… **would you like to leave a message?** I think he'll be back soon.
Mo: You think? You mean you don't know?
M: I'm… very sorry, sir, but…
Joe: Miyuki, I'll take the phone. Hello. Can I help you?
Mo: I hope so. Dave promised he'd call me by three o'clock.
J: I'm afraid Dave had an outside emergency. **May I ask what this is in regard to?**
Mo: He was going to give me some flight information.
J: I see. Can I have your name, sir?
Mo: It's Andrew Moloney.
J: OK, Mr. Moloney. **Can you hold a moment?**
Mo: Well, all right.

J: Thanks. Moloney, Moloney… Ah, here. **Thank you for holding**, Mr. Moloney.
Dave: Moloney? I'll take that, Joe.
J: Wait a sec—
D: Mr. Moloney, Dave Collier here. **Sorry to keep you waiting.** I was out having a smoke.
J: Oops. Oh, well.
M: Joe, I'm sorry about—
J: Miyuki… when someone is upset, **it doesn't help to** apologize over and over. **The important thing is to** keep your cool and try to solve the problem logically. If you can't solve it, **you need to** ask someone.
M: I know. I'm sor—um… never mind.
J: That's OK. Oh, **one more thing. Never** try to cover up for Dave, like I did. **It could backfire.**
D: Cover up for me? What did I do?
J: You should tell us where you're going and when you'll be back.
D: Every time I go out for a smoke?
M: Maybe you should stop smoking.
J: Excellent problem-solving!
D: Miyuki… **what's got into you?**

Thank you for holding.
「お待たせいたしました」。Can you hold a moment(, please)? とセットで覚えておこう。

Sorry to keep you waiting.
「お待たせして申し訳ありません」。電話を保留した後などにも使える。

It doesn't help to…
「いくら……にしても仕方がない」という意味。ここでは、「いくら謝っても、仕方がない」。

- The important thing is to…
- You need to…
「肝心なのは……することだ」というアドバイスをする際の言い回し。

-One more thing. -Never…
「最後にもうひとつ。決して……するな」という説得力のあるアドバイスの言い方。

It could backfire.
いくらがんばっても、「逆効果になる」「裏目に出る」という意味。

What's got(ten) into you?
相手が苛立っていたり、機嫌が悪い様子のとき、「どうしちゃったの?」という表現。

Can you hold (for) a moment?
電話を保留にして相手を待たせる表現。Hold on, please.、Just a moment, please. ともいえる。電話を転送する場合には、Let me transfer you to….(……に転送します)といえばよい。

Miyuki: Good afternoon. Hit the Road Travel.
Moloney: Hello. Is Dave there?
M: I'm sorry, he's out of the office now.
Mo: He's out? He said he'd call me by three today. It's almost three now.
M: Oh. I'm sorry, but… would you like to leave a message? I think he'll be back soon.
Mo: You think? You mean you don't know?
M: I'm… very sorry, sir, but…
Joe: Miyuki, I'll take the phone. Hello. Can I help you?
Mo: I hope so. Dave promised he'd call me by three o'clock.
J: I'm afraid Dave had an outside emergency. May I ask what this is in regard to?
Mo: He was going to give me some flight information.
J: I see. Can I have your name, sir?
Mo: It's Andrew Moloney.
J: OK, Mr. Moloney. Can you hold a moment?
Mo: Well, all right.
J: Thanks. Moloney, Moloney… Ah, here. Thank you for holding, Mr. Moloney.
Dave: Moloney? I'll take that, Joe.
J: Wait a sec—
D: Mr. Moloney, Dave Collier here. Sorry to keep you waiting. I was out having a smoke.
J: Oops. Oh, well.
M: Joe, I'm sorry about—
J: Miyuki… when someone is upset, it doesn't help to apologize over and over. The important thing is to keep your cool and try to solve the problem logically. If you can't solve it, you need to ask someone.
M: I know. I'm sor—um… never mind.
J: That's OK. Oh, one more thing. Never try to cover up for Dave, like I did. It could backfire.
D: Cover up for me? What did I do?
J: You should tell us where you're going and when you'll be back.
D: Every time I go out for a smoke?
M: Maybe you should stop smoking.
J: Excellent problem-solving!
D: Miyuki… what's got into you?

ミユキ：こんにちは。ヒット・ザ・ロード・トラベルです。
モロニー（電話の相手）：もしもし。デーブはいる？
ミユキ：申し訳ございません、彼はいま外出中です。
モロニー：外出？　彼はきょうの3時までに電話するっていったんだよ。もうすぐ3時だよ。
ミユキ：あ、申し訳ございません……伝言を残されますか？　もうすぐ戻ると思うのですが。
モロニー：思う？　つまり知らないってこと？
ミユキ：も……本当に申し訳ないのですが……
ジョー：ミユキ、僕が電話をとるよ。もしもし。何かお役に立てることは。
モロニー：だといいけどね。デーブは3時までに電話をするって約束したんだ。
ジョー：申し訳ございませんが、デーブは緊急の用事で外出しております。どういったご用件かうかがってもよろしいですか。
モロニー：彼は航空便について情報をくれることになっていたんだ。
ジョー：わかりました。お名前をいただけますか。
モロニー：アンドリュー・モロニーだ。
ジョー：承知しました、モロニー様。少々お待ちいただけますか。
モロニー：まあ、いいよ。
ジョー：ありがとうございます。モロニー、モロニー……ああ、これだ。モロニー様、お待たせしております。
デーブ：モロニー？　ジョー、僕がとるよ。
ジョー：ちょっと待て……
デーブ：モロニー様、デーブ・コリアーです。お待たせして申し訳ありません。外で一服していたんですよ。
ジョー：おっと。まあいいか。
ミユキ：ジョー、すいません……
ジョー：ミユキ……相手が機嫌が悪いときは、何回も誤ってもどうにもならないんだよ。重要なのは、冷静を保って、論理的に問題を解決すること。自分で解決できなかったら、誰かに頼まなきゃだめだ。
ミユキ：そうですね。ごめ……何でもありません。
ジョー：いいんだよ。あ、もうひとつ。決してデーブをかばおうとしないこと、僕みたいに。逆効果になりかねない。
デーブ：僕をかばう？　僕が何かした？
ジョー：君はどこに行くのか、いつ帰ってくるのか、僕たちに伝えるべきだよ。
デーブ：タバコを吸いにいくたびに？
ミユキ：たぶん、禁煙するべきですよ。
ジョー：すばらしい解決法だ。
デーブ：ミユキ、君はいったいどうしたっていうんだ。

Chapter 8
November

Exercises

Part A Track 16

①リスニング、②パラレル・リーディング(音を聞きながらテキストを音読)、③プロソディ・シャドーイング（音の再現）④コンテンツ・シャドーイング（意味を意識）の順で会話を再現してみましょう。下記の Key Phrases を意識しながら、最低でも7回は会話を聞いてみましょう。

Key Phrases:
- Good afternoon.
- I'm sorry, he's out of the office now.
- Would you like to leave a message?
- I'm afraid…
- May I ask what this is in regard to?
- Can you hold (for) a moment?
- Thank you for holding.
- Sorry to keep you waiting.
- It doesn't help to…
- The important thing is to…
- You need to…
- One more thing. Never…
- It could backfire.
- What's got(ten) into you?

Part B

相手の問いやコメントに対して、自分なりの答えを考えてみましょう。

1) **Ian:** Good afternoon. Hit the Road Travel. Ian White speaking. How may I help you?
   You: _____

2) **Ian:** I'm afraid Mr. Graham is away from his desk at the moment.
   You: _____

3) **Ian:** Would you like to leave a message?
   You: _____

今度は相手に質問してみましょう。

4) グラハムさんと話したいときに使う表現は？
   You: _____
   Ian: I'm sorry, but Mr. Graham is away on business. He will be back next Thursday.

5) 電話の相手が誰か知りたいときのたずね方は？
   You: _____
   Ian: Certainly. My name is Ian White.

6) 電話を保留にしたとき、相手にいう表現は？
   You: _____
   Ian: Sure, no problem.

Exercises の解答例と訳

1) May I speak to Mr. Graham, please?
2) Then may I leave a message?
3) Yes. Please tell him that I will call back at three o'clock.
4) May I speak to Mr. Graham, please?
5) May I ask who is calling?
6) Can you hold, please?

問題と答えの訳

1) イアン：こんにちは。ヒット・ザ・ロード・トラベルのイアン・ホワイトです。ご用件は何でしょうか。
   あなた：グラハムさんはいらっしゃいますか。
2) イアン：恐れ入ります、グラハムは席を外しております。
   あなた：では伝言をお願いできますか。
3) イアン：伝言を承りましょうか。
   あなた：はい。3時にかけ直しますとお伝えください。
4) あなた：グラハムさんはいらっしゃいますか。
   イアン：申し訳ありませんが、グラハムは出張しております。木曜日には戻ってきます。
5) あなた：お名前をお伺いしてもよろしいでしょうか。
   イアン：はい。イアン・ホワイトといいます。
6) あなた：お待ちいただけますか。
   イアン：もちろんです。

コラム　謝罪に対する意識

　一般的に欧米人は日本人と比べると簡単には謝りません。交通事故などのときに "I'm sorry." と下手に自分の非を認めてしまうと、後で不利な立場になるという意識が根強くあるからでしょう。一方、日本ではとりあえず謝って、なるべく事が穏便に収まるようにすることが賢明であるとされています。そのため、日本人は何度も何度も頭を下げて謝罪することがありますが、このような態度は欧米人からすると奇異に映るものです。

　北米では、謝り続けられると、たいていの人が困惑します。そして謝っている人に対して大丈夫だよといってあげることを期待されているかのように感じます。

　また、ただ謝ってばかりいると、その人には問題を解決する能力や意志がないと見なされることもあります。謝り続ける暇があるのなら、前向きに問題を解決する方法を考えろ、というのが欧米的なプラグマティズム（実用主義）なのです。

　ですから、一般的に、欧米人は過去の失敗や間違いについて日本人ほどくよくよ考えることはなく、実際、厳密な意味で日本語の「反省」にあたることばは英語にはありません。

Chapter 8 November

Skit B

ストーリーについて

　11月も終わりに近づきました。ミユキはリチャードの誕生日のために、特別なディナーを準備しました。ふたりの仲は順調に進行中、でも問題にぶつかることもたまにはあります。ミユキがデーブと出張するというニュースに、リチャードは少々ご不満の様子。

ここで扱う表現について

　ここでは「自分の気持ちを表現する」ことを中心に学びましょう。

　ミユキの自宅に招待されたリチャード。初めて会ったときに飲んだワイン、リチャードの好物のローストチキン、それにプレゼントまで用意したミユキに、That's my favorite dish!（僕の大好物だ！）、That was the luckiest day of my life.（人生でいちばん幸運な日だった）とリチャードは感激しっぱなしです。日本人にはちょっとオーバーな表現に聞こえるかもしれませんが、英語ではよく耳にします。ミユキは、これに対して What a sweet thing to say.（何てすてきなことをいってくれるの）と素直にうれしさを表現していますね。自分の感情を表現するのが苦手なミユキですが、少しずつ自分の気持をことばで表すように努力していますね。

　会話の後半、ミユキがデーブと出張に行くことを知って、動揺するリチャード。それに気づいてミユキが What's the matter?（どうしたの）と聞いています。I'm just surprised that...（ただ……で驚いているんだ）と打ち明けるリチャード。その反面ミユキは、「わたしが逆の立場に立たされたとしても、I have faith in you.（あなたを信頼している）、だから心配はしないわ」と訴えます。I trust you completely. もも同じで completely で意味を強めています。彼女の雄弁さに、つい Your English is amazing.（君の英語はすばらしいよ）とコメントしてしまうリチャードですが、Don't change the subject.（話題を変えないで）と叱責されています。どうやらリチャードよりもミユキのほうが強そうですね。相手のいうことが本質から外れているときには、That isn't the point. といって指摘することができます。

Chapter 8 November

Skit B

Track 17

うれしくも気がかりな誕生日

Miyuki: Happy birthday!
Richard: Thanks! Hey, **something smells good.**
M: I'm making roast chicken.
R: Really? **That's my favorite dish!**
M: I know. *Kampai*! We drank this wine the day we met.
R: That's right! **That was the luckiest day of my life.**
M: Wow. **What a sweet thing to say.** Um… here's your present.
R: Wait, Miyuki. I just told you how I feel. **Can you tell me how you feel?**
M: Richard… **I'm trying to.** Please open the present.
R: Oh. OK. Miyuki, this bowl is beautiful—thank you.
M: I made it for you. The shape is like a heart.

Something smells good.:
何かいい匂いがするよ

That's my favorite dish!:
私の大好物です

That's right!:
その通り

sweet: すてきな

try to…:
〜するように努力する

Do you see?

R: I see. My favorite dish, the wine, the gift…

M: It's hard for me to talk about my feelings, so…

R: You tell me in other ways. From now on, I'll listen better.

M: And I'll try to talk more.

R: It's a deal.

M: Oh—**I have some news.** Joe is sending me to Canada on business next month.

R: Really? That's exciting! For how long?

M: About a week. We're going to Vancouver, Toronto, Ottawa—

R: We? Who're you going with?

M: Dave. You remember Dave.

R: Yeah. So it's… just the two of you?

M: Well, yes. **What's the matter?**

R: I'm just surprised that Joe is sending you to Canada with… a guy.

M: But **that's silly.** Dave is… a little crazy, but he's a gentleman. And I'm a grownup.

R: I know, but you'll be traveling together for a week.

M: What are you saying? Don't you trust me?

R: Sure I do. It's the situation I don't trust.

M: That means you don't trust me. Oh, I don't believe it!

R: Miyuki, calm down! Just think for a minute.

M: OK. Let's be logical. **If it was the reverse situation, I'd be… a little uncomfortable.** But I wouldn't worry, because I have faith in you.

R: Miyuki… your English is amazing.

M: Thank you, but don't change the subject.

R: Hey, is something burning?

M: Oh, no! The chicken!

Do you see?: わかる？

It's hard for me to…: 私にとって〜するのは難しい

From now on: これからは

It's a deal.: 約束よ。それで結構です

send… to 〜 on business: （人）を〜へ出張させる

For how long?: どれくらいの期間？

What's the matter?: どうしたの？

silly: バカげている

grownup: 大人（adultよりもややくだけた「大人」の意味で、会話中によく使われる）

What are you saying?: どういう意味？

Sure I do.: （前の文を受けて）信頼しているよ

Calm down.: 落ち着いて

If it was the reverse situation: もし逆の状況だったら

uncomfortable: 不安な

have faith in…: 〜を信頼する

Don't change the subject.: 話を変えるな

ポイント解説

Chapter 8 November Skit B

ミユキはリチャードの誕生日を祝うためにディナーを振る舞います。相手の気持ちを確認するや相手の言動を非難する表現、「努力はしているが難しい」といったときに便利な表現が使われています。

- That's my favorite dish!
- That was the luckiest day of my life.
- What a sweet thing to say.

上から「私の大好物です」「あれは僕の人生の中で最も幸運な日だった」「そんな素敵なことをいってくれるなんて」。いずれも素直に感情を表している。食事に招待されたときに、That's my favorite dish! というと相手も喜ぶだろう。このように素直に感情を表現する方法を文脈から学ぼう。

Can you tell me how you feel?

日本人は感情表現が苦手だが、Please tell me how you feel.（どう思っているのか教えてください）や How do you feel about it?（どう思う？）と聞かれたら、少しずつ自分の考えを伝えられるようにしよう。

- I'm trying to.
- It's hard for me to talk about my feelings.

どうしてもはじめはことばで自分の感情を表現するのが難しいかもしれない。だまっているよりは正直に「努力はしています」や「感情を話すのはむずかしいです」と伝えたほうが相手に理解される。

Something smells good.

食事に招待されたら「何かいいにおいがする」と伝えればホストもうれしい。Smells good.（いいにおい）だけでも OK。

Miyuki: Happy birthday!
Richard: Thanks! Hey, **something smells good.**
M: I'm making roast chicken.
R: Really? **That's my favorite dish!**
M: I know. *Kampai*! We drank this wine the day we met.
R: That's right! **That was the luckiest day of my life.**
M: Wow. **What a sweet thing to say.** Um… here's your present.
R: Wait, Miyuki. I just told you how I feel. **Can you tell me how you feel?**
M: Richard… **I'm trying to.** Please open the present.
R: Oh. OK. Miyuki, this bowl is beautiful—thank you.
M: I made it for you. The shape is like a heart. Do you see?
R: I see. My favorite dish, the wine, the gift…
M: **It's hard for me to talk about my feelings,** so…
R: You tell me in other ways. From now on, I'll listen better.
M: And I'll try to talk more.
R: **It's a deal.**
M: Oh—**I have some news.** Joe is sending me to Canada on business next month.
R: Really? That's exciting! For how long?

M: About a week. We're going to Vancouver, Toronto, Ottawa—
R: We? Who're you going with?
M: Dave. You remember Dave.
R: Yeah. So it's… just the two of you?
M: Well, yes. **What's the matter?**
R: I'm just surprised that Joe is sending you to Canada with… a guy.
M: But **that's silly.** Dave is… a little crazy, but he's a gentleman. And I'm a grownup.
R: I know, but you'll be traveling together for a week.
M: **What are you saying?** Don't you trust me?
R: Sure I do. It's the situation I don't trust.
M: That means you don't trust me. Oh, I don't believe it!
R: Miyuki, calm down! Just think for a minute.
M: OK. Let's be logical. **If it was the reverse situation, I'd be… a little uncomfortable.** But I wouldn't worry, because I have faith in you.
R: Miyuki… your English is amazing.
M: Thank you, but don't change the subject.
R: Hey, is something burning?
M: Oh, no! The chicken!

What's the matter?
「どうかしたの?」。What's wrong?、Is something wrong? も同じ。

That's silly.
「ばかばかしい」という意味。これよりもかなり強い表現である That's stupid! もよく使われるが、とても失礼な言い方なので要注意。

What are you saying?
What do you mean? と同じ、「何いってるの?」「どういう意味?」と苛立ちが込められた表現。

If it was the reverse situation, I'd be… a little uncomfortable.
If it was the reverse situation は「逆の状況だったら」。自分が相手の状況に置かれたと仮定して考えるときに用いる表現。ここでは「逆の立場だったら不安になる」としている。

It's a deal.
「約束だ」、「決まりだね」。否定形 It's not a big deal. は「大したことじゃない」とまったく意味が変わる。他にも good を加えただけで It's a good deal. となると「お買い得ですよ」となるので、気をつけよう。

I have some news.
I have something to tell you. (伝えることがあります) となると、やや深刻なニュアンス。

訳

Miyuki: Happy birthday!
Richard: Thanks! Hey, something smells good.
M: I'm making roast chicken.
R: Really? That's my favorite dish!
M: I know. *Kampai*! We drank this wine the day we met.
R: That's right! That was the luckiest day of my life.
M: Wow. What a sweet thing to say. Um… here's your present.
R: Wait, Miyuki. I just told you how I feel. Can you tell me how you feel?
M: Richard… I'm trying to. Please open the present.
R: Oh. OK. Miyuki, this bowl is beautiful—thank you.
M: I made it for you. The shape is like a heart. Do you see?
R: I see. My favorite dish, the wine, the gift…
M: It's hard for me to talk about my feelings, so…
R: You tell me in other ways. From now on, I'll listen better.
M: And I'll try to talk more.
R: It's a deal.
M: Oh—I have some news. Joe is sending me to Canada on business next month.
R: Really? That's exciting! For how long?
M: About a week. We're going to Vancouver, Toronto, Ottawa—
R: We? Who're you going with?
M: Dave. You remember Dave.
R: Yeah. So it's… just the two of you?
M: Well, yes. What's the matter?
R: I'm just surprised that Joe is sending you to Canada with… a guy.
M: But that's silly. Dave is… a little crazy, but he's a gentleman. And I'm a grownup.
R: I know, but you'll be traveling together for a week.
M: What are you saying? Don't you trust me?
R: Sure I do. It's the situation I don't trust.
M: That means you don't trust me. Oh, I don't believe it!
R: Miyuki, calm down! Just think for a minute.
M: OK. Let's be logical. If it was the reverse situation, I'd be… a little uncomfortable. But I wouldn't worry, because I have faith in you.
R: Miyuki… your English is amazing.
M: Thank you, but don't change the subject.
R: Hey, is something burning?
M: Oh, no! The chicken!

ミユキ: ハッピー・バースデー！
リチャード: ありがとう。お、何かいい匂いがする。
ミユキ: ロースト・チキンを作ってるのよ。
リチャード: 本当？　僕の大好物だよ。
ミユキ: 知ってるわよ。乾杯。これは私たちが最初に会った日に飲んだワイン。
リチャード: そうだ。あれは僕の人生でいちばんラッキーな日だったね。
ミユキ: わあ。そんな素敵なことをいってくれるなんて。えーと……これがプレゼント。
リチャード: 待った、ミユキ。いま僕は自分が感じていることをいった。君がどう感じているかいってくれる？
ミユキ: リチャード……私もそうしようと努力しているの。どうぞプレゼントを開けて。
リチャード: ああ、OK。ミユキ、素敵な器だね、ありがとう。
ミユキ: あなたのために作ったの。ハートみたいな形なの。わかる？
リチャード: そうか。好物の料理、ワインにプレゼント……
ミユキ: 私にとって、気持ちを話すのは難しいの、だから……
リチャード: 別の方法で話せばいいんだよ。これからは、もっと君の話を聞くようにするよ。
ミユキ: じゃあ私はもっとしゃべるようにするわ。
リチャード: よし。
ミユキ: そうだ、ニュースがあるの。ジョーが来月私をカナダに出張させることになったの。
リチャード: 本当？　楽しみじゃないか。どれくらい行くの？
ミユキ: 1週間くらい。私たちが行くのはバンクーバー、トロント、オタワ……
リチャード: 「私たち」？　誰といっしょに行くんだ？
ミユキ: デーブよ。デーブは覚えているでしょ。
リチャード: うん。じゃあ……ってことは君たちふたりだけ？
ミユキ: まあ、そうね。どうしたの。
リチャード: ジョーが君をカナダに男といっしょに行かせることに驚いただよ。
ミユキ: でもそれっておかしいわよ。デーブは……少し変わってるけど、紳士よ。それに私だって大人だし。
リチャード: わかってるけど、君たちは1週間もいっしょに旅行するんだろ。
ミユキ: 何をいおうとしてるの？　私を信用してないの？
リチャード: もちろん信用してるよ。僕が信用してないのはその状況だよ。
ミユキ: ということは、私を信用していないってことよ。もう、信じられない！
リチャード: ミユキ、落ち着けよ。ちょっと考えて。
ミユキ: OK。ロジカルに考えましょう。もし私が逆の立場だったら……少し不安になるわ。でも心配しないでしょうね、私はあなたのことを信頼してるから。
リチャード: ミユキ……君の英語はすばらしいよ。
ミユキ: ありがとう。でも話を変えないで。
リチャード: おい、何か焦げてる？
ミユキ: 大変！　チキンよ。

Chapter 8
November

Exercises

Part A `Track 17`

①リスニング、②パラレル・リーディング(音を聞きながらテキストを音読)、③プロソディ・シャドーイング（音の再現）④コンテンツ・シャドーイング（意味を意識）の順で会話を再現してみましょう。下記の Key Phrases を意識しながら、最低でも7回は会話を聞いてみましょう。

Key Phrases:
- Something smells good.
- That's my favorite dish!
- That was the luckiest day of my life.
- What a sweet thing to say.
- Can you tell me how you feel?
- I'm trying to.
- It's hard for me to talk about my feelings.
- It's a deal.
- I have some news.
- What's the matter?
- That's silly.
- What are you saying?
- If it was the reverse situation, (I'd be a little uncomfortable.)

Part B

相手の問いかけや語りかけに対して、自分なりの答えを考えてみましょう。

1) **Janice:** Oh, I'm not sure about that. By the way, how is Brian doing?
   You: _____

2) **Janice:** Aaagh! I can't believe I have to write this essay by tomorrow! I will never finish in time!
   You: _____

3) **Janice:** What do you mean? Can you tell me exactly how you feel?
   You: _____

今度は相手の応答にふさわしい語りかけをしてみましょう。

4) 交通事故が起きたことを聞いたときの反応は？
   You: _____
   Janice: Calm down! It looks like everyone's OK.

5) JaneとAlanが結婚する！
   You: _____
   Janice: I don't believe it! They've only been dating for a couple of months!

6) Janiceの着ているドレスがとてもよく似合っている……。
   You: _____
   Janice: What a sweet thing to say! Thank you.

Exercisesの解答例と訳

1) Don't change the subject.
2) Calm down.
3) It's hard for me to express my feelings.
4) Oh, no! There's been a car accident!
5) Jane and Alan are getting married.
6) That dress looks really nice on you.

問題と答えの訳

1) ジャニス：よくわからないわ。ところでブライアンはどうしているの。
   あなた：話をそらさないで。
2) ジャニス：ああ。このエッセイを明日までに書かないといけないなんて信じられない！
   あなた：落ち着いて。
3) ジャニス：つまりどういうこと？ あなたの気持ちを聞かせて。
   あなた：自分の気持ちを表現するのはむずかしいよ。
4) あなた：何てことだ。交通事故だ！
   ジャニス：落ち着いて。みんな大丈夫そうよ。
5) あなた：ジェーンとアランが結婚するらしい。
   ジャニス：信じられない。2、3カ月デートしただけなのに。
6) あなた：そのドレスはとても君に似合うよ。
   ジャニス：なんて素敵なことをいってくれるの。ありがとう。

コラム　バレンタインデー

バレンタインデー (Valentine's Day) はローマ初期の聖職者である聖バレンタイン (Saint Valentine) にちなんだ名前です。なぜ彼の名前がロマンティックな愛と関係づけられているのかについてはいろいろな説がありますが、まだはっきりしたことはわかっていません。

日本ではバレンタインデーには女性から男性にチョコレートをあげる習慣がありますが、欧米ではお互いにあげ合うか、むしろ男性から女性に花（愛の象徴である紅いバラが人気があります）やチョコレートなどをあげるのが普通です。

また、日本ではバレンタインデーは、女性が意中の男性にチョコレートを渡しながら愛の告白をする日でもありますが、欧米ではすでに付き合っている男女が愛を確認し合う日です。

欧米のバレンタインデーの雰囲気とよく似ているのが、付き合っているカップルがデートをして過ごすことが多い日本のクリスマスイブなのです。ですから、バレンタインデーには、男性から女性にアクセサリーなど多少高価なプレゼントをあげる人や、リッチなレストランでデートをする人もいます。

Chapter 8 の 重要表現リスト

Skit A

- ☐ **Good afternoon.** こんにちは
- ☐ **I'm sorry, he's out of the office now.** すいません、彼はいま外出しております
- ☐ **Would you like to leave a message?** メッセージを残されますか
- ☐ **I hope so.** そうだといいけど
- ☐ **I'm afraid…** 残念ながら〜なのですが
- ☐ **May I ask what this is in regard to?** 何のご用件かうかがってもよろしいでしょうか
- ☐ ***How may I help you?** どのようなご用件ですか
- ☐ ***Can I help you?** お役に立てることは?
- ☐ **Can you hold (for) a moment?** 少々お待ちいただけますか
- ☐ **Thank you for holding.** お待たせいたしました
- ☐ **Sorry to keep you waiting.** お待たせして申し訳ありませんでした
- ☐ **It doesn't help to…** いくら〜しても仕方がない
- ☐ **over and over** 何度も何度も
- ☐ **The important thing is to…** 肝心なのは〜すること
- ☐ **You need to…** 〜する必要がある
- ☐ **keep one's cool** 冷静さを保つ
- ☐ **Never mind.** 気にするな
- ☐ **One more thing. Never…** 最後にもうひとつ。決して〜するな
- ☐ **cover up for…** 〜をかばう
- ☐ **It could backfire.** 裏目に出る
- ☐ **What's got(ten) into you?** どうしちゃったの

Skit B

- ☐ **Something smells good.** 何かいいにおいがする
- ☐ **That's my favorite dish!** 私の大好物です
- ☐ **That was the luckiest day of my life.** あれは僕の人生で最もラッキーな日だった
- ☐ **What a sweet thing to say.** そんな素敵なことをいってくれるなんて
- ☐ **That's right!** そのとおり
- ☐ **Can you tell me how you feel?** どう思っているのか教えてください
- ☐ ***How do you feel about…?** 〜についてどう思う?
- ☐ **I'm trying to.** 努力はしています
- ☐ **It's hard for me to talk about my feelings.** 感情を話すのは難しいです
- ☐ **Do you see?** わかる?
- ☐ **from now on** これからは
- ☐ **It's a deal.** 約束だ、決まりだね
- ☐ ***It's not a big deal.** 大したことじゃない
- ☐ ***It's a good deal.** お買い得ですよ
- ☐ **I have some news.** ニュースがある
- ☐ ***I have something to tell you.** 伝えることがあります
- ☐ **What's the matter?** どうかしたの
- ☐ ***What's wrong?** どうかしたの
- ☐ ***Is something wrong?** どうかしたの
- ☐ **That's silly.** ばかばかしい
- ☐ **What are you saying?** 何いってるの
- ☐ **If it was the reverse situation, (I'd be a little uncomfortable.)** 逆の立場だったら少し不安になる
- ☐ **have faith in…** 〜を信頼する

Chapter 9
December

Skit A	
場面・状況	トロント出張でホテルを相手に商談する
表現のテーマ	質問する／ほめる／感想を述べる
Skit B	
場面・状況	テレビの前で男３人がアメフト観戦
表現のテーマ	ジョーク／非難する／応援する／断る

Chapter 9 December

Skit A

ストーリーについて

　12月中旬、ミユキは初めての出張でカナダにやってきました。当初の予定が変わり、ミユキに同伴しているのはデーブではなくジェニファーです。現地のホテル、ツアーやレストランをいっしょに調べてまわり、ふたりは絶好の仕事仲間としてだけでなく、気の合う友人同士になりました。いまふたりがいるトロントは、ジェニファーの出身地でもあります。

ここで扱う表現について

　商用でカナダに出張中のジェニファーとミユキ。現地のホテルと交渉です。Can you tell us...?、How about...? と質問攻めのジェニファー。ミユキも Are there...? と加担しています。このような商談などの場面では、質問したほうが積極性を評価されます。逆に商談に積極的でないのであれば、あまり質問すると相手に期待させてしまうので注意しましょう。

　商談の後のふたりの会話はやはりジェニファーのほめ言葉から始まります。もちろん思ってもいないことを口にするのは論外ですが、相手のよいところを見つけ、積極的にいうのが人間関係をスムーズにするコツでしょう。

　トロントについての感想を求められ、It's a cool city. It's also a cold city. とミユキは答えていますが、ここの意味はわかりますか？　最初の cool は気温のことではなく「カッコイイ」といった意味ですが、最後の cold のほうが気温を指しているのです。cool と cold を合わせたことば遊びが見られます。

　商談のあとは、プライベートな話に移行します。話題はミユキとリチャードのこと。ついでにジェニファーのデーブへの気持ちがバレてしまいます。あわてるジェニファーにミユキが I knew it! (やっぱり！) と確信。I think he likes you, too. と伝えると No way! と驚きを隠せないジェニファー。でもつい期待して Um...really? とユーモラスな結末でスキットが終わります。

Chapter 9 December

Skit A

Track 18

初めての海外出張──トロントで商談

Hotel manager: … so **we believe** our hotel is the ideal choice for your clients.
Jennifer: **As you know,** many Japanese travelers prefer twin rooms. **Can you tell us** how many there are?
HM: We have 35 twin rooms.
J: I see. How about smoking and non-smoking rooms?
HM: Ninety percent are non-smoking. In other words, there are 30 smoking rooms.
Miyuki: You mentioned Japanese-speaking staff. Are there Japanese speakers on duty at all times?
HM: Yes, we always have at least one Japanese speaker here. Now, can I show you around the hotel?
J: That sounds good!

その夜、ミユキとジェニファーはダウンタウンのフュージ

---

ideal: 理想的な
client: 顧客
as you know:
ご存じのように

in other words:
つまり

on duty: 当番で
at all times:
いつも（ややフォーマルな表現）

That sounds good!:
いいですね

ョン料理のレストランでディナーをすることにしました。

J: Miyuki, **you did a great job** today.

M: Oh, thanks—but I get a little nervous in meetings.

J: It doesn't show. By the way, **how do you like** Toronto?

M: It's a cool city. It's also a cold city.

J: Yeah, that's why Dave didn't want to take this trip. He hates the cold.

M: Is that the reason? I was afraid he was mad at me.

J: Why?

M: One day he went out for a cigarette at a bad time, so I said he should stop smoking. I meant it as a joke, but he seemed a little upset.

J: But I always tell him that—and I'm serious! I'm sure Dave isn't angry. He's a bit crazy, but he's very nice.

M: That's what I said to Richard. When I told him I was going to Canada with a guy, he wasn't happy at all.

J: Oh. **Is he the jealous type?**

M: Not usually. I was shocked. He said he trusted me, but not the situation.

J: Isn't that just like a guy? **What if the situation were reversed?**

M: That's what I said!

J: And what was his answer?

M: He said he was impressed with my English.

J: But he probably understood your point. And **I can tell** you love him.

M: Well… yeah. And I can tell you like Dave.

J: Well, yeah I mean, uh…

M: I knew it! You do like him. I think he likes you, too.

J: No way! Um… really?

---

do a great job:
うまくやる、いい仕事をする

It doesn't show.:
そうは見えない

How do you like…?:
〜はどう思いますか？

cool:
いかした、格好いい

be mad at…:
〜に対して怒る（be angry at... も同じ）

upset:
機嫌が悪い、がっかりして

I'm serious!:
本気よ、マジメよ

Not usually.:
ふだんはそんなことはない

What if…?:
もし〜だったら

reversed: 逆転した

be impressed with…:
〜に感心する

Chapter 9 December Skit A

ポイント解説

出張でカナダ・トロントにやってきたミユキとジェニファー。前半はビジネスでクライアントと交渉するときに使う表現を学びます。後半では相手をほめたり、それに対する応答の表現などを覚えていきましょう。

As you know…
「ご存じの通り」も商談などでよく使われるフレーズ。

Can you tell us…?
「……を教えてもらえますか」。相手から情報を引き出す質問。うしろに how many (sv)、how much…、how long… などを使ってたずねれば、具体的な数字をともなう情報を引き出すことができる。

That sounds good!
「……はいかがですか?」という相手の申し出には、That would be great. もしくは、シンプルに Yes, thank you. と返事をしてもいい。

You did a great job.
「よくやったね」というほめ文句。Great job!、You did great! といってもよい。

It doesn't show.
相手が「実は緊張しているの」などネガティブなことを打ち明けたとき、「そうは見えないわよ」と励ます言い回し。

We believe
「……ということを私どもは確信しています」。代表して自分の会社のよさをアピールするときの表現。

Hotel manager: … so **we believe** our hotel is the ideal choice for your clients.
Jennifer: **As you know,** many Japanese travelers prefer twin rooms. **Can you tell us** how many there are?
HM: We have 35 twin rooms.
J: I see. How about smoking and non-smoking rooms?
HM: Ninety percent are non-smoking. In other words, there are 30 smoking rooms.
Miyuki: You mentioned Japanese-speaking staff. Are there Japanese speakers on duty at all times?
HM: Yes, we always have at least one Japanese speaker here. Now, can I show you around the hotel?
J: That sounds good!

J: Miyuki, **you did a great job** today.
M: Oh, thanks—but I get a little nervous in meetings.
J: It doesn't show. By the way, **how do you like** Toronto?
M: It's a cool city. It's also a cold city.
J: Yeah, that's why Dave didn't want to take this trip. He hates the cold.
M: Is that the reason? I was afraid

he was mad at me.
J: Why?
M: One day he went out for a cigarette at a bad time, so I said he should stop smoking. I meant it as a joke, but he seemed a little upset.
J: But I always tell him that—and I'm serious! I'm sure Dave isn't angry. He's a bit crazy, but he's very nice.
M: That's what I said to Richard. When I told him I was going to Canada with a guy, he wasn't happy at all.
J: Oh. **Is he the jealous type?**
M: Not usually. I was shocked. He said he trusted me, but not the situation.
J: Isn't that just like a guy? **What if the situation were reversed?**
M: That's what I said!
J: And what was his answer?
M: He said he was impressed with my English.
J: But he probably understood your point. And I can tell you love him.
M: Well… yeah. And **I can tell** you like Dave.
J: Well, yeah I mean, uh…
M: I knew it! You do like him. I think he likes you, too.
J: No way! Um… really?

Is he the jealous type?
the jealous type で「焼きもち焼き」「嫉妬深い人」という意味。

What if the situation were reversed?
What if…? は「もし……だったら」。現実と反対のことを仮定する仮定法なので、was ではなく were と用いている。「もし逆の状況だったらどうなってたの?」。

That's what I said!
「それはまさに私がいったこと!」。That's exactly / just what I said. と exactly や just を加えるとさらに強調される。That's not what I said. だと「私はそうはいっていません」つまり「誤解しています」となる。

I can tell…
「……ということがいえる」「きっと……ということだろう」「……ということにちがいない」という意味。I can tell you love him. (あなたは彼のことが好きなんでしょう)のようにいえる。

No way!
「とんでもない!」、「信じられない!」、「無理だ!」などの感情を表す表現。

How do you like…?
「……はどうですか」と相手の感想や意見を聞くのに手軽に使える表現。

I knew it!
「やっぱり」。I knew it. は it がつく場合は単独で使うが、I knew you liked him. (やっぱり君は彼のことが好きなんだ)のように、it を節に変えて続けることができる。

Hotel manager: … so we believe our hotel is the ideal choice for your clients.
Jennifer: As you know, many Japanese travelers prefer twin rooms. Can you tell us how many there are?
HM: We have 35 twin rooms.
J: I see. How about smoking and non-smoking rooms?
HM: Ninety percent are non-smoking. In other words, there are 30 smoking rooms.
Miyuki: You mentioned Japanese-speaking staff. Are there Japanese speakers on duty at all times?
HM: Yes, we always have at least one Japanese speaker here. Now, can I show you around the hotel?
J: That sounds good!

J: Miyuki, you did a great job today.
M: Oh, thanks—but I get a little nervous in meetings.
J: It doesn't show. By the way, how do you like Toronto?
M: It's a cool city. It's also a cold city.
J: Yeah, that's why Dave didn't want to take this trip. He hates the cold.
M: Is that the reason? I was afraid he was mad at me.
J: Why?
M: One day he went out for a cigarette at a bad time, so I said he should stop smoking. I meant it as a joke, but he seemed a little upset.
J: But I always tell him that—and I'm serious! I'm sure Dave isn't angry. He's a bit crazy, but he's very nice.
M: That's what I said to Richard. When I told him I was going to Canada with a guy, he wasn't happy at all.
J: Oh. Is he the jealous type?
M: Not usually. I was shocked. He said he trusted me, but not the situation.
J: Isn't that just like a guy? What if the situation were reversed?
M: That's what I said!
J: And what was his answer?
M: He said he was impressed with my English.
J: But he probably understood your point. And I can tell you love him.
M: Well… yeah. And I can tell you like Dave.
J: Well, yeah I mean, uh…
M: I knew it! You do like him. I think he likes you, too.
J: No way! Um… really?

ホテル支配人：……ですので、私どものホテルは、御社のお客様方には理想的な選択となると思います。
ジェニファー：ご存じだとは思いますが、日本人の旅行者の多くはツインルームを好みます。ツインは何室あるか教えていただけますか。
支配人：ツインルームは35室です。
ジェニファー：わかりました。喫煙室、禁煙室については？
支配人：90%が禁煙室です。つまり、30室の喫煙室があるということです。
ミユキ：日本語を話すスタッフについて触れていらっしゃいましたね。日本語を話せる常駐スタッフはいますか。
支配人：はい、日本語を話すスタッフは最低でもひとりはいつもいます。では、ホテルの中をお見せしましょうか。
ジェニファー：よろしくお願いします。

ジェニファー：ミユキ、あなたきょうはよくやったわね。
ミユキ：ありがとう—でも会議中はいつも少し緊張するの。
ジェニファー：そうは見えないわよ。ところで、トロントはどう？
ミユキ：クールな町ね。それにコールド（寒い）な町だわ。
ジェニファー：そうね、だからデーブは今回来たくなかったのよ。彼は寒いのが嫌いだから。
ミユキ：それが理由なの？ 彼は私に怒ってるのかと思ったわ。
ジェニファー：どうして？
ミユキ：この前、彼は都合が悪いときに外にタバコを吸いに行ってたものだから、タバコを止めるべきだっていったの。冗談のつもりだったのに、少し機嫌を損ねたみたいだったわ。
ジェニファー：でも私もいつも彼にそういっているわ。それも本気で！ 絶対にデーブは怒っていないわ。彼は少しクレイジーだけど、とてもいい人よ。
ミユキ：私は同じことをリチャードにいったの。私がカナダに男の人と行くっていったら、彼、すごく不愉快になったの。
ジェニファー：そう。彼って嫉妬するタイプ？
ミユキ：普段はそうでもないんだけど。ショックだったわ。私のことは信用するけど、その状況は信用しないっていったのよ。
ジェニファー：それってすごく男っぽくない？ 状況が逆だったらどう？
ミユキ：私もそういったのよ！
ジェニファー：それで彼の答えは？
ミユキ：私の英語に感心した、って。
ジェニファー：でも彼はたぶんあなたの言い分はわかったんじゃない。それにあなたが彼のことが好きだって私はわかるもの。
ミユキ：まあ……そうね。そして、私には、あなたがデーブのことが好きだってわかるわ。
ジェニファー：えーと、う……ていうかその……
ミユキ：やっぱり。彼のこと本当に好きなんだ。彼もあなたのこと好きだと思うわ。
ジェニファー：まさか。あ……本当に？

Chapter 9
December

Exercises

Part A Track 18

①リスニング、②パラレル・リーディング(音を聞きながらテキストを音読)、③プロソディ・シャドーイング（音の再現）④コンテンツ・シャドーイング（意味を意識）の順で会話を再現してみましょう。下記の Key Phrases を意識しながら、最低でも7回は会話を聞いてみましょう。

Key Phrases:

- We believe…
- As you know…
- Can you tell us…?
- That sounds good!
- You did a great job.
- It doesn't show.
- How do you like…?
- Is he the jealous type?
- What if the situation were reversed?
- That's what I said!
- I can tell…
- I knew it!
- No way!

Part B

相手の問いかけやコメントに対して、自分なりの答えを考えてみましょう。

1) **Keith:** You look a bit pale. Are you OK?
   You: _____

2) **Keith:** Dave said he didn't want to go to Canada. Do you know why?
   You: _____

3) **Keith:** I'm impressed with your English!
   You: _____

今度は相手の応答にふさわしい語りかけや質問をしてみましょう。

4) 「ご一行様は何名ですか」とていねいにたずねてみましょう。
   You: _____
   Keith: Yes, there are eight of us. We need four twin rooms.

5) 「彼の演技に感銘を受けた」といってみましょう。
   You: _____
   Keith: Yes, so was I.

6) 彼が怒っているのではないかと気にしていました。
   You: _____
   Keith: Don't worry. He's not mad at all.

Exercises の解答例と訳

1) Yes. I just get nervous in meetings.
2) Yes. He hates the cold.
3) Thank you. I've been studying for three years.
4) Can you tell us how many there are in your group?
5) I was impressed with his performance.
6) I was afraid he was mad at me.

問題と答えの訳

1) キース：少し顔色が悪いですね。大丈夫ですか。
   あなた：はい。会議で緊張するんです。
2) キース：デーブはカナダに行かないっていっていたよ。なぜか知ってる？
   あなた：ええ。彼は寒いのが嫌いなんです。
3) キース：あなたの英語は素晴らしいですね。
   あなた：ありがとう。3年間勉強してきていますから。
4) あなた：ご一行様は何名いらっしゃいますか。
   キース：はい、8人います。ツインルームが4部屋必要です。
5) あなた：彼のパフォーマンスには感銘を受けました。
   キース：ええ、私もです。
6) あなた：彼が私に怒っているのでは、と気にしていました。
   キース：心配しないで。彼はまったく君のことを怒っていないよ。

コラム　気持ちを伝える

　日本は「察しの文化」といわれ、いわれなくても相手の気持ちを察して行動することが美徳であるとされています。「以心伝心」という言葉も日本独特のものではないでしょうか。

　しかし、欧米人との人間関係においては、こういった感覚はあまり通用しません。欧米では、自分の気持ちをわかってもらうためには、それを伝えるのは本人の責任であると考えられています。ですから、何か問題があるときには、相手が察してくれるのを期待するのではなく、一般的にはこちらから問題があると伝えなければいけません。例えば、自分が話したくないことをきかれた場合、日本人なら相手の態度でなんとなく察してくれるものですが、欧米人に対しては "I'd rather not talk about it." などとはっきりといわない限り、伝わらないことが多いでしょう。

　効果的な異文化コミュニケーションを実践するためには、こういった感覚のちがいを知ることも非常に重要です。

Chapter 9 December

Skit B

ストーリーについて

　ジョーとアナの家には、クリスマスを前にリチャードやタケシなど友人らが集まりました。男性陣はテレビの前を陣取って、ビールを飲みながらアメリカンフットボールを観ています。リチャードは真冬のカナダに出張中のミユキが心配で、試合中継にも集中できない様子です。

ここで扱う表現について

　ミユキが出張中に、ジョー宅でフットボールの試合をテレビ観戦中の男性陣。アメリカでは、フットボール試合を見ながら男性が集まって談笑する、というのはごく一般的な休日の過ごし方です。

　選手たちが群がって取っ組み合いをしているのを見て、「寒いからだ」というリチャードのジョークに、Good one, Levinson. と喜ぶジョー。ウィットに富んだジョークに対し、(That's a) Good one! と返すのは相手にとっては賞讃。さらにファーストネームではなく、ラストネーム（苗字）である Levinson とすることで、親密さが増します。男性同士がラストネームだけで呼び合うのはよくあることです。ただし、女性同士では一般的ではありません。

　リチャードはジョーにミユキとのけんかのことを聞かれて、I'd rather not talk about it... (できれば話したくない) と答えています。本当に話したくない場合はこのようにきっぱり断ってかまいません。

　けんかの原因はジョーにある、It was partly your fault. (あなたのせいでもあったんだ) とジョーに訴えるリチャード。It was your fault. はよく使われますし、冗談ぽくいうのはいいのですが、真剣にいうのはおすすめしません。ジョーも少し反応が頑なになっているのにお気づきですか？　What's wrong with that? (何が悪いっていうんだ？) や、But that seems a little unfair. (でもそれはフェアじゃないような気がする) と反論しています。何でもストレートに表現するアメリカ人ですが、やはり相手を攻めるようにものをいうと関係に亀裂が入る可能性があります。相手への批判はもう少しやんわりと伝えたいものです。

Chapter 9 December

Skit B

Track 19

男性陣、テレビの前に集合！

Joe: Look, it's snowing. The players must be freezing.
Richard: That's why they're huddling.
J: Ha! Good one, Levinson.
Takeshi: Hey, where did the ball go?
R: **I bet** it's snowing in Toronto. Hope Miyuki doesn't catch a cold.
J: I guess you miss her, huh? I feel guilty about sending her away.
T: No problem. **As long as** she brings back maple syrup.
R and J: Oh! / Ouch!
R: Did you see that tackle? That had to hurt.
J: He's still lying there. The snow is covering him up.

---

be freezing: 凍える（coldも「寒い」だが、少し大げさに「凍えるような寒さ」を表すfreezingもよく使われる）
huddle: 群がる
Good one.: うまい！
I bet…: 〜にちがいない
catch a cold: 風邪を引く
miss…: 〜を寂しく思う
feel guilty: 悪く思う
No problem.: ご心配なく
hurt: 傷む

T: I'm glad I play baseball. I don't like cold weather, and I don't like fighting.

R: **I wish I could say the same for** your sister—uh, **forget I said that.**

J: Nope, too late.

T: You mean she likes to argue? Yes, I know.

J: So, Richard, what did you and Miyuki argue about?

R: I'd rather not talk about it in front of her little brother.

J: Cover your ears, Takeshi.

T: OK.

J: You can't hear, can you?

T: No, not at all.

J: Go ahead, Richard.

R: Actually, it was partly your fault. You were going to send her to Canada with **what's-his-name**.

J: Dave? **What's wrong with that?** Ah, **I get it.** You were jealous.

R: No, I just… wasn't completely comfortable with the situation.

J: But that seems a little unfair. I mean, what if the situation were reversed?

R: That's exactly what Miyuki said! She was so cool and… logical. It was scary.

J: I can imagine. I wonder where she learned to be cool and logical.

R: I… think I have an idea.

J: Anyway, Dave is a good guy. Also, I'm pretty sure he's in love with Jennifer.

T: Is Jennifer the one who Miyuki went to Canada with?

R: **You might as well** take your hands off your ears, Takeshi.

T: Don't worry. I didn't hear anything.

J, R, T: Hey… who won?

I wish I could say the same for…: ～もそうだったらいいのに
Forget I said that.: 今のは聞かなかったことにして
argue: 口論する
I'd rather not…: できれば～したくない

Go ahead.: どうぞ
fault: 責任、過ち
what's-his-name: 「彼の名前は何だっけ」さん
What's wrong with that?: それの何が悪い？
I get it.: わかった
be jealous: 嫉妬する

scary: 怖い

You might as well…: ～してもいい

ポイント解説

Chapter 9 December Skit B

クリスマスを前に、ジョーとアナの家に友人が集まりフランクに会話をしています。ここでは「……にちがいない」と自信を持っていうときの表現や、人の名前がわからないときに使う便利な代用語が登場します。

I bet...
Bet は「賭ける」。I bet... で「……ということに賭けてもいい」つまり「……にちがいない」ということ。

As long as...
「……さえすれば」「……である限り」。You won't get metabolic syndrome as long as you exercise regularly.（規則的に運動しさえすれば、メタボリック症候群になることはないでしょう）のように使える。

I wish I could say the same for...
「……もそうだったらいいのに」。セットフレーズとして覚えよう。I like reading. I wish I could say the same for my son.（私は読書が好き。息子もそうだといいんだけど）のように単語を入れ替えることによっていろいろと応用がきく。

Forget I said that.
日本語でいえば「聞かなかったことにして」「今のは忘れて」といったところ。

Joe: Look, it's snowing. The players must be freezing.
Richard: That's why they're huddling.
J: Ha! Good one, Levinson.
Takeshi: Hey, where did the ball go?
R: **I bet** it's snowing in Toronto. Hope Miyuki doesn't catch a cold.
J: I guess you miss her, huh? I feel guilty about sending her away.
T: No problem. **As long as** she brings back maple syrup.
R and J: Oh! / Ouch!
R: Did you see that tackle? That had to hurt.
J: He's still lying there. The snow is covering him up.
T: I'm glad I play baseball. I don't like cold weather, and I don't like fighting.
R: I wish I could say the same for your sister—uh, **forget I said that.**
J: Nope, too late.
T: You mean she likes to argue? Yes, I know.
J: So, Richard, what did you and Miyuki argue about?
R: I'd rather not talk about it in front of her little brother.
J: Cover your ears, Takeshi.
T: OK.

J: You can't hear, can you?
T: No, not at all.
J: Go ahead, Richard.
R: Actually, it was partly your fault. You were going to send her to Canada with **what's-his-name**.
J: Dave? **What's wrong with that?** Ah, **I get it.** You were jealous.
R: No, I just… wasn't completely comfortable with the situation.
J: But that seems a little unfair. I mean, what if the situation were reversed?
R: That's exactly what Miyuki said! She was so cool and… logical. It was scary.
J: I can imagine. I wonder where she learned to be cool and logical.
R: I… think I have an idea.
J: Anyway, Dave is a good guy. Also, I'm pretty sure he's in love with Jennifer.
T: Is Jennifer the one who Miyuki went to Canada with?
R: **You might as well** take your hands off your ears, Takeshi.
T: Don't worry. I didn't hear anything.
J, R, T: Hey… who won?

what's-his-name

-（ハイフン）でつなげることによって、ひとつの代用語とすることができる。この場合はリチャードがジョーに「あなたはミユキを『彼の名前は何だっけ』さんといっしょにカナダにいかせようとした」といっている。Can you get me that what-do-you-call-it?（あの「何とかいう名前のもの」を取ってくれる？）。once-in-a-lifetime experience で「一生に一度の経験」。

What's wrong with that?

自分や誰かのやったことやいったことを否定、非難されたときにいう「それの何が悪いんだ？」というフレーズ。

I get it.

「わかった」という、覚えておくと便利なフレーズだが、砕けた印象がある。フォーマルな席では代わりに I understand. といったほうが印象がいい。

You might as well…

「……してもいい」。「……したほうがいい」という意味にも使われる。

Joe: Look, it's snowing. The players must be freezing.
Richard: That's why they're huddling.
J: Ha! Good one, Levinson.
Takeshi: Hey, where did the ball go?
R: I bet it's snowing in Toronto. Hope Miyuki doesn't catch a cold.
J: I guess you miss her, huh? I feel guilty about sending her away.
T: No problem. As long as she brings back maple syrup.
R and J: Oh! / Ouch!
R: Did you see that tackle? That had to hurt.
J: He's still lying there. The snow is covering him up.
T: I'm glad I play baseball. I don't like cold weather, and I don't like fighting.
R: I wish I could say the same for your sister—uh, forget I said that.
J: Nope, too late.
T: You mean she likes to argue? Yes, I know.
J: So, Richard, what did you and Miyuki argue about?
R: I'd rather not talk about it in front of her little brother.
J: Cover your ears, Takeshi.
T: OK.
J: You can't hear, can you?
T: No, not at all.
J: Go ahead, Richard.
R: Actually, it was partly your fault. You were going to send her to Canada with what's-his-name.
J: Dave? What's wrong with that? Ah, I get it. You were jealous.
R: No, I just… wasn't completely comfortable with the situation.
J: But that seems a little unfair. I mean, what if the situation were reversed?
R: That's exactly what Miyuki said! She was so cool and… logical. It was scary.
J: I can imagine. I wonder where she learned to be cool and logical.
R: I… think I have an idea.
J: Anyway, Dave is a good guy. Also, I'm pretty sure he's in love with Jennifer.
T: Is Jennifer the one who Miyuki went to Canada with?
R: You might as well take your hands off your ears, Takeshi.
T: Don't worry. I didn't hear anything.
J, R, T: Hey… who won?

ジョー：見ろ、雪だよ。選手たちは寒いだろうな。
リチャード：だから彼らは群がってるんだ。
ジョー：ハハ！　うまいな、レヴィンソン。
タケシ：ちょっと、ボールはどこに行ったんだ？
リチャード：トロントは雪にちがいない。ミユキは風邪を引かなきゃいいけど。
ジョー：彼女がいなくて寂しいんだろ。彼女を遠くに行かせちゃって悪いな。
タケシ：大丈夫。メープルシロップを持って帰ってきてくれさえすればいいんだから。
リチャード＆ジョー：あ！／痛っ！
リチャード：あのタックル見たか。ありゃ痛いよ。
ジョー：彼はまだあそこに倒れてるよ。彼の上に雪が積もってる。
タケシ：僕は野球でよかった。寒いのは嫌だし、けんかも嫌です。
リチャード：同じことを僕も君のお姉さんにいえたらな……あ、いまいったことは忘れて。
ジョー：だめだよ、もう遅い。
タケシ：姉さんが口論するのが好きかってことですか。ええ、知ってますよ。
ジョー：それでリチャード、君とミユキは何のことで言い合ったんだ。
リチャード：できれば彼女の弟さんの前ではそのことは話したくないね。
ジョー：タケシ、耳をふさいで。
タケシ：OK。
ジョー：聞こえないだろ、どう？
タケシ：はい、まったく聞こえません。
ジョー：よしいいよ、リチャード。
リチャード：実際のところ、あなたのせいでもあったんですよ。彼女をカナダにナントカ君といっしょに行かせようとしたでしょう。
ジョー：デーブか。それの何が悪いんだ。ああ、わかった。嫉妬したんだな。
リチャード：いや、ただ……その状況を完全に納得しなかっただけです。
ジョー：でもそれはちょっとフェアじゃないんじゃないか。つまり、もし状況が逆だったら？
リチャード：まったく同じことをミユキもいってた！　彼女はすごく冷静で……論理的で。怖かったですよ。
ジョー：想像つくな。彼女はどこであんなに冷静でロジカルになることを学んだんだろう。
リチャード：少し……思い当たるふしはあるよ。
ジョー：とにかく、デーブはいいやつだよ。それに、かなりの可能性で彼はジェニファーに気があるね。
タケシ：ジェニファーって、ミユキがカナダにいっしょに行った人？
リチャード：耳から手を離してもいいよ、タケシ。
タケシ：ご心配なく。僕は何も聞いてません。
皆：ちょっと……どっちが勝った？

Chapter 9
December

Exercises

Part A Track 19

①リスニング、②パラレル・リーディング(音を聞きながらテキストを音読)、③プロソディ・シャドーイング（音の再現）④コンテンツ・シャドーイング（意味を意識）の順で会話を再現してみましょう。下記の Key Phrases を意識しながら、最低でも7回は会話を聞いてみましょう。

Key Phrases:
- I bet…
- As long as…
- I wish I could say the same for…
- Forget I said that.
- what's-his-name
- What's wrong with that?
- I get it.
- You might as well…

Part B

相手の語りかけや問いかけに対して、自分なりの答えを考えてみましょう。

1) **Leslie:** The next time I see him, I'm going to punch him in the face!
   You: _____

2) **Leslie:** What if I go to the meeting with you?
   You: _____

3) **Leslie:** You might as well stay for dinner. I don't think he's coming home anytime soon.
   You: _____

今度は相手に語りかけたり質問をしてみましょう。

4) 「考えがある。彼が日本にいる間は私の家にいては」と提案してみてください。
   You: _____
   Leslie: Oh, no, I wouldn't want to put you to all that trouble.

5) 待ち合わせの場所をどこにするかたずねてください。
   You: _____
   Leslie: I have an idea. Why don't we all meet at the station?

6) 提出しなければならないレポートの書き方がわかりません……。
   You: _____
   Leslie: I'm sure your professor will be able to help you.

Exercises の解答例と訳

1) That seems a little extreme.
2) Thank you! That would be great.
3) Are you sure you don't mind?
4) I have an idea. He can stay with us while he's in Japan.
5) Where should we meet?
6) I don't know how to write my report.

問題と答えの訳

1) レスリー：今度会ったらあいつの顔を殴ってやる！
   あなた：それはちょっとやりすぎじゃないかしら。
2) レスリー：ミーティングに同席しましょうか。
   あなた：ありがとう！それはいいですね。
3) レスリー：晩御飯を食べていってください。彼がすぐに戻って来るとは思わないから。
   あなた：本当にいいんですか。
4) あなた：考えがあるわ。彼が日本にいる間はうちにいていいわよ。
   レスリー：ええダメだよ、君に迷惑をかけたくない。
5) あなた：どこで会おうか。
   レスリー：そうだ。駅で待ち合わせしたらどうかな。
6) あなた：レポートの書き方がわからないの。
   レスリー：君の教授ならきっとあなたを助けてくれるよ。

コラム　スポーツTV観戦

アメリカではバスケットやアメリカンフットボール、野球などのプロスポーツが盛んです。各チームはそれぞれ本拠地を持ち、熱狂的な地元ファンがいます。そのため、週末になると男性数人が誰かの家に集まって、地元チームの試合をみんなでテレビ観戦するということがよくあります。たいていはビールを飲んだり、たとえば宅配ピザを食べながら、テレビにくぎ付けになって応援します。

地元チームの選手がいいプレイをすれば、"Way to go, Michael!"（いいぞ、マイケル）などと称賛し、ミスをすれば、"What are you doing?!"（なにやってんだよ）などと画面に向かってヤジを飛ばしたりします。

また、親戚の集まりやカジュアルなホームパーティーでも、気がつくと男性陣だけテレビの前にたむろして、スポーツの試合に熱中しているということがよくあります。

Chapter 9 の 重要表現リスト

Skit A

- [ ] **We believe...**
  〜を私どもは確信しております
- [ ] **As you know...** ご存じのように
- [ ] **Can you tell us...?**
  〜を教えてもらえますか
- [ ] **in other words** つまり
- [ ] **on duty** 当番
- [ ] **at all times** いつも (ややフォーマル)
- [ ] **That sounds good!**
  いいですね (よろしくお願いします)
- [ ] ***That would be great.** いいですねえ
- [ ] **You did a great job.** よくやったね
- [ ] **It doesn't show.** そうは見えない
- [ ] **How do you like...?**
  〜はどう思いますか
- [ ] **be mad at...** 〜に対して怒る
- [ ] ***be angry at...** 〜に対して怒る
- [ ] **I'm serious.** 本気よ
- [ ] **Is he the jealous type?**
  彼は焼きもち焼きなの?
- [ ] **Not usually.**
  ふだんはそんなことはない
- [ ] **What if the situation were reversed?**
  もし逆の状況だったらどうなっているの
- [ ] **That's what I said!**
  それはまさに私がいったことです
- [ ] ***That's not what I said.**
  誤解している
- [ ] **be impressed with...**
  〜に感心する
- [ ] **I can tell...** きっと〜ということだろう
- [ ] **I knew it!** やっぱり
- [ ] ***I knew that...** やっぱり〜だ
- [ ] **No way!** とんでもない

Skit B

- [ ] **Good one.** うまい!
- [ ] **I bet...** 〜にちがいない
- [ ] **feel guilty** 悪く思う
- [ ] **No problem.** ご心配なく
- [ ] **As long as...** 〜さえすれば
- [ ] **I wish I could say the same for...**
  〜もそうだったらいいのに
- [ ] **Forget I said that.**
  今のは聞かなかったことにして
- [ ] **I'd rather not...**
  できれば〜したくない
- [ ] **what's-his-name** ナントカ君
- [ ] **What's wrong with that?**
  それの何が悪いんですか
- [ ] ***But that seems a little unfair.**
  でもそれはフェアじゃないような気がする
- [ ] **I get it.** わかった
- [ ] ***I understand.**
  わかった (フォーマルな席で)
- [ ] **You might as well...**
  〜しほうがよい

Chapter 10

January

場面・状況	**ミユキの家で新年会を開く**
表現のテーマ	**質問する／驚く／喜ぶ／お礼をいう**

Skit A

場面・状況	**老舗の料亭で本社の副社長をもてなす**
表現のテーマ	**接待でのやりとり**

Skit B

Chapter 10 January

Skit A

ストーリーについて

　ジョーとアナ、エミリーはクリスマスを実家のあるサンフランシスコで過ごし、東京へ戻ってきました。きょうは新年のお祝いにツカザワ家にやってきました。そこにはリチャードも参加。一時は危ぶまれたミユキとリチャードの仲でしたが、ミユキがカナダから帰ってくると、そんなことはすっかり忘れてしまったようです。

ここで扱う表現について

　お正月にミユキ宅に招かれたリチャードとジョー一家。用意された食事に称賛が絶えないジョーとアナ。Can you tell me what everything is?（これらが何か説明していただけますか）のように、積極的に質問することで、相手に自分が興味があることを伝えています。これが礼儀です。ただ黙々と食事するのは味気ないですし、相手を不安にさせますよね。

　ロスへの転勤が決まったジョー一家。発表する際、We have some news. と切り出しています。Chapter 8 Skit B でミユキがリチャードにカナダへの出張が決まったことを伝える際にも I have some news. といっていましたね。吉報の場合は、We have some good news.、逆に悪い場合は We have some bad news.、もし両方であれば、We have both good and bad news. となります。News は複数形なので、a news とはなりません。注意しましょう。

　ジョーの転勤、そしてミユキとリチャードの結婚報告に対して This is so sudden!（すごく急ですね）、I can hardly believe it.（とても信じられない）、Oh, my gosh!（びっくり）と驚きのセリフが続きます。その後は、This is so exciting!（わくわくするわ）、That's great!（すばらしい）、Congratulations!（おめでとう）と喜びの表現に。よい知らせには、思いっきりお祝いのことばを発しましょう。

Chapter 10 January

Skit A

Track 20

ミユキの家に全員集合！

Miyuki: Richard, sit next to me.
Richard: Well… **if you insist.**
Takeshi: Be careful, Richard. She spills soy sauce.
Joe: The food looks delicious.
Anna: And it's so beautifully arranged. Can you tell me what everything is?
Masako: This is *kamaboko*—fish cake. And… *kinpira gobo*. **What is that in English?**
M: Simmered… *gobo*. **I'm sorry, I don't know the English word.**
Hiroshi: We have special *sake*. Here you are, Joe-*san*… Anna-*san*…
A: Just a sip, please.
H: Ah, yes, a sip. We learned this word in Australia—in wine country.
T: My father had many sips. Then he left his wallet on a train.
H: My son talks too much. The train people

---

if you insist: どうしてもというのなら
spill: こぼす

simmer: 煮る

Here you are.: どうぞ

just a sip: ひと口だけ

found it, so… no worries!

Emily: Can I have a sip? I'm eight now.

J: Sorry, kid. Yesterday was Emily's birthday, everyone.

Everyone: Happy birthday, Emily!

Ma: We have so many things to celebrate!

H: First… Happy New Year!

Everyone: *Akemashite omedeto gozaimasu!* Happy New Year!

M: So this is the the first time you've been in Japan for the New Year?

A: That's right. We came back from the States early this time.

J: We wanted to experience *oshogatsu* before we leave.

R: Leave? What do you mean?

J: We… have some news. I was offered a job at the agency's parent company in Los Angeles.

A: So it looks like we'll be moving back to America.

M: This is so sudden! I can hardly believe it.

Ma: You are going back to America?

A: We'll be very sad to leave.

J: But we'll be here until the end of March.

R: Oh, that's good, because… you tell them, Miyuki.

M: Well… we're getting married at the end of February.

A: Oh, my gosh! This is so exciting! And I introduced you!

R: Yes—thanks!

J: That's great! Congratulations! Takeshi, how long have you known about this?

T: Oh, I knew before Miyuki and Richard knew.

R and M: What?

T: I told you, Richard. Younger brothers understand everything.

Can I have a sip?:
ひとくちだけ飲んでもいい？
kid:
親しい呼びかけ

What do you mean?:
どういうこと？
We have some news.:
お知らせしたいことがあります
offer: オファーする、提供する
parent company:
親会社
It looks like…:
どうやら〜のようだ
This is so sudden!:
そんな急に！
I can hardly believe it.:
とても信じられません
That's good.:
それならよかった
This is (so) exciting!:
すごく楽しみ！

ポイント解説

Chapter 10 January Skit A

ジョー一家が新年にミユキの家にやってきます。6月のSkit Bで登場した英語で何というか尋ねる表現や、10月のSkit Aで登場した「どういう意味ですか?」といった表現が再登場するので、おさらいしておきましょう。

if you insist

insistは「強く主張する」。if you insistは、「どうしてもというのであれば」のような意味合いを含み、どちらかというとネガティブな表現。便利な表現だが、あまり多用しないほうがいいかもしれない。ここではリチャードは照れ隠しのために、「しょうがないなあ」というニュアンスを込めていっている。

- What is that in English?
- I'm sorry, I don't know the English word.

日本独自の食材や料理には、英語名がないものも多い。わからない場合は素直にそのことを伝え、どういうものなのかを説明するといい。ゴボウは burdock root だが、英語圏の人でもピンとこないかもしれないので、This is called *gobo*. It's a Japanese root vegetable. (これはゴボウです。日本の根菜です)といえばいい。ちなみに豆腐 *tofu*、枝豆 *edamame*、山葵 *wasabi* などは日本語のまま使われている。

Just a sip, please.

a sipは「ひとくち」。Would you like some sake? とすすめられたときの「ではひとくちだけ」というフレーズ。あまり飲めない場合は無理しないで、No, thank you. I can't / don't drink. と断ればいい。

Miyuki: Richard, sit next to me.
Richard: Well… **if you insist.**
Takeshi: Be careful, Richard. She spills soy sauce.
Joe: The food looks delicious.
Anna: And it's so beautifully arranged. Can you tell me what everything is?
Masako: This is *kamaboko*—fish cake. And… *kinpira gobo*. **What is that in English?**
M: Simmered… *gobo*. **I'm sorry, I don't know the English word.**
Hiroshi: We have special *sake*. Here you are, Joe-*san*… Anna-*san*…
A: **Just a sip, please.**
H: Ah, yes, a sip. We learned this word in Australia—in wine country.
T: My father had many sips. Then he left his wallet on a train.
H: My son talks too much. The train people found it, so… no worries!
Emily: Can I have a sip? I'm eight now.
J: Sorry, kid. Yesterday was Emily's birthday, everyone.
Everyone: **Happy birthday,** Emily!
Ma: We have so many things to celebrate!
H: First… Happy New Year!

Everyone: *Akemashite omedeto gozaimasu!* Happy New Year!
M: So **this is the first time** you've been in Japan for the New Year?
A: That's right. We came back from the States early this time.
J: We wanted to experience *oshogatsu* before we leave.
R: Leave? What do you mean?
J: We… have some news. I was offered a job at the agency's parent company in Los Angeles.
A: So **it looks like** we'll be moving back to America.
M: This is so sudden! **I can hardly believe it.**
Ma: You are going back to America?
A: We'll be very sad to leave.
J: But we'll be here until the end of March.
R: Oh, that's good, because… **you tell** them, Miyuki.
M: Well… we're getting married at the end of February.
A: Oh, my gosh! **This is so exciting!** And I introduced you!
R: Yes—thanks!
J: That's great! Congratulations! Takeshi, how long have you known about this?
T: Oh, I knew before Miyuki and Richard knew.
R and M: What?
T: I told you, Richard. Younger brothers understand everything.

This is the first time…

肯定文だが、文末をあげることで質問文になる。Is this the first time…? と同じ。「……するのは初めてです」というフレーズ。This is the first time I've been to the U.S. (アメリカを訪れるのは初めてです) など。

It looks like…

断言はできないがほぼ確実、あまり気が乗らないのだが、というニュアンスが込められた「どうやら……ということのようだ」という表現。

I can hardly believe it.

hardly は「とても……ない」。I can't believe it. よりも「信じられない」という思いが込められている。

You tell…

「君がいってくれよ」と you (あなた) が強調される。

This is so exciting!

exciting は興奮やうれしさ、楽しみなどを伝えるよく使われる単語。This is so exciting! には「すばらしい」「楽しみだ」「わくわくする」などのニュアンスが含まれる。

Happy birthday!

誕生日は日本人同様、アメリカ人にとっても大切な記念日。誕生日を迎える人には Happy birthday! とひとこと。もしお祝いをいうのが後日になってしまった場合は、Happy belated birthday.。

訳

Miyuki: Richard, sit next to me.
Richard: Well… if you insist.
Takeshi: Be careful, Richard. She spills soy sauce.
Joe: The food looks delicious.
Anna: And it's so beautifully arranged. Can you tell me what everything is?
Masako: This is *kamaboko*—fish cake. And… *kinpira gobo*. What is that in English?
M: Simmered… *gobo*. I'm sorry, I don't know the English word.
Hiroshi: We have special *sake*. Here you are, Joe-*san*… Anna-*san*…
A: Just a sip, please.
H: Ah, yes, a sip. We learned this word in Australia—in wine country.
T: My father had many sips. Then he left his wallet on a train.
H: My son talks too much. The train people found it, so… no worries!
Emily: Can I have a sip? I'm eight now.
J: Sorry, kid. Yesterday was Emily's birthday, everyone.
Everyone: Happy birthday, Emily!
Ma: We have so many things to celebrate!
H: First… Happy New Year!
Everyone: *Akemashite omedeto gozaimasu!* Happy New Year!
M: So this is the the first time you've been in Japan for the New Year?
A: That's right. We came back from the States early this time.
J: We wanted to experience *oshogatsu* before we leave.
R: Leave? What do you mean?
J: We… have some news. I was offered a job at the agency's parent company in Los Angeles.
A: So it looks like we'll be moving back to America.
M: This is so sudden! I can hardly believe it.
Ma: You are going back to America?
A: We'll be very sad to leave.
J: But we'll be here until the end of March.
R: Oh, that's good, because… you tell them, Miyuki.
M: Well… we're getting married at the end of February.
A: Oh, my gosh! This is so exciting! And I introduced you!
R: Yes—thanks!
J: That's great! Congratulations! Takeshi, how long have you known about this?
T: Oh, I knew before Miyuki and Richard knew.
R and M: What?
T: I told you, Richard. Younger brothers understand everything.

ミユキ: リチャード、私の隣に座って。
リチャード: まあ……君がそういうなら。
タケシ: 気をつけたほうがいいよ、リチャード。彼女は醤油をこぼすよ。
ジョー: おいしそうな料理ですね。
アナ: それにとてもきれいにアレンジされてる。どれが何なのか教えてくださいますか。
マサコ: これはカマボコ、フィッシュケーキよ。それと……キンピラゴボウ。これは英語で何ていうのかしら。
ミユキ: 煮た……ゴボウ（笑）。ごめんなさい、英語の名前がわからないわ。
ヒロシ: 特別なお酒がありますよ。どうぞ、ジョーさん、アナさん。
アナ: ほんのひと口だけ、お願いします。
ヒロシ: ああ、はい、ひと口ね。この単語はオーストラリアで覚えたんだ、ワインの国でね。
タケシ: 父さんはひと口をたくさん飲んだんだ。それで電車の中に財布を置いてきたんだよ。
ヒロシ: 息子はおしゃべりなんです。電車の人たちが見つけてくれたから、ご心配なく。
エミリー: 私もひと口飲んでいい？ 私もう8歳よ。
ジョー: 残念だね、お嬢さん。みなさん、昨日はエミリーの誕生日だったんです。
全員: お誕生日おめでとう、エミリー！
マサコ: お祝いすることがいっぱいね！
ヒロシ: まず……ハッピーニューイヤー！
全員: アケマシテ、オメデトウゴザイマス！／ハッピーニューイヤー！
ミユキ: では、あなたたちにとってこれが日本での初めてのお正月ね。
アナ: そう。今回は早めにアメリカから戻ってきました。
ジョー: 離れる前にお正月を体験したかったので。
リチャード: 離れる？ どういうこと？
ジョー: あの……お知らせがあります。ロサンゼルスの親会社のほうから仕事の機会を与えられて。
アナ: なので、アメリカにまた戻ることになりそうね。
ミユキ: そんな急に。とても信じられないわ。
マサコ: アメリカに戻られるの？
アナ: 日本を離れるなんてとても悲しくなるわ。
ジョー: でも3月の終わりまではいるから。
リチャード: ああ、それはよかった、だって……ミユキ、君がいってくれよ。
ミユキ: その……私たち、2月の末に結婚するんです。
アナ: それはびっくり。すごく楽しみだわ。それに私が紹介したのよ。
リチャード: そう。ありがとう。
ジョー: すばらしい！ おめでとう。タケシ、君はこのことをいつから知ってたの。
タケシ: ああ、ミユキとリチャードよりも前から知ってましたよ。
リチャードとミユキ: え？
タケシ: いったよね、リチャード、弟は何でもわかってるんだよ。

Chapter 10
January

Exercises

Part A `Track 20`

①リスニング、②パラレル・リーディング(音を聞きながらテキストを音読)、③プロソディ・シャドーイング（音の再現）④コンテンツ・シャドーイング（意味を意識）の順で会話を再現してみましょう。下記の Key Phrases を意識しながら、最低でも7回は会話を聞いてみましょう。

Key Phrases:
- if you insist
- -What is that in English?
  -I'm sorry, I don't know the English word.
- Just a sip, please.
- Happy birthday!
- This is the first time…
- It looks like…
- I can hardly believe it.
- You tell…
- This is so exciting!

Part B

相手の質問に対して、自分なりの答えを考えてみましょう。

1) **Bill:** So this is "*chirashi-zushi*." Can you tell me what everything is?
   You: _____

2) **Bill:** So you and your family are going back to Japan? This is so sudden!
   You: _____

3) **Bill:** How long have you known about your transfer?
   You: _____

今度は相手に質問してみましょう。

4) 「サンマ」は英語で何というかたずねてみましょう。
   You: _____
   Bill: "*Sanma*"? Oh, I'm sorry, I don't know the English word for it.

5) ふたりが婚約したこと、いつ知った？
   You: _____
   Bill: I first heard about it in June.

6) 来月に昇進、妊娠3カ月というダブルのオメデタをBillに告げましょう。
   You: _____
   Bill: How exciting! You have so many things to celebrate!

Exercises の解答例と訳

1) Let's see. "*Ikura*" — fish roe. This is squid, this is shrimp, and this is tuna.
2) We're very sad to leave.
3) I was told about it two weeks ago.
4) "*Sanma*" — what is that in English?
5) How long have you known they were engaged?
6) I'm getting promoted next month. Also, I just found out that I'm three months pregnant.

問題と答えの訳

1) ビル：これが「ちらし寿司」ですか。どれが何なのか教えてくれますか？
 あなた：ええと。これが「イクラ」——魚の卵です。これがイカ、これがエビで、これがマグロです。
2) ビル：それで君は家族と日本へ帰るのかい？ずいぶん急な話だね！
 あなた：離れるのはとてもさびしいわ。
3) ビル：異動についてはどのくらい前から知っていたのですか。
 あなた：2週間前にいわれました。
4) あなた：「サンマ」——英語で何というのですか。
 ビル：ああ、ごめん、英語で何ていうのかはわからないんだ。
5) あなた：彼らが婚約したといつから知っていましたか。
 ビル：そのことは6月にはじめて聞きました。
6) あなた：来月に昇進します。また、妊娠3カ月ということもわかりました。
 ビル：すごい！お祝いしないといけないことがいっぱいありますね！

コラム

クリスマスとお正月

アメリカやカナダでは、日本のように年末年始のお正月休みというものがありません。お正月よりクリスマスに重きが置かれており、24日と25日にはクリスマス休暇があります。日本ではクリスマスにケーキを食べることがお約束ですが、北米ではケーキの代わりにパンプキンパイを食べるのが習慣となっています。他には七面鳥 (turkey) の丸焼きやマッシュポテトなどが定番メニューです。人々の多くはちょうどクリスマスの1カ月前にある感謝祭 (Thanksgiving Day) とまったく同じものを食べるので、ある種の déjà vu のような感覚になる人もいます。

クリスマスになると、日本人がお正月に故郷に帰省するように、北米でも多くの人々が別の土地に住む家族を訪れます。

クリスマス・イブにデートをするのは、北米では日本のように一般的ではありません。クリスマス・イブは家族や友だちと過ごすのが普通です。一方、大晦日は1年で最大の「デートのための夜」です。

クリスマスはもちろんご存じのようにクリスチャンの祝日です。そのため、クリスチャンではない人の多くはクリスマスのお祝いをしませんが、非宗教的な家族の祝日として祝う人もいます。

Chapter 10 January

Skit B

ストーリーについて

　ジョー一家はアメリカへ帰国のための引っ越しの準備を始め、ミユキとリチャードは結婚式の段取りに追われています。ジョーとミユキは会社でも大忙し。ヒット・ザ・ロード・トラベルのアメリカ本社の副社長が来社することになったからです。ジョーと社員たちは、副社長を連れて、老舗の和食料理屋に夕食を食べにきました。

ここで扱う表現について

　本社から訪問中の副社長を接待するミユキとジョー。初対面ゆえ、相手をファーストネームでなく Mr. Robinson と呼ぶミユキですが、それに対して副社長は、Please—call me Brian. (お願いです、ブライアンと呼んでください) といっていますね。相手からそう促された場合は、そうするのがマナーであり、頑なに Mr. Robinson と呼び続けるのはかえって失礼にあたります。ただし相手からそういった申し出がなかった場合には、Mr. Robinson と呼ぶべきです。

　Can you recommend a good sake? (何かいい酒をすすめてくれないか) というジョーの依頼に対し、デーブが I'd be happy to. (よろこんで) と答えています。このように何か頼まれた場合はこのように返すと相手の心象もよくなります。もし応えられない場合は I'm sorry, but... (申し訳ないのですが……) と断りましょう。ここでは、I'm sorry, but I'm afraid I don't know much about sake. (申し訳ありませんが、あまり酒には詳しくないので) とすればいいでしょう。

　このスキットでも Excellent.、You did a first-rate job.、I'm very impressed by your initiative.、You've come very far. などと、相手をほめる表現が複数出てきますね。それに対して Thank you. と素直に認めるもよし、ミユキのように I still have a long way to go. (まだまだ道のりは長いです) と謙遜してもいいでしょう。ただあちらがずっとほめているのにそれを頑なに拒否するのは問題です。適度に相手の称賛に対し、感謝の意を表しましょう。

Chapter 10 January

Skit B

Track 21

日本料理はどうですか？

Joe: **This restaurant is known for** its seafood.
Brian: Wonderful! **I've been looking forward to** the seafood in Japan.
Miyuki: Do you know what you'd like to drink, Mr. Robinson?
B: Please—call me Brian. **Some sake would be nice.**
J: Dave, can you recommend a good sake?
Dave: I'd be happy to. This is on the company, right?
J: Uh… yes.
D: **Just making sure.** How about this sake from Aomori? Exquisite balance, extravagant price.
B: Excellent.
M: Is everyone ready to order drinks?
Others: Yes. / Oh yes, I'll have a beer. / Me, too. / I think so.
Jennifer: Dave, **are you feeling OK?** You look pale.
D: I'm fine, thanks, Jen. It's the, uh, cold weath-

---

be known for…:
〜で有名だ

look forward to…:
〜を楽しみにしている

…would be nice.:
〜ならうれしいです

recommend:
すすめる
I'd be happy to.:
喜んでします
This is on…:
これは〜のおごりです
make sure:
確認する
exquisite: 絶妙の
extravagant:
非常に高価な
I'll have…:
〜をもらいます、注文します
look pale:
顔色が青い

er—makes me turn blue.
Je: **Good thing** you didn't go to Canada. Talk about cold.
D: Well… you did a first-rate job over there.
Je: Thanks. You would have done a great job, too.
D: **That goes without saying.**
J: Everyone, it's time for a toast. Brian, welcome to Japan! *Kampai*!
Everyone: *Kampai*!

その後

B: So, Miyuki, tell me more about your tourism database.
M: OK. Um, to explain briefly, I input information about 30 different features and services. Then the travel consultants can match the features with the clients' needs.
B: Sounds very efficient.
M: Basically, it's a way to narrow down options. At that point, the consultants use their own knowledge and judgment.
J: Miyuki collected a lot of valuable information on her trip to Canada.
B: I don't doubt it. I'm very impressed by your initiative. And by your English.
M: Thank you. But I still have a long way to go.
J: You're too modest, Miyuki. You've come very far in less than a year.
B: Joe, may I make a suggestion?
J: Please do.
B: Before you… hit the road, so to speak, maybe you should promote Ms. Tsukazawa to travel consultant.
J: That's just what I was thinking. What do you think, Ms. Tsukazawa?
M: Um… I think it's a good idea! But please call me Miyuki!

Good thing…:
〜でよかった
Talk about cold.:
本当に寒かった
first-rate:
すばらしい、一流の
would have done…: きっと〜しただろう
That goes without saying.:
いうまでもない
did/have (has, had) done a great (good) job:
よくやった
tourism: 観光
to explain briefly:
ざっと説明すると
feature:
見所、主要なもの
sounds…:
〜そうだ
It's a way to…:
それは〜するための方法だ
narrow down:
範囲を絞る
at that point:
その時点で
be impressed by…: 〜に感心させられる
initiative: イニシアチブ、率先力
have a long way to go: まだまだ先は長い
modest:
謙虚な、腰の低い
have come very far: よくここまでやってきた
hit the road:
出発する
so to speak: いってみれば
promote:
昇進させる
That's just what I was thinking.:
まさにそう思っていました

ポイント解説

Chapter 10 January Skit B

ジョーとミユキたちがアメリカの副社長ブライアンを接待するシーンです。ここでは何かを説明するときに使える表現や、人に飲み物をすすめる表現が使われています。相手を気遣う表現もいっしょに覚えておきましょう。

This restaurant is known for...

be known for...「……で知られている」は、英語で何かを説明するときに覚えておくと便利なフレーズ。be famous for...（……で有名です）も同じ。Kyoto is famous for its many old temples.（京都はたくさんの古い寺で有名です）など。

I've been looking forward to...

be looking forward to...で「……を楽しみにする」。I'm looking forward to...（……が楽しみです）の現在進行形よりも、「これまでずっと楽しみにしていました」という気持ちが込められたセリフ。

Some sake would be nice.

What would you like to drink?（お飲み物は何がいいですか）や Would you like sake or wine?（日本酒とワインとどちらがいいですか）などとすすめられたとき、「……をいただきます」という返事には ...would be nice.。

Just making sure.

「念のため」という意味。Just wanted to make sure. も同様に使われる。

Joe: **This restaurant is known for** its seafood.

Brian: Wonderful! **I've been looking forward to** the seafood in Japan.

Miyuki: Do you know what you'd like to drink, Mr. Robinson?

B: Please—call me Brian. **Some sake would be nice.**

J: Dave, can you recommend a good sake?

Dave: I'd be happy to. This is on the company, right?

J: Uh… yes.

D: **Just making sure.** How about this sake from Aomori? Exquisite balance, extravagant price.

B: Excellent.

M: Is everyone ready to order drinks?

Others: Yes. / Oh yes, I'll have a beer. / Me, too. / I think so.

Jennifer: Dave, **are you feeling OK?** You look pale.
D: I'm fine, thanks, Jen. It's the, uh, cold weather—makes me turn blue.
Je: **Good thing** you didn't go to Canada. Talk about cold.
D: Well… you did a first-rate job over there.
Je: Thanks. You would have done a great job, too.
D: That goes without saying.
J: Everyone, it's time for a toast. Brian, welcome to Japan! *Kampai*!
Everyone: *Kampai*!

B: So, Miyuki, tell me more about your tourism database.
M: OK. Um, to explain briefly, I input information about 30 different features and services. Then the travel consultants can match the features with the clients' needs.
B: Sounds very efficient.
M: Basically, it's a way to narrow down options. At that point, the consultants use their own knowledge and judgment.
J: Miyuki collected a lot of valuable information on her trip to Canada.
B: I don't doubt it. I'm very impressed by your initiative. And by your English.
M: Thank you. But I still have a long way to go.
J: You're too modest, Miyuki. You've come very far in less than a year.
B: Joe, may I make a suggestion?
J: Please do.
B: Before you… hit the road, so to speak, maybe you should promote Ms. Tsukazawa to travel consultant.
J: That's just what I was thinking. What do you think, Ms. Tsukazawa?
M: Um… I think it's a good idea! But please call me Miyuki!

Are you feeling OK?
誰かの具合が悪そうだったら、Are you all right? や Are you OK? と尋ねる。

Good thing…
Good thing… で「……でよかった 」。Good thing you don't have to work on Sundays.（日曜日に働かなくてよかったね）など。

That goes without saying.
「それはいうまでもないでしょう」「当たり前でしょう」という決まり文句。It goes without saying that drunk driving is illegal.（飲酒運転が禁止なのはいうまでもない）などとしても応用できる。

Joe: This restaurant is known for its seafood.
Brian: Wonderful! I've been looking forward to the seafood in Japan.
Miyuki: Do you know what you'd like to drink, Mr. Robinson?
B: Please—call me Brian. Some sake would be nice.
J: Dave, can you recommend a good sake?
Dave: I'd be happy to. This is on the company, right?
J: Uh… yes.
D: Just making sure. How about this sake from Aomori? Exquisite balance, extravagant price.
B: Excellent.
M: Is everyone ready to order drinks?
Others: Yes. / Oh yes, I'll have a beer. / Me, too. / I think so.
Jennifer: Dave, are you feeling OK? You look pale.
D: I'm fine, thanks, Jen. It's the, uh, cold weather—makes me turn blue.
Je: Good thing you didn't go to Canada. Talk about cold.
D: Well… you did a first-rate job over there.
Je: Thanks. You would have done a great job, too.
D: That goes without saying.
J: Everyone, it's time for a toast. Brian, welcome to Japan! *Kampai!*
Everyone: *Kampai!*

B: So, Miyuki, tell me more about your tourism database.
M: OK. Um, to explain briefly, I input information about 30 different features and services. Then the travel consultants can match the features with the clients' needs.
B: Sounds very efficient.
M: Basically, it's a way to narrow down options. At that point, the consultants use their own knowledge and judgment.
J: Miyuki collected a lot of valuable information on her trip to Canada.
B: I don't doubt it. I'm very impressed by your initiative. And by your English.
M: Thank you. But I still have a long way to go.
J: You're too modest, Miyuki. You've come very far in less than a year.
B: Joe, may I make a suggestion?
J: Please do.
B: Before you… hit the road, so to speak, maybe you should promote Ms. Tsukazawa to travel consultant.
J: That's just what I was thinking. What do you think, Ms. Tsukazawa?
M: Um… I think it's a good idea! But please call me Miyuki!

ジョー：この店はシーフードで有名なんですよ。
ブライアン：いいね。日本でシーフードを食べることを楽しみにしてたんだ。
ミユキ：ミスター・ロビンソン、飲み物は何にされるかお決まりですか。
ブライアン：ブライアンと呼んでください。日本酒なんかいいね。
ジョー：デーブ、おすすめの何かいい日本酒を選んでくれないか。
デーブ：よろこんで。会社のツケ、ですよね。
ジョー：えー……そうだな。
デーブ：念のため。この青森県の日本酒はどうですか。絶妙なバランスで、お値段も張ります。
ブライアン：それはいいね。
ミユキ：みなさん、飲み物の注文は決まりましたか。
社員たち：はい。／ああ、僕はビール。／私も。／（注文が）決まったよ。
ジェニファー：デーブ、気分は大丈夫？　顔色が悪いけど。
デーブ：大丈夫だよ。ありがとう、ジェン。その、この寒さのせいで顔が青白いんだ。
ジェニファー：カナダに行かなくてよかったわね。本当に寒かった。
デーブ：まあ……君はあっちでは最高の仕事をやったな。
ジェニファー：ありがとう。きっとあなただっていい仕事をしたわよ。
デーブ：当たり前さ。
ジョー：みなさん、乾杯の時間です。ブライアン、日本へようこそ。乾杯！！
全員：乾杯！

ブライアン：それでミユキ、観光業界のデータベースについてもっと教えてくれないか。
ミユキ：はい。えーと、手短にご説明しますと、30の異なる見所とサービスに関する情報を入力しました。これで旅行コンサルタントは、クライアントの要望と見所をマッチさせることができます。
ブライアン：とても効率的な感じだね。
ミユキ：基本的に、これで選択肢を絞れるわけです。後はコンサルタント自身の知識と判断になります。
ジョー：ミユキはカナダへの出張で、役立つ情報をたくさん集めてきたんですよ。
ブライアン：確かに。君の率先力にとても感心させられたよ。それと君の英語にもね。
ミユキ：ありがとうございます。でもまだ先は長いです。
ジョー：謙虚すぎるよ、ミユキ。1年もたっていないのに、君はこれほどまでになったんだから。
ブライアン：ジョー、ひとつ提案してもいいか。
ジョー：どうぞ。
ブライアン：君が……その、いってみれば「ヒット・ザ・ロード（出発する）」する前に、ツカザワさんを旅行コンサルタントに昇進させたらいいんじゃないかな。
ジョー：まさに私も考えていたことです。ツカザワさん、あなたはどう思いますか。
ミユキ：えーと……とてもいいお話だと思います。でもお願いですから「ミユキ」と呼んでください。

Chapter 10
January

Exercises

Part A `Track 21`

①リスニング、②パラレル・リーディング(音を聞きながらテキストを音読)、③プロソディ・シャドーイング（音の再現）④コンテンツ・シャドーイング（意味を意識）の順で会話を再現してみましょう。下記の Key Phrases を意識しながら、最低でも７回は会話を聞いてみましょう。

Key Phrases:

- This (restaurant) is known for…
- I've been looking forward to…
- (Some sake) would be nice.
- Just making sure.
- Are you feeling OK?
- Good thing…
- That goes without saying.

Part B

相手の語りかけに対して、自分なりの答えを考えてみましょう。

1) **Nancy:** Can you recommend a good coffee shop in Ginza?
   You: _____
2) **Nancy:** That was superb! You did a first-rate job.
   You: _____
3) **Nancy:** You've come very far.
   You: _____

今度は相手に質問したり語りかけたりしてみましょう。

4) 相手に借りた本が面白かったと感想を述べてお礼をいいましょう。
   You: _____
   Nancy: I'm glad you enjoyed it. This author is famous for his beautiful writing style.
5) トロントに行く予定のあなたは、Nancyにおすすめの場所をたずねてください。
   You: _____
   Nancy: I'd be happy to. My favorite place in Toronto is the Harbor Front.
6) 気分が悪そうな相手に「大丈夫か」とたずねてみてください。
   You: _____
   Nancy: I feel like I'm catching a cold. I think I may have a fever.

Exercisesの解答例と訳

1) I'd be happy to. My favorite coffee shop is "West".
2) Thank you. You would have done a great job, too.
3) Thank you, but I still have a long way to go.
4) I really enjoyed the book. Thank you for lending it to me.
5) Can you recommend a good place to visit in Toronto?
6) Do you know what you'd like to do this weekend?

問題と答えの訳

1) ナンシー：銀座でおすすめのコーヒーショップを教えてください。
   あなた：よろこんで。私のおすすめのコーヒーショップは「ウエスト」です。
2) ナンシー：素晴らしかったわ！　最高の仕事をやり遂げたわね。
   あなた：ありがとう。きっとあなたでもいい仕事をしたでしょう。
3) ナンシー：とても成長したわね。
   あなた：ありがとう。でもまだまだです。
4) あなた：その本、本当に面白かったです。貸してくれてありがとう。
   ナンシー：楽しんでもらえてよかった。この著者はきれいな文体で有名なんですよ。
5) あなた：トロントで訪れるのにおすすめの場所を教えてください。
   ナンシー：よろこんで。トロントで私のお気に入りの場所はハーバー・フロントです。
6) あなた：大丈夫ですか。
   ナンシー：ちょっと風邪気味なの。熱があるかもしれないわ。

コラム　お酒の席

　欧米の個人主義はお酒の席でも垣間見ることができます。日本ではお酌をし合うのがお酒の席におけるある種のマナーとなっていて、杯が空になる度に注ぎ足し合ったりしますが、欧米では自分のお酒は自分で注ぐのが普通です。ボトル・ワインを飲むようなときには、ひとりが全員の分をつぐことはありますが、日本のように「お酌は女性がやるもの」という考えはなく、むしろたいていの場合、男性が率先してつぎます。

　日本ではまずビールで乾杯するのがお決まりですが、欧米では各自が好きなものを頼みます。ただ、友だちが集まった場合には、ときどきビールをピッチャーで頼んでシェアすることもあります。

　そして、水を注文することも珍しくありません。また、飲みたくない人に無理にお酒をすすめることもほとんどありません。

Chapter 10の 重要表現リスト

Skit A

- [ ] **If you insist.**
  どうしてもというのなら
- [ ] **-What is that in English?**
  それは英語では何というの
  -I'm sorry, I don't know the English word.
  ごめんなさい。英語のことばはわかりません。
- [ ] **Here you are.** どうぞ
- [ ] **Just a sip, please.** ではひとくちだけ
- [ ] ***Would you like some (sake)?**
  (お酒は)いかがですか
- [ ] ***No, thank you. I can't...**
  ありがとう、でもいいわ。〜できないんです
- [ ] **Happy birthday!** 誕生日おめでとう
- [ ] **This is the first time...**
  〜するのははじめてです
- [ ] **We have some news.**
  お知らせしたいことがあります
- [ ] **It looks like...**
  どうやら〜ということのようだ
- [ ] ***This is so sudden!** すごく急ですね
- [ ] ***Oh, my gosh!** びっくり
- [ ] **I can hardly believe it.**
  とても信じられません
- [ ] **That's good.** それならよかった
- [ ] **You tell...** 君がいってくれよ
- [ ] **This is so exciting!** すごく楽しみ

Skit B

- [ ] **This (restaurant) is known for...**
  〜で知られている
- [ ] ***be famous for...** 〜で有名な
- [ ] **I've been looking forward to...**
  〜を楽しみにしています
- [ ] ***What would you like to drink?**
  お飲み物は何がいいですか
- [ ] ***Would you like sake or wine?**
  お酒とワイン、どちらがいいですか
- [ ] **(Some sake) would be nice.**
  (お酒を)いただきます
- [ ] **Can you recommend a good (sake)?** 何かよい(酒)をすすめてくれますか
- [ ] **I'd be happy to.** よろこんでします
- [ ] **I'm sorry, but I'm afraid I don't know much about (sake).**
  申し訳ないのですが、あまり(酒)にはくわしくないのです
- [ ] **This is on...** これは〜のおごりです
- [ ] **Just making sure.** 念のため
- [ ] **Are you feeling OK?** 気分は大丈夫?
- [ ] **-Are you all right?**
  -Are you OK? 大丈夫?
- [ ] **Good thing...** 〜でよかった
- [ ] **Talk about cold.** 本当に寒かった
- [ ] **do a good job** よくやった
- [ ] **That goes without saying.**
  それは当たり前でしょう
- [ ] **To explain briefly** ざっと説明すると
- [ ] **It's way to...** それは〜するための方法だ
- [ ] **narrow down** 範囲を絞る
- [ ] **at that point** その時点で
- [ ] **be impressed by...** 〜に感心させられる
- [ ] **have a long way to go**
  まだまだ先は長い
- [ ] **have come very far**
  よくここまでやってきた
- [ ] **hit the road** 出発する
- [ ] **so to speak** いわば
- [ ] **That's just what I was thinking.**
  まさにそう思っていました

Chapter 11
February

Skit A	
場面・状況	ミユキとリチャードの両親が初めて対面する
表現のテーマ	初対面のあいさつ／紹介する／スモールトーク
Skit B	
場面・状況	ミユキとリチャードの結婚式当日
表現のテーマ	祝う／感謝の気持ちを伝える

Chapter 11 February

Skit A

ストーリーについて

　リチャードの両親アダム Adam とダイアン Diane が結婚式に出席するためにシカゴからやってきました。ふたりはすでにミユキとは会い、きょうは初めてミユキの両親と対面します。高層ビルの最上階にあるレストランでのランチの約束に、最初に到着したのはミユキ、リチャードと彼の両親のアダムとダイアン。東京の景色を眺めながら、ヒロシとマサコを待つことにしました。

ここで扱う表現について

　結婚が決まり、リチャードの両親が日本にあいさつに来ました。このシーンもいわゆる会話を始める際の small talk (世間話) で始まります。東京に来てその大きさに驚く父アダム。東京の広さについて聞かれ困ったリチャードは、I can't say offhand. (急にいわれてもわからない) といっていますね。他にも I can't say off the top of my head. といった表現もあります。まったくわからなければ I have no idea / clue. (見当もつかない)、I should look it up. (調べておかなきゃ) といっておきましょう。

　アダムとダイアンのことを、はじめは Mr. and Mrs. Levinson と呼ぶミユキ。このように相手から許しがあるまでは、ファーストネームで呼ばないほうが無難です。気が早いダイアンは Why can't she call us Mom and Dad? といっていますが。日本でも結婚したら義理の両親に対して「お父さん」「お母さん」と呼ぶのが一般的であり、同様に英語でも Mom、Dad になるわけですが、実際このように呼ぶのは北米では少ないようです。ファーストネームで呼ぶことも珍しくないでしょう。

　ミユキの両親と会うとアダムは、I'm Adam と自己紹介をすると同時に、and this is Diane. と妻のことも紹介しています。このように、同伴している人を相手に紹介することは相手に対しても、また同伴している人に対してもマナーです。自分の紹介だけに留まらず、いっしょにいる配偶者や友人も紹介しましょう。

Chapter 11 February

Skit A

Track 22

両家の両親、ゴタイメ〜ン

Adam: It sure is a huge city. **What's the area of Tokyo in square miles?**
Richard: Gee, Dad, I can't say offhand.
A: How about square kilometers? Miyuki?
Diane: Adam, **what difference does it make?**
Miyuki: I'm sorry, Mr. Levinson, I'm not sure.
A: Hey, no more "Mr. and Mrs. Levinson." Call us Adam and Diane.
D: Why can't she call us Mom and Dad?
R: Ah, **here they are.** Good timing.
M: Um, **these are my parents,** Hiroshi and Masako.
Masako and Hiroshi: Nice to meet you!
A: Happy to meet you, too! **I'm Adam and this is Diane.**
D: We're sorry we don't speak any Japanese.
Ma and H: No worries!
A and D: Pardon?

sure:
確かに、本当に

Gee:
うーん、ちぇっ

I can't say offhand.:
即座にはいえません

What difference does it make?:
そんなことどうでもいいでしょう？

Here they are.:
彼らが来ました

Good timing.:
ちょうどよかった

No worries!:
ご心配なく（オーストラリア英語）

Pardon?:
何といいましたか？

その後……

A: **We were very excited** when Richard told us the news.

D: Oh, **we were thrilled.** But frankly, **we wondered why** they set the wedding so soon.

R: I told you, Mom. We'll both be too busy in the spring.

Ma: **We were surprised,** too… not much time. But it's a… simple wedding, so…

M: My parents wanted us to have a formal reception. But we wanted something more personal.

R: Miyuki planned it all perfectly.

M: We planned it together. Richard has excellent taste.

D: I'm sure it'll be lovely. **I only wish I could** have helped.

R: Mom, you can help plan our wedding in Chicago this summer.

D: You're… having a wedding back home, too? And I can help?

A: My boy, you've made your mother very happy—**I should say** happier.

R: Actually, it was Miyuki's idea.

D: It was? Hiroshi, Masako, you have a wonderful daughter!

Ma: Thank you. She is sometimes a little stubborn, but…

H: Your son is very nice, too.

D: **Isn't he?**

A: Uh, Richard, can you hand me the bill?

H: Wait, Adam-*san*. I will shout you lunch.

A: Pardon?

M: It's Australian English. It means "**I'll treat you to** lunch."

A: Oh… that's very nice of you, Hiroshi!

D: I thought there'd be a language barrier, but this isn't what I was expecting.

---

be excited: 興奮する
be thrilled: わくわくする
frankly: 率直にいって、実のところ
wonder why…: なぜ〜なのか疑問 に思う
I told you: ほらいったでしょ
reception: 披露宴
personal: 個人的な

taste: 趣味、センス
lovely: すてきな
I only wish…: 〜だったらいいのに

My boy: 息子に対する親しみを込めた呼びかけ
I should say: 〜というべきだ
actually: 現に、実は

stubborn: 頑固な
bill: 勘定書、請求書
shout: おごる（オーストラリア英語。shout someone lunch / dinner）
treat: おごる
That's very nice of you.: ご親切にありがとうございます
language barrier: ことばの壁
This isn't what I was expecting.: 「想像していたこと（ことばの壁）とはちがう」

Chapter 11 February Skit A

ポイント解説

リチャードの両親とミユキの両親がレストランで食事をします。両家の両親は初対面なので、ここでもまず会話を始めるための世間話から始まっています。両親を紹介する表現なども覚えておきましょう。

What's the area of Tokyo in square miles / kilometers?
「東京は何平方マイルなのか」という質問だが、単純に How big is Tokyo? （東京はどれくらい大きいのか）と尋ねてもいい。アメリカやイギリスではマイル単位が使われることがほとんど。1マイルは約1.6キロメートル。

What difference does it make?
「そんなことどうでもいいでしょう」というフレーズ。

Here they are.
これまでによく出てきた Here you are. は何かを差し出すときの「どうぞ」という意味だったが、ここでの Here they are. や Here she / he is. は「……がきた」ということ。何かを見つけて Here it is. (Here they are.)「ここにあった」とも使われる。

These are my parents.
「両親」を紹介する場合は複数なので These are...、片方の親の場合はもちろん This is...。 I'd like to introduce my parents. は少しかしこまった紹介の仕方。

I'm Adam and this is Diane.
アダム氏は、I'm Adam と自己紹介するだけではなく、妻も this is Diane と紹介している。この簡単な表現で同伴者が誰であれ、相手に気軽に紹介できる。

Adam: It sure is a huge city. **What's the area of Tokyo in square miles?**

Richard: Gee, Dad, I can't say offhand.

A: How about square kilometers? Miyuki?

Diane: Adam, **what difference does it make?**

Miyuki: I'm sorry, Mr. Levinson, I'm not sure.

A: Hey, no more "Mr. and Mrs. Levinson." Call us Adam and Diane.

D: Why can't she call us Mom and Dad?

R: Ah, **here they are.** Good timing.

M: Um, **these are my parents**, Hiroshi and Masako.

Masako and Hiroshi: Nice to meet you!

A: Happy to meet you, too! **I'm Adam and this is Diane.**

D: We're sorry we don't speak any Japanese.

Ma and H: No worries!

A and D: Pardon?

A: We were very excited when Richard told us the news.

D: Oh, **we were thrilled.** But frankly, **we wondered why** they set the wedding so soon.

R: I told you, Mom. We'll both be too busy in the spring.
Ma: **We were surprised**, too… not much time. But it's a… simple wedding, so…
M: My parents wanted us to have a formal reception. But we wanted something more personal.
R: Miyuki planned it all perfectly.
M: We planned it together. Richard has excellent taste.
D: I'm sure it'll be lovely. **I only wish I could** have helped.
R: Mom, you can help plan our wedding in Chicago this summer.
D: You're… having a wedding back home, too? And I can help?
A: My boy, you've made your mother very happy—**I should say** happier.
R: Actually, it was Miyuki's idea.
D: It was? Hiroshi, Masako, you have a wonderful daughter!
Ma: Thank you. She is sometimes a little stubborn, but…
H: Your son is very nice, too.
D: **Isn't he?**
A: Uh, Richard, can you hand me the bill?
H: Wait, Adam-*san*. I will shout you lunch.
A: Pardon?
M: It's Australian English. It means "**I'll treat you** to lunch."
A: Oh… that's very nice of you, Hiroshi!
D: I thought there'd be a language barrier, but this isn't what I was expecting.

I only wish I could…
「……だったらいいのに」と願望を表す wish に続く節の動詞は過去形か過去完了形。only を加えることで願う気持が強調される。

I should say…
「……といえる」。特にこの場面の場合は「いや……といったほうがいいだろう」というニュアンス。

Isn't he?
息子のことをほめられて、Is he?（そうかしら?）ではなく「そうですね」と認めている。日本人は家族のことをほめられると謙遜するが、外国では I'm proud of my son.（息子を誇りに思う）と素直に自分の家族のことをほめることが多い。

I'll treat you to…
treat ＋人＋ to… で「食事をおごる」という意味。This is my treat. で「私のおごりです」。以前の会話に出てきた This is on the company. のように、This is on me. でも同じ意味。

We were very excited. / We were thrilled. / We were surprised.
驚き、興奮の表現として、excited や surprised のほかに thrilled もよく使われる単語。喜びの意味を込めた delighted も覚えておくと便利。happy でもいいが、やや感動に欠ける。

We wondered why…
wonder why… で「なぜ……なのか疑問に思う」。

訳

Adam: It sure is a huge city. What's the area of Tokyo in square miles?
Richard: Gee, Dad, I can't say offhand.
A: How about square kilometers? Miyuki?
Diane: Adam, what difference does it make?
Miyuki: I'm sorry, Mr. Levinson, I'm not sure.
A: Hey, no more "Mr. and Mrs. Levinson." Call us Adam and Diane.
D: Why can't she call us Mom and Dad?
R: Ah, here they are. Good timing.
M: Um, these are my parents, Hiroshi and Masako.
Masako and Hiroshi: Nice to meet you!
A: Happy to meet you, too! I'm Adam and this is Diane.
D: We're sorry we don't speak any Japanese.
Ma and H: No worries!
A and D: Pardon?

A: We were very excited when Richard told us the news.
D: Oh, we were thrilled. But frankly, we wondered why they set the wedding so soon.
R: I told you, Mom. We'll both be too busy in the spring.
Ma: We were surprised, too… not much time. But it's a… simple wedding, so…
M: My parents wanted us to have a formal reception. But we wanted something more personal.
R: Miyuki planned it all perfectly.
M: We planned it together. Richard has excellent taste.
D: I'm sure it'll be lovely. I only wish I could have helped.
R: Mom, you can help plan our wedding in Chicago this summer.
D: You're… having a wedding back home, too? And I can help?
A: My boy, you've made your mother very happy—I should say happier.
R: Actually, it was Miyuki's idea.
D: It was? Hiroshi, Masako, you have a wonderful daughter!
Ma: Thank you. She is sometimes a little stubborn, but…
H: Your son is very nice, too.
D: Isn't he?
A: Uh, Richard, can you hand me the bill?
H: Wait, Adam-*san*. I will shout you lunch.
A: Pardon?
M: It's Australian English. It means "I'll treat you to lunch."
A: Oh… that's very nice of you, Hiroshi!
D: I thought there'd be a language barrier, but this isn't what I was expecting.

アダム：まったく巨大な町だなあ。東京の面積は何平方マイルなんだろう。
リチャード：うーん、父さん、見ただけではわからないよ。
アダム：平方キロメートルではどうだ。ミユキ？
ダイアン：アダム、そんなことはどうでもいいでしょう。
ミユキ：ごめんなさい、ミスター・レヴィンソン、私はよく知りません。
アダム：おい、「ミスター＆ミセス・レヴィンソン」はもうやめよう。アダムとダイアンって呼んで。
ダイアン：お母さんとお父さんはだめかしら。
リチャード：ほら、きたよ。グッド・タイミングだ。
ミユキ：えーと、これが私の両親、ヒロシとマサコです。
マサコとヒロシ：はじめまして。
アダム：こちらこそはじめまして。私はアダムで、これがダイアンです。
ダイアン：私たちは日本語が話せなくてごめんなさい。
マサコとヒロシ：ノー・ウォリーズ（ご心配なく）！
アダムとダイアン：え？

アダム：リチャードが私たちに（結婚の）ニュースを知らせてきたときは、とても興奮しましたよ。
ダイアン：もうわくわくしちゃって。でも本当のところ、どうしてそんなに急いで結婚式をするのかが疑問だったんです。
リチャード：いっただろう、母さん。僕たちはふたりとも春はすごく忙しくなるんだ。
マサコ：私たちも驚きました……そんなに（準備の）時間がないのに。でも、シンプルな結婚式なので……
ミユキ：私の両親はフォーマルな披露宴をしてほしかったんです。でも私たちは何かもっと自分たちらしいものにしたかったんです。
リチャード：ミユキがすべて完璧に準備したんだ。
ミユキ：ふたりでいっしょに計画したんです。リチャードはすごく趣味がいいんです。
ダイアン：きっとすてきな結婚式になるわよ。手伝うことができたらよかったのに。
リチャード：母さんは夏のシカゴでの結婚式を手伝ってよ。
ダイアン：え……うちのほうでも結婚式をするの？　それで私が手伝えるの？
アダム：お前ってやつは、母さんをこんなにハッピーにさせて……いや、ハッピーじゃなくてもっとハッピーだな。
リチャード：実はこれはミユキのアイディアだったんだ。
ダイアン：そうなの。ヒロシさん、マサコさん、あなたたちはすばらしいお嬢さんをお持ちだわ。
マサコ：ありがとうございます。たまに少し頑固ですけれども……
ヒロシ：あなた方の息子さんもとてもいい人ですよ。
ダイアン：そうでしょう。
アダム：えーとリチャード、勘定を取ってくれ。
ヒロシ：待って、アダムさん。ランチは私がシャウトします（私のおごりです）。
アダム：はい？
ミユキ：オーストラリア英語です。「ランチは私がおごります」という意味です。
アダム：ああ……とてもご親切に、ヒロシさん。
ダイアン：ことばの壁があるんじゃないかと思ってましたが、これは予想してませんでしたよ。

Chapter 11
February

Exercises

Part A Track 22

①リスニング、②パラレル・リーディング(音を聞きながらテキストを音読)、③プロソディ・シャドーイング(音の再現)④コンテンツ・シャドーイング(意味を意識)の順で会話を再現してみましょう。下記の Key Phrases を意識しながら、最低でも7回は会話を聞いてみましょう。

Key Phrases:
- What's the area of (Tokyo) in square miles (kilometers)?
- What difference does it make?
- Here they are.
- These are my parents.
- I'm (Adam) and this is (Diane).
- -We were very excited
- -We were thrilled.
- -We were surprised.
- We wondered why…
- I only wish I could…
- I should say…
- Isn't he?
- I'll treat you to…

Part B

相手の語りかけに対して、自分なりの答えを考えてみましょう。

1) **Oliver:** Who arranged the party?
   You: _____

2) **Oliver:** Your boss told me that you and your wife are expecting a baby! Congratulations!
   You: _____

3) **Oliver:** Tokyo has several urban centers.
   You: _____

今度は相手の応答にふさわしい語りかけをしてみましょう。

4) どうしてそんなに急いで結婚式を挙げたのか、たずねてみましょう。
   You: _____
   Oliver: We really wanted a June wedding.

5) Oliverの奥さんのセンスをほめてあげましょう。
   You: _____
   Oliver: Thank you. She's been studying flower arrangement for five years.

6) 素晴らしい娘さんを持ちましたね、とほめてあげましょう。
   You: _____
   Oliver: Thank you. You have a wonderful daughter, too!

Exercises の解答例と訳

1) The secretary—she planned it all perfectly.
2) Thank you. We were thrilled when we heard the news.
3) It sure is a huge city.
4) We wondered why the wedding was so soon.
5) Your wife has excellent taste!
6) You have a wonderful daughter!

問題と答えの訳

1) オリバー：誰がパーティーの準備をしたのでしょうか。
   あなた：秘書です—彼女がすべて完璧に計画しました。
2) オリバー：上司からあなたと奥さんの間に子どもが生まれると聞きました。おめでとう！
   あなた：ありがとう。その知らせを聞いたときは興奮しました。
3) オリバー：東京にはいくつもの都心があります。
   あなた：確かに巨大な街ですね。
4) あなた：私たちは結婚式がなぜそんなに早いのか不思議でした。
   オリバー：本当にジューン・ブライドがよかったものですから。
5) あなた：あなたの奥さんはとてもセンスがいいですね！
   オリバー：ありがとう。彼女は5年間フラワー・アレンジメントを勉強しているんです。
6) あなた：素晴らしい娘さんをお持ちですね！
   オリバー：ありがとう。あなたも素晴らしい娘さんをお持ちで！

コラム　結婚とお墓

　日本では女性が結婚し、名字が、例えば「鈴木」から夫の姓の「佐藤」に変わると、その女性は「佐藤家」の一員になり、亡くなった後には「佐藤家のお墓」に入ることになります。

　一方、アメリカでは「〇〇家のお墓」というものは普通はありません。個人がそれぞれのお墓を持つのが普通なので、「〇〇さんのお墓」ということになります。しかし、一族のお墓のエリアをもつこともあります。また、夫婦単位などでお墓を隣同士に並べるということはよくあります。

　アメリカと日本とは埋葬形態もちがいます。日本ではすべて火葬 (cremation) されますが、アメリカでは土葬 (burial) のほうがより一般的です。しかし都市部では火葬がそれほど珍しいものではありません。とはいえ、日本と異なり、粉々になるまで焼かれ、日本における火葬のように骨の原型をとどめていません。概していえば、アメリカ人は遺骨に対する執着心が強くないので、散布することも珍しくありません。

Chapter 11 February

Skit B

ストーリーについて

きょうはミユキとリチャードの結婚式。日本の伝統的な式は、両家の親族の出席のもと、午前中にミユキの両親宅で執り行われました。おいしい料理と和やかな雰囲気で楽しいパーティーにしたいというふたりの希望で、夕方の披露宴はふたりが初めてデートをしたレストランで行うことになりました。

ここで扱う表現について

いよいよ結婚式当日となりました。お祝いのことば Congratulations! は、かならず覚えてください。最後には複数形の s がつきます。

You look so beautiful.（とてもきれいだよ）は花嫁に向けてぜひいってほしいお祝いのことばです。アナはリチャードにも You look beautiful, too. といいますが、それを皮肉ったリチャードの答えが Well, they say all grooms do.（まあ、花婿はみんなそうだっていうからね）。結婚式の主役はなんといっても花嫁とわかっていての、彼のユーモアのある発言です。

新郎新婦を祝福するフレーズとして、レナの I know you two will be very happy.（あなたたちはきっととても幸せになるわ）のほかにも、You make a beautiful couple.（すてきなカップルですね）、I wish you lots of happiness.（たくさんの幸せがありますように）なども覚えておきましょう。

参列してくれた人たちに感謝の気持ちを伝えるべく、ミユキも We're really glad you could all be here.（みなさんにここにおいでいただくことができて、本当にうれしいです）といっています。Thank you so much for coming!（来てくださって本当にありがとうございます）でも気持ちは十分に伝わります。このことばに対するアナの返答は、We wouldn't have missed it for anything.（私たちは絶対に欠席したくなかったのよ）ですが、この for anything には「何に変えても」「絶対に」という意味があります。何としても参加したかった、という彼女の気持ちが伝わってきますね。

Chapter 11 February

Skit B

Track 23

結婚披露パーティー、始まる

Joe: Congratulations, you two! We're very happy for you.
Anna: Miyuki, **you look so beautiful.**
Miyuki: Thank you, Anna. We're really glad you could all be here.
A: We wouldn't have missed it for anything. Richard… you look beautiful, too.
Richard: Well, **they say** all grooms do.
J: Emily, it's your turn.
Emily: Congratulations, Miyuki and Richard!
M and R: Thank you, Emily!
Lena: I know you two will be very happy. By the way, Richard—that's a nice tie.
R: Thanks. Miyuki picked it out.
L: I knew it the day you two met—**it was meant to be.**

一方、別のテーブルでは……

Dave: So, uh, you're looking very nice tonight, Jen.

…happy for you!:
(あなたたちが幸せで)うれしいです！

…glad you could be here.:
来てくださってうれしいです

for anything:
絶対に、何があっても

They say…:
〜だそうだ、〜らしい

It's your turn.:
君の番だよ

pick out: 選ぶ
It was meant to be.:
そうなる運命だったんだ

Jennifer: Um… thanks. You, too. I'm glad you got over that cold. I was worried about you.
D: Actually, it wasn't a cold. It was nicotine withdrawal. I quit smoking.
J: You quit?! That's great, Dave! How— I mean… why?
D: Well, you always said it was bad for me.
J: I didn't know you were listening.
D: I listen to everything you tell me, Jen. You're my spiritual advisor.
J: That's quite a responsibility.
D: Also… I didn't think you'd go out with a guy who smoked. I mean, maybe you won't go out with me anyway, but—
J: Of course I will. I would've before.
D: No kidding?
J: No kidding. But don't start smoking again, OK?
D: Whatever you say, Jen.

主賓テーブルで……

M: Look… Jennifer and Dave! How wonderful!
A: Oh, it's just like a movie.
J: Well, it's about time! See, Richard? I told you you didn't need to worry about Da—
R: Hey, Miyuki, let's go see the parents, OK?
M: OK. What was Joe saying?
Adam: Ah, here are the bride and groom. Come sit down, you two.
Diane: Richard, Miyuki… it's a beautiful reception! I'm so happy!
M: We're so happy you're here… Mom and Dad.
R: Um… yeah. *Otosan, okasan… arigato.*
Ad, D, Hiroshi, Masako: No worries!
Takeshi: There they go again.

---

get over…: 〜から快復する
withdrawal: 禁断症状
quit: 止める

That's quite a responsibility.: それはかなり責任重大だ
go out: 付き合う

No kidding?: 冗談でしょ?、ホントに?
No kidding.: 本当よ、その通り
Whatever you say.: いうとおりにするよ

It's about time!: もうそろそろ時間 (頃) だ!
See?: ほらね

Here are(is)…: 〜が来た

There… go(goes) again.: ああまただ

ポイント解説

Chapter 11 February Skit B

ミユキとリチャードの結婚式当日です。結婚式らしく、単純な「おめでとう」からちょっと気の利いた表現まで、じつにさまざまなお祝いの表現がたくさん出てきます。表現にバリエーションをつけましょう。

We're very happy for you.
直訳すると「私たちはあなたのことをとてもうれしく思う」だが、「よかったわね」「おめでとう」を表す、覚えておくと便利なお祝いのフレーズ。

You look so beautiful.
「とてもきれいね」と相手をほめる表現。beautiful のかわりに nice / cute（すてき／かわいい）も使える。また、You look so pale.（顔が青ざめている）などと相手を気づかうときにも使える。

They say…
They は一般の人を指しているので、they say で「……ということだ」「……らしい」という言い回しになる。

I know you two will be very happy.
「あなたたちはきっとすごく幸せになるわ」。ふたりを祝福することば。I know や I'm sure よりも強く確信を持って表現している。

It was meant to be.
「なるべくしてなった」つまり「そういう運命だった」という決まり文句。

Congratulations!
「おめでとう」という定番のお祝いのことば。Congratulations! と複数形になっていることに注意。入学試験に合格したときなどにも使える。

Joe: **Congratulations,** you two! **We're very happy for you.**
Anna: Miyuki, **you look so beautiful.**
Miyuki: Thank you, Anna. We're really glad you could all be here.
A: We wouldn't have missed it for anything. Richard… you look beautiful, too.
Richard: Well, **they say** all grooms do.
J: Emily, it's your turn.
Emily: Congratulations, Miyuki and Richard!
M and R: Thank you, Emily!
Lena: **I know you two will be very happy.** By the way, Richard—that's a nice tie.
R: Thanks. Miyuki picked it out.
L: I knew it the day you two met—**it was meant to be.**

Dave: So, uh, you're looking very nice tonight, Jen.
Jennifer: Um… thanks. You, too. I'm glad you got over that cold. I was worried about you.
D: Actually, it wasn't a cold. It was nicotine withdrawal. I quit smoking.
J: You quit?! That's great, Dave! How—I mean… why?
D: Well, you always said it was bad for me.

J: I didn't know you were listening.
D: I listen to everything you tell me, Jen. You're my spiritual advisor.
J: That's quite a responsibility.
D: Also… I didn't think you'd go out with a guy who smoked. I mean, maybe you won't go out with me anyway, but—
J: Of course I will. I would've before.
D: No kidding?
J: No kidding. But don't start smoking again, OK?
D: Whatever you say, Jen.

M: Look… Jennifer and Dave! How wonderful!
A: Oh, it's just like a movie.
J: Well, **it's about time!** See, Richard? I told you you didn't need to worry about Da—
R: Hey, Miyuki, let's go see the parents, OK?
M: OK. What was Joe saying?
Adam: Ah, here are the bride and groom. Come sit down, you two.
Diane: Richard, Miyuki… it's a beautiful reception! **I'm so happy!**
M: We're so happy you're here… Mom and Dad.
R: Um… yeah. *Otosan, okasan… arigato.*
Ad, D, Hiroshi, Masako: No worries!
Takeshi: There they go again.

-No kidding? / -No kidding.
kidは「ふざける」。No kidding? (=Really?)と文末を上げて「ふざけてないよね」、No kidding.と下げることで「ふざけていません、ホントです」。

Whatever you say.
「あなたのいう通りにします」。なげやりに「好きにしてくれ」という意味にもなる。

It's about time!
「そろそろ……すべき時期だ」。

I'm so happy!
うれしさ、よろこびを伝える表現として This is the happiest day of my life.(きょうは人生で最も幸せな日です)、I'll never forget this day.(きょうのことは決して忘れません)は難しくないので覚えておこう。

There they go again.
There… go / goes again.で「また始まった」。「飽きれた」というニュアンス。

Joe: Congratulations, you two! We're very happy for you.
Anna: Miyuki, you look so beautiful.
Miyuki: Thank you, Anna. We're really glad you could all be here.
A: We wouldn't have missed it for anything. Richard… you look beautiful, too.
Richard: Well, they say all grooms do.
J: Emily, it's your turn.
Emily: Congratulations, Miyuki and Richard!
M and R: Thank you, Emily!
Lena: I know you two will be very happy. By the way, Richard—that's a nice tie.
R: Thanks. Miyuki picked it out.
L: I knew it the day you two met—it was meant to be.

Dave: So, uh, you're looking very nice tonight, Jen.
Jennifer: Um… thanks. You, too. I'm glad you got over that cold. I was worried about you.
D: Actually, it wasn't a cold. It was nicotine withdrawal. I quit smoking.
J: You quit?! That's great, Dave! How—I mean… why?
D: Well, you always said it was bad for me.
J: I didn't know you were listening.
D: I listen to everything you tell me, Jen. You're my spiritual advisor.
J: That's quite a responsibility.
D: Also… I didn't think you'd go out with a guy who smoked. I mean, maybe you won't go out with me anyway, but—
J: Of course I will. I would've before.
D: No kidding?
J: No kidding. But don't start smoking again, OK?
D: Whatever you say, Jen.

M: Look… Jennifer and Dave! How wonderful!
An: Oh, it's just like a movie.
J: Well, it's about time! See, Richard? I told you you didn't need to worry about Da—
R: Hey, Miyuki, let's go see the parents, OK?
M: OK. What was Joe saying?
Adam: Ah, here are the bride and groom. Come sit down, you two.
Diane: Richard, Miyuki… it's a beautiful reception! I'm so happy!
M: We're so happy you're here… Mom and Dad.
R: Um… yeah. *Otosan, okasan… arigato.*
Ad, D, Hiroshi, Masako: No worries!
Takeshi: There they go again.

ジョー：ふたりともおめでとう。僕たちもとてもうれしいよ。
アナ：ミユキ、あなた、とてもきれいだわ。
ミユキ：ありがとう、アナ。あなたたちにきてもらえてとてもうれしいわ。
アナ：どんなことがあっても、絶対に欠席したくなかったのよ。リチャード……あなたもとてもすてきよ。
リチャード：まあ、新郎はみんなそうだっていうからね。
ジョー：エミリー、きみの番だよ。
エミリー：おめでとう、リチャード、ミユキ。
ミユキとリチャード：ありがとう、エミリー。
レナ：あなたたちはきっととても幸せになるわね。ところですてきなネクタイね。
リチャード：ありがとう。ミユキが選んだんだ。
レナ：あなたたちが初めて会ったときからわかってたわ、こうなる運命だったのよ。

デーブ：それで、えーと、今夜はすごくきれいだね、ジェン。
ジェニファー：あ……ありがとう。あなたこそ。あなたの風邪が治ってよかったわ。心配したのよ。
デーブ：実は、風邪じゃなかったんだ。あれは脱ニコチン症状。タバコを止めたんだ。
ジェニファー：止めたの？　すごいわ、デーブ。どうやって……ていうか、どうして？
デーブ：まあ、タバコは僕によくないってきみはいつもいってただろ。
ジェニファー：聞いてるとは思ってなかったわ。
デーブ：きみのいうことはすべて聞いているよ、ジェン。きみは僕の心のアドバイザーだよ。
ジェニファー：それは責任重大だわ。
デーブ：それに……きみはタバコを吸う男とは付き合わないだろうと思ったから。ていうか、きみはどっちにしろ僕とは付き合ってくれないだろうけど……
ジェニファー：もちろん付き合うわよ。タバコを止める前でも付き合っていたわ。
デーブ：本当？
ジェニファー：本当よ。でもまたタバコは始めないで、いい？
デーブ：きみのいうとおりにするよ、ジェン。

ミユキ：見て、ジェニファーとデーブを。よかったわ。
アナ：あら、まるで映画みたいね。
ジョー：まあ、そろそろそんな時期なんだよ。ほらな、リチャード。デーブのことは心配しなくてもいいっていった……
リチャード：ねえ、ミユキ、両親に会いにいこう、いい？
ミユキ：オーケー。ジョーは何ていってたの？
アダム：ああ、新郎新婦のお出ましだ。ふたりとも、こっちに座りなさい。
ダイアン：リチャード、ミユキ、すばらしい披露宴だわ。私はとてもうれしいわ。
ミユキ：きていただいて、私たちはとてもうれしいです、お母さん、お父さん。
リチャード：あ……そうだ。オトーサン、オカーサン、アリガト。
アダム、ダイアン、ヒデオ、マサコ：ノー・ウォリーズ！
タケシ：あーまただ。

Chapter 11
February

Exercises

Part A **Track 23**

①リスニング、②パラレル・リーディング(音を聞きながらテキストを音読)、③プロソディ・シャドーイング（音の再現）④コンテンツ・シャドーイング（意味を意識）の順で会話を再現してみましょう。下記の Key Phrases を意識しながら、最低でも7回は会話を聞いてみましょう。

Key Phrases:
- Congratulations!
- We're very happy for you.
- You look so beautiful.
- They say…
- I know you two will be very happy.
- It was meant to be.
- -No kidding?
  -No kidding.
- Whatever you say.
- It's about time!
- I'm so happy!
- There they go again.

Part B
相手の語りかけに対して、自分なりの答えを考えてみましょう。

1) **Patricia:** I just learned that I got into medical school!
   You: Wow! _____

2) **Patricia:** Guess what. I'm finally getting promoted!
   You: _____

3) **Patricia:** Thank you so much for coming to my wedding! It means a lot to me.
   You: _____

今度は相手の応答にふさわしい語りかけをしてみましょう。

4) 「みんなに来てもらえて、私たちは本当にうれしい」といってみましょう。
   You: _____
   Patricia: Thank you. I'm excited to be here, too!

5) 「風邪が治ってよかったですね」といってみましょう。
   You: _____
   Patricia: Thank you. It took a long time, but I'm finally feeling better.

6) 「結婚します」と報告してみましょう。
   You: _____
   Patricia: That's wonderful! Congratulations!

Exercises の解答例と訳

1) How wonderful!
2) Congratulations! I'm really happy for you!
3) I wouldn't have missed it for anything.
4) We're really glad you could all be here.
5) I'm glad you got over that cold.
6) I'm getting married!

問題と答えの訳

1) パトリシア：さっき知ったんだけど、私、医療学校に受かったのよ！
   あなた：わあすごい！
2) パトリシア：あのね。私ついに昇進するのよ！
   あなた：おめでとう！　私も本当にうれしいです。
3) パトリシア：私の結婚式に来てくれてどうもありがとう。本当にうれしいわ。
   あなた：どんなことがあっても欠席したくなかったよ。
4) あなた：みんなに来てもらえて私たちは本当にうれしいです。
   パトリシア：ありがとう。私もこの場にいられて興奮しています。
5) あなた：あなたの風邪が治ってうれしいです。
   パトリシア：ありがとう。長引いたけれど、だいぶよくなりました。
6) あなた：私、結婚します。
   パトリシア：素晴らしい。おめでとう！

コラム　結婚式 & gift registry

　日本では結婚式の披露宴後に来賓に引出物を贈りますが、欧米ではゲストのほうから新郎新婦にプレゼントを贈ります。その際、ゲストは gift registry という方法を使って贈り物をすることが多いようです。

　結婚を控えたカップルはデパートなどで希望する商品のリストを作って登録し、デパート、あるいは両親がそのリストをゲストに公開します。希望するアイテムが購入される度にリストから消去される仕組みになっているので、贈り物が重複してしまったり、不要なものを贈ってしまったりということを防げるわけです。カップルはほしくて必要なものだけをもらえるし、ゲストも贈り物選びに悩まなくてすむので、双方にとって有益なシステムであるといえます。

　しかし、ゲストはかならず希望商品リストからものを購入するようにと求められているわけではありません。リストにはないけれども、自分が好ましいと思ったものを、ゲストはふたりにプレゼントすることができるのです。

　また、結婚式の前に新婦の女友だちが集まってホームパーティーを開き、新婦にプレゼントを贈るウェディング・シャワー (wedding shower) というイベントもあります。

Chapter 11の 重要表現リスト

Skit A

- [ ] **What's the area of (Tokyo) in square miles (kilometers)?**
  東京は何平方マイル（キロメートル）あるの？
- [ ] ***How big is Tokyo?**
  東京はどのくらい大きいの？
- [ ] **I can't say offhand.**
  即座にはいえません
- [ ] **What difference does it make?**
  そんなことどうでもいいでしょう
- [ ] **I'm not sure.** よく知りません
- [ ] **Here they are.** 彼らが来ました
- [ ] ***Here it is.** ここにあった
- [ ] **Good timing.** ちょうどよかった
- [ ] **I'm (Adam) and this is (Diane).**
  私が（アダム）で、こちらが（ダイアン）です。
- [ ] **I told you…** ほら、いったでしょ
- [ ] **These are my parents.**
  私の両親です
- [ ] ・**We were very excited.**
  非常に興奮した
- [ ] ・**We were thrilled.** もうわくわくした
- [ ] ・**We were surprised.** 驚いた
- [ ] **We wondered why…**
  なぜ〜なのか疑問に思う
- [ ] **I only wish I could…**
  〜だったらいいのに
- [ ] **I should say…**
  （いや）〜といったほうがいいだろう
- [ ] **Isn't he?** そうですね
- [ ] **I'll treat you to…** 私がおごりましょう
- [ ] ***・This is my treat.**
  ***・This is on me.**
  これは私のおごりです
- [ ] **That's very nice of you.**
  ご親切にありがとうございます
- [ ] **This isn't what I was expecting.**
  想像していたこととはちがう

Skit B

- [ ] **Congratulations!** おめでとう
- [ ] **We're very happy for you.**
  （あなたたちが幸せで）うれしいです
- [ ] **We're very glad you could all be here.** 来てくださってうれしいです
- [ ] **We wouldn't have missed it for anything.**
  何としても出席したかったのよ
- [ ] **They say…** 〜だそうだ
- [ ] **It's your turn.** 君の番だよ
- [ ] **I know you two will be very happy.** そうなる運命だったんだ
- [ ] ***You look so beautiful.**
  とてもきれいだよ
- [ ] ***I know you two will be very happy.**
  あなたたちはとても幸せになるわ
- [ ] ***You make a beautiful couple.**
  すてきなカップルですね
- [ ] ***I wish you lots of happiness.**
  たくさんの幸せが訪れますように
- [ ] **pick out** 選ぶ
- [ ] **It was meant to be.**
  そうなる運命だったんだ
- [ ] **get over** 回復する
- [ ] **That's quite a responsibility.**
  それはかなり責任重大だ
- [ ] **-No kidding?** 冗談でしょ？
  -No kidding. 本当よ
- [ ] **Whatever you say.**
  君のいうとおりにするよ
- [ ] **It's about time!** そろそろ時間だ
- [ ] **I'm so happy!** とても幸せだよ
- [ ] **There they go again.**
  ああ、また始まった

March

Chapter 12

場面・状況	花見をしながらジョーとアナの送別会
表現のテーマ	お礼をいう／質問をする／写真を撮る／別れを惜しむ

Skit A

場面・状況	ミユキは昇進し、新人が入社する
表現のテーマ	総まとめ

Skit B

Chapter 12 March

Skit A

ストーリーについて

　3月も最後の週になり、ジョーの家族がそろそろ日本を去るときが近づきました。彼らは友人たちを近くの公園に誘い、「お別れピクニック」をすることにしました。桜が咲き始め、温かい日差しに肌寒さが混じりあった陽気、まるで去ることのさみしさと、新しい生活が始まるうれしさが混じりあった彼らの複雑な気分を表しているかのようです。

ここで扱う表現について

　ジョー一家のために特別なお寿司を作ってきたヒデオ一家。お寿司を囲んで記念撮影となります。日本語でも「はい、笑って」、「いいですか?」、「では、もう1枚」など写真を撮る際の言い回しがあるように、ここでも、Hey, let's take a picture with...(ねえ、……といっしょに写真を撮ろうよ)、Get together.(寄って)、Let me take one.(私にも1枚撮らせて)、Smile.(笑って)などが使われています。写真を撮ったあとは、Great! Thanks.(最高! ありがとう)とお礼をいうと印象がいいですね。誰かに写真を撮ってもらうときはCould you take a picture of us, please?と頼み、You just press here.(ここを押すだけです。)と説明します。海外旅行に行くと写真を撮る機会も多いでしょうから、覚えておくと便利です。また、日本で外国人旅行者が観光名所の写真を撮ろうとしていたら、Do you want me to take a picture of all of you?(みなさんの写真を撮りましょうか)と親切に尋ねてみるのもいいですね。

　ジョー一家が主役の送別会。会話も彼ら中心となるべきで、ヒデオも帰国後のジョー一家の生活について質問したりしています。

　タケシがアメリカを後にしたときと同様に、ここでも別れを惜しむ表現がたくさん出てきますね。We'll really miss Japan.、We wish you a wonderful life in Los Angeles.、We'll see you again, right?、You guys should come to L.A. などがそうです。このような表現がすらすらと出てくるようになったら、もう英語上級者といえましょう。

Chapter 12 March

Skit A

Track 24

花見をしながら送別会

Joe: **We're lucky to** see cherry blossoms before we leave.
Emily: **They look like** pink popcorn!
Richard: Emily, I always said you were a poet.
E: But I'm not good in math.
R: I'll tell you a secret—neither am I.
Lena: Hi, everyone! Sorry we're late.
Takako: We were making a special dish.
Hideo: Go ahead, Mai-*chan*.
Mai: **Ta-da!**
J: Interesting sushi! It has letters! A-N… "Anna, Joe, Emily, we'll miss you!"
Anna: Oh, my gosh! **How did you do this?** I'm going to cry.
Miyuki: No, **I won't let you!** I'll start crying,

---

be lucky to…: 〜ができて幸せだ、〜ができてよかった

be good in…: 〜が得意だ
math: 算数
Neither am I.: I'm not good in math. に呼応して「僕も苦手なんだ」
Go ahead.: ほらどうぞ
Ta-da!: じゃーん

I won't let you!: そうはさせません！

too.

Dave: Then I'll cry, and **that's not a pretty sight.**

Jennifer: I saw you cry at the end of *The Wizard of Oz*. It was cute.

D: That was, uh, hay fever, Jen.

J: Hey, let's take a photo with the sushi. Get together, everyone. OK!

L: Wait… Let me take one, too. Smile!

R: Lena, **are you sure** you have film in your camera?

L: Perhaps I should double-check. Wait—it's a digital camera. Oh, Richard!

R: **Gotcha!**

E and Mai: Can we eat the sushi now?

H: So… **what will you do when you get to Los Angeles?**

J: Well, I'll be starting my new job. And Anna will look for a job at an elementary school, and—hey, **look who's here!**

Takeshi: Hi, you guys! Um… this is Rachel.

Everyone: Hi, Rachel!

Rachel: Hi! It's nice to meet you all. I'm, like, so excited to be in Japan!

A: That's just how we felt when we came here. Remember, Joe?

J: I sure do. We'll really miss Japan… and our great friends here.

L: We wish you a wonderful life in Los Angeles.

M: And we'll see you again, right?

Ra: Hey, you guys should all come to L.A. Takeshi's coming to visit this summer!

E: I knew Rachel was your girlfriend!

T: Um… what can I say?

D: How about "*kampai*"?

Everyone: *Kampai*!

That's not a pretty sight.:
あまり美しい光景ではない、お見せできるような光景ではない
cute:
かわいらしい

double-check:
再確認する

Gotcha!:
（この場合は文脈上）ひっかかった！

Look who's here.:
誰かと思ったら

I sure do.: もちろん。
doはrememberの代わりに用いられている

Chapter 12 March Skit A

ポイント解説

ジョーの家族は友人といっしょに公園でピクニックをします。写真を撮るときに使われる決まり文句のほか、何かを別のことに例える表現、旅立つ人へ今後の予定を聞く際に使う表現などが使われています。

We're lucky to...

「……できて運がよかった」という表現。I was lucky to find this apartment.（運よくこの部屋が見つかりました）。You are lucky to have a nice boss.（上司がいい人でよかったですね）など。

They look like...

何かを見て「まるで……みたいだ」と描写するときは look like を使う。ここの場合は cherry blossoms が複数なので主語が they になっている。They are like... といっても同じ意味。

Ta-da!

何か驚かせるものを披露するときの、「じゃーん！」という表現。お祝いの際のラッパの音を真似たもの。

How did you do this?

ここの場面では、「どうやって作ったの？」のほかにも、「よくここまでやってくださって」という感動と驚きが込められている。

Joe: **We're lucky to** see cherry blossoms before we leave.
Emily: **They look like** pink popcorn!
Richard: Emily, I always said you were a poet.
E: But I'm not good in math.
R: I'll tell you a secret—neither am I.
Lena: Hi, everyone! Sorry we're late.
Takako: We were making a special dish.
Hideo: Go ahead, Mai-*chan*.
Mai: **Ta-da!**
J: Interesting sushi! It has letters! A-N… "Anna, Joe, Emily, we'll miss you!"
Anna: Oh, my gosh! **How did you do this?** I'm going to cry.
Miyuki: No, **I won't let you!** I'll start crying, too.
Dave: Then I'll cry, and **that's not a pretty sight.**
Jennifer: I saw you cry at the end of *The Wizard of Oz*. It was cute.
D: That was, uh, hay fever, Jen.
J: Hey, let's take a photo with the sushi. Get together, everyone. OK!
L: Wait… Let me take one, too. Smile!
R: Lena, **are you sure** you have film in your camera?

L: Perhaps I should double-check. Wait—it's a digital camera. Oh, Richard!
R: Gotcha!
E and Mai: Can we eat the sushi now?
H: So… **what will you do when you get to Los Angeles?**
J: Well, I'll be starting my new job. And Anna will look for a job at an elementary school, and—hey, **look who's here!**
Takeshi: Hi, you guys! Um… this is Rachel.
Everyone: Hi, Rachel!
Rachel: Hi! It's nice to meet you all. I'm, like, so excited to be in Japan!
A: That's just how we felt when we came here. Remember, Joe?
J: I sure do. We'll really miss Japan… and our great friends here.
L: We wish you a wonderful life in Los Angeles.
M: And we'll see you again, right?
Ra: Hey, you guys should all come to L.A. Takeshi's coming to visit this summer!
E: I knew Rachel was your girlfriend!
T: Um… what can I say?
D: How about "*kampai*"?
Everyone: *Kampai*!

Gotcha!

I got you. の略。このシーンの場合は、リチャードのいたずらにひっかかったレナにいう「やーい、ひっかかった！」というニュアンス。「捕まえた！」というときにも使われる。

What will you do when you get to Los Angeles?

旅立つ人には、このほかにも Are you excited about going…?（……へいくのは楽しみですか？）、How do you feel about going back to the U.S.?（アメリカに帰ることをどう感じていますか？）、Where will you live?（どこに住むのですか？）などさまざまな質問で会話を広げることができる。

Look who's here.

パーティや会食、集まりなどで親しい仲間がやってきたときの、「おや、誰かと思ったら」というニュアンスの表現。

That's not a pretty sight.

「それはいい光景ではないな」、「あまり見たくない状況だな」とあえて遠回しな表現。けんかや浮気など、思わしくない現場を目撃してしたり、想像したときの反応。

I won't let you!

「そうはさせないよ！」。試合などの前に I'll beat you this time.（今回は勝たせてもらうよ。）と対戦相手にいわれたときももちろん、I won't let you! と言い返せる。

Are you sure…?

相手に確認をとるためのフレーズ。Are you sure you locked the front door?（ちゃんと家のドアの鍵をかけましたか？）。また Are you sure?「本当に？」は日常よく使われる。

Joe: We're lucky to see cherry blossoms before we leave.
Emily: They look like pink popcorn!
Richard: Emily, I always said you were a poet.
E: But I'm not good in math.
R: I'll tell you a secret—neither am I.
Lena: Hi, everyone! Sorry we're late.
Takako: We were making a special dish.
Hideo: Go ahead, Mai-*chan*.
Mai: Ta-da!
J: Interesting sushi! It has letters! A-N… "Anna, Joe, Emily, we'll miss you!"
Anna: Oh, my gosh! How did you do this? I'm going to cry.
Miyuki: No, I won't let you! I'll start crying, too.
Dave: Then I'll cry, and that's not a pretty sight.
Jennifer: I saw you cry at the end of *The Wizard of Oz*. It was cute.
D: That was, uh, hay fever, Jen.
J: Hey, let's take a photo with the sushi. Get together, everyone. OK!
L: Wait… Let me take one, too. Smile!
R: Lena, are you sure you have film in your camera?
L: Perhaps I should double-check. Wait—it's a digital camera. Oh, Richard!
R: Gotcha!
E and Mai: Can we eat the sushi now?
H: So… what will you do when you get to Los Angeles?
J: Well, I'll be starting my new job. And Anna will look for a job at an elementary school, and—hey, look who's here!
Takeshi: Hi, you guys! Um… this is Rachel.
Everyone: Hi, Rachel!
Rachel: Hi! It's nice to meet you all. I'm, like, so excited to be in Japan!
A: That's just how we felt when we came here. Remember, Joe?
J: I sure do. We'll really miss Japan… and our great friends here.
L: We wish you a wonderful life in Los Angeles.
M: And we'll see you again, right?
Ra: Hey, you guys should all come to L.A. Takeshi's coming to visit this summer!
E: I knew Rachel was your girlfriend!
T: Um… What can I say?
D: How about "*kampai*"?
Everyone: *Kampai*!

訳

ジョー： 日本を発つ前に桜を見ることができてよかった。
エミリー： ピンクのポップコーンみたい。
リチャード； エミリー、僕はきみのことを詩人だっていつもいってたよね。
エミリー： でも、算数は苦手。
リチャード： 秘密を教えるよ……ぼくもダメなんだ。
レナ： ハーイ、みんな！　遅れてごめんなさい。
タカコ： 特別な料理を作ってたの。
ヒデオ： ほら、マイちゃん。
マイ： じゃーん！
ジョー： おもしろいスシだ。文字が書いてある。A……N……「アナ、ジョー、エミリー、お元気で」
アナ： わあすごい。どうやったの？　泣いちゃいそうだわ。
ミユキ： だめ、泣かせないわ。わたしも泣いちゃうもの。
デーブ： そしたら僕も泣くよ、お見せできる光景じゃないよ。
ジェニファー： あなたが『オズの魔法使い』の最後で泣いたの見たわよ。あれはかわいかった。
デーブ： あれは、その、花粉症だよ、ジェン。
ジョー： ねえ、おスシといっしょに写真を撮ろう。みんな寄って、いいね。
レナ： 待って……わたしにも撮らせて。笑って。
リチャード： レナ、そのカメラはちゃんとフィルム入ってるの？
レナ： たぶんもう1度確認したほうがいいわね。待って、これデジタルカメラよ。もう、リチャードったら。
リチャード： ひっかかった。
エミリーとマイ： もうおスシ食べてもいい？
ヒデオ： それで、きみはロサンゼルスに着いたら何をするの。
ジョー： 僕は新しい仕事を始めます。そしてアナは小学校の仕事を探すつもりなんだ。それで……あ、誰かと思ったら。
タケシ： ハーイ、みんな。えーと……レイチェルです。
全員： ハーイ、レイチェル。
レイチェル： ハーイ。みなさん、はじめまして。日本にいれてすごくわくわくしています。
アナ： わたしたちがここにきたときも、まさにそう感じたわ。覚えてる、ジョー？
ジョー： もちろん。日本のことが本当に懐かしくなるだろうな、それとここにいるすばらしい友だちも。
レナ： ロサンゼルスですばらしい生活を。
ミユキ： それと、また会えるわよね？
レイチェル： ねえみなさん、ぜひLAに来てください。タケシはこの夏にくるんですよ。
エミリー： やっぱりレイチェルはあなたのガールフレンドなのね。
タケシ： うーん……何ていったらいいんだ？
デーブ：「カンパイ」でどう？
全員： カンパイ！

Chapter 12
March

Exercises

Part A Track 24

①リスニング、②パラレル・リーディング(音を聞きながらテキストを音読)、③プロソディ・シャドーイング（音の再現）④コンテンツ・シャドーイング（意味を意識）の順で会話を再現してみましょう。下記の Key Phrases を意識しながら、最低でも７回は会話を聞いてみましょう。

Key Phrases:
- We're lucky to…
- They look like…
- Ta-da!
- How did you do this?
- I won't let you!
- That's not a pretty sight.
- Are you sure…?
- Gotcha!
- What will you do when you get to (Los Angeles)?
- Look who's here.

Part B

相手の語りかけや質問に対して、自分なりの答えを考えてみましょう。

1) **Rod:** I'll be leaving for college this fall.
   You: _____

2) **Rod:** What will you do when you get to Seoul?
   You: _____

3) **Rod:** What will you be doing after you graduate?
   You: _____

今度は相手の応答にふさわしい語りかけや質問をしてみましょう。

4) 「あなたのご両親と写真を撮りましょう」といってみましょう。
   You: _____
   Rod: OK, let's do that. I'll go and get them.

5) カメラの中にフィルムが入っているのか、聞いてみましょう。
   You: _____
   Rod: Actually, this is a digital camera, so it doesn't need film.

6) 大阪に着いたらまず何をするのか、聞いてみましょう。
   You: _____
   Rod: I'll look for a place to live.

Exercises の解答例と訳

1) I'll miss you!
2) I'll look for a good Korean language school.
3) I'll be starting my new job.
4) Let's take a photo with your parents.
5) Are you sure you have film in your camera?
6) What will you do when you get to Osaka?

問題と答えの訳

1) ロッド：この秋に大学に行きます。
   あなた：さびしくなりますね！
2) ロッド：ソウルに行ったら何をするつもりですか。
   あなた：いい韓国語の語学学校を探すつもりです。
3) ロッド：卒業後は何をするつもりですか。
   あなた：新しい仕事を始めます。
4) あなた：あなたのご両親といっしょに写真を撮りましょう。
   ロッド：いいですよ。そうしましょう。呼んできます。
5) あなた：本当にカメラにフィルムが入っているんですね？
   ロッド：実際これはデジカメなので、フィルムはいらないんです。
6) あなた：大阪に着いたら何をしますか。
   ロッド：住むところを探します。

コラム　写真

　日本では行事ごとに写真を撮らなければならないという意識が強く、親は子どもの入学式や運動会には必ずカメラを持っていきます。欧米でもそういった行事で写真を撮ることはもちろんありますが、日本ほどではなく、カメラを持ってこない人もけっこういます。また、もっとも大きなちがいが見られるのは、日常生活における写真のあり方でしょう。欧米では家族や友だち、ペットなどの写真を冷蔵庫に貼ったり、職場でも自分のデスクの上に飾ったりして、常に見えるところに置いておきます。また、欧米の人は家族の写真を財布の中に入れておき、人に見せることもよくあります。

　仕事で疲れたりストレスを感じたりしたときに、家族の写真を見ると気分転換ができたり、元気づけられることもあるでしょう。家族のことを誇りに思っており、他の人に自分の家族を見せたいと思っているのかもしれません。また、それらの写真がきっかけとなって、お互いの家族の話などで盛り上がることもあるでしょう。たとえば次のように。

A: How old are your kids?
お子さんはおいくつですか。

B: Fifteen and 11. Nancy is starting high school this fall.
15歳と11歳です。ナンシーはこの秋から高校生です。

A: Oh, really? My son is a freshman now.
えっそうですか。うちの息子はいま高校1年生です。

Chapter 12 March

Skit B

ストーリーについて

　春とともにヒット・ザ・ロード・トラベル社にも変化が訪れました。ジョーは親会社のディレクターとして LA に旅立ち、シニア旅行コンサルタントのジェニファーは、ジョーの後任として支部長に昇格。デーブは自分の酒輸出業に専念するために、近々退社することになり、ミユキは一人前の旅行コンサルタントとして働き始めました。そして、ミユキの後任にはいったい誰が？

ここで扱う表現について

　1年が過ぎました。ミユキも今では立派な中堅のビジネスウーマンです。そして彼女には後輩ができました。This is…、Please call me…、Happy to meet you. など紹介、初対面でのあいさつはもうおなじみですね。1年前はおどおどとしていた彼女でしたが、ここでは流暢に英語で自己紹介しています。If you have any questions, please feel free to ask. (もし質問があれば、気軽に聞いてください) と頼もしい先輩ぶりを発揮しています。Let me know if you need any help. (何か助けが必要なら知らせてね) ともいえます。

　また、彼に対して I heard you worked at a travel agency in Moscow? (以前モスクワの旅行代理店で働いてたって聞いたけど) など、質問をすることで彼女のほうから積極的に会話をしようとしています。こうすることで相手もリラックスし、彼女の仲良くしよう、という気持ちが伝わります。

　以前のミユキのように、自分の英語能力に自信がないようなマックスですが、ミユキは No, it's great! (そんなことないわ、大丈夫よ！) と励まします。電話にもてきぱきと対処するミユキ。クライアントの依頼にも、I'll call you as soon as it comes in. (情報が入り次第すぐにお電話します) とその場を上手く切り抜けています。

　このユニットは、自己紹介、会話を広げるためのコツ、電話の対応、ほめる／励ます、などこれまでの12章で練習してきた会話の総まとめ、そして応用になっています。はじめは違和感のあった英語独特の受け答えも、だいぶ自然に耳に入るようになってきたのではないでしょうか。実際にその状況にいないとニュアンスがつかめないフレーズもあるかもしれませんが、要点として解説されている表現はもう1章に戻って復習してください。あとは実行あるのみです。

Chapter 12 March

Skit B

Track 25

ミユキの昇進と新人登場！

Miyuki: Good morning, everyone.
Dave, Jennifer, others: Morning! / Hi, Miyuki!
Max: Hello. *Hajimemashite*.
J: Miyuki, this is our new assistant travel consultant, Maksim… Ku—
Max: Kudryavtsev. But **please call me Max.**
M: Thank you! I'm Miyuki Tsukazawa. Please call me Miyuki.
Max: Thank you also. Happy to meet you.
M: Nice to meet you. If you have any questions, please feel free to ask.
Max: That is kind of you.
M: I heard you worked at a travel agency in Moscow?
Max: Yes. But I am afraid my English is…uh…rusty.
M: No, it's great! Excuse me. Hit the Road

rusty: さびた、下手になった

Travel. **Miyuki speaking.**
Moloney: Miyuki, this is Andrew Moloney. Do you have that information yet?
M: I'm sorry, Mr. Moloney, I'm still waiting. **I'll call you as soon as** it comes in.
Mo: Well… OK. Thank you.
M: Thank you for calling. Goodbye. Whew!
Max: Miyuki, I have a question already.
M: Yes, Max?
Max: Your English is excellent. Where did you learn it?
M: Well, from Dave and Jennifer… and our friends, Joe and Anna…
D: Aren't you forgetting your husband, Miyuki?
M: I could never forget Richard. Oh, he's calling. **I'll be right back.**
Max: I think they are newlyweds, yes?
D: Very perceptive, Max.
Max: Uh… may I ask… You and Jennifer are married?
D: Not yet, but… I reckon **it's a matter of time.** Oh, hiya, Jen!
Jennifer: What's a matter of time?
D: Uh…learning to appreciate good sake. Say—let's all go to my favorite sake bar after work.
Max: I like this idea.
J: Me, too. But I don't think Miyuki can join us. Today is her one-month anniversary.

建物の外で、ミユキはリチャードと電話で会話中。

M: What time shall we meet at the restaurant?
Richard: I was thinking—why don't I make a special dinner at home?
M: That sounds great!
R: And I'll pick up a bottle of "our" wine.
M: You think of everything.
R: I do, don't I? Uh…Miyuki…
M: I know, Richard. I love you, too.

I'll be right back :
すぐに戻ります
newlyweds:
新婚夫婦
perceptive:
敏感な、鋭い

It's a matter of time.:
時間の問題だ

I was thinking…:
考えたのですが……
That sounds great!:
いいね！

Chapter 12 March Skit B

ポイント解説

1年が経ち、ミユキの会社に新入社員が入社します。初対面でのあいさつ、電話での応答表現、相手を励ます表現など過去に登場した表現がたくさん出てくるので、最後にもう一度総復習しておきましょう。

Please call me Max.

外国人の名前は、複雑だったり発音し難いものもある。相手が自分の名前を覚え難そうな場合は、単純に Please call me Ken. (ケンと呼んでください) でもいいが、My real name is Kenichi, but everyone calls me Ken. (本名はケンイチですが、ケンと呼ばれています) と伝えることもできる。

Miyuki speaking.

自分のデスクを持ったということで、「ミユキです」と自分の名前を名乗っている。仕事の電話では、…speaking. や This is… といって自分の名前を名乗る。

I'll call you as soon as…

「……次第すぐにお電話します」。I'll call you as soon as I get back from vacation. (休暇から戻り次第すぐにお電話します) など。

Miyuki: Good morning, everyone.
Dave, Jennifer, others: Morning! / Hi, Miyuki!
Max: Hello. *Hajimemashite*.
J: Miyuki, this is our new assistant travel consultant, Maksim… Ku—
Max: Kudryavtsev. But **please call me Max.**
M: Thank you! I'm Miyuki Tsukazawa. Please call me Miyuki.
Max: Thank you also. Happy to meet you.
M: Nice to meet you. If you have any questions, please feel free to ask.
Max: That is kind of you.
M: I heard you worked at a travel agency in Moscow?
Max: Yes. But I am afraid my English is…uh…rusty.
M: No, it's great! Excuse me. Hit the Road Travel. **Miyuki speaking.**
Moloney: Miyuki, this is Andrew Moloney. Do you have that information yet?
M: I'm sorry, Mr. Moloney, I'm still waiting. **I'll call you as soon as** it comes in.
Mo: Well… OK. Thank you.
M: Thank you for calling. Goodbye. Whew!

Max: Miyuki, I have a question already.
M: Yes, Max?
Max: Your English is excellent. Where did you learn it?
M: Well, from Dave and Jennifer… and our friends, Joe and Anna…
D: Aren't you forgetting your husband, Miyuki?
M: I could never forget Richard. Oh, he's calling. **I'll be right back.**
Max: I think they are newlyweds, yes?
D: Very perceptive, Max.
Max: Uh… may I ask… You and Jennifer are married?
D: Not yet, but… I reckon **it's a matter of time.** Oh, hiya, Jen!
Jennifer: What's a matter of time?
D: Uh…learning to appreciate good sake. Say—let's all go to my favorite sake bar after work.
Max: I like this idea.
J: Me, too. But I don't think Miyuki can join us. Today is her one-month anniversary.

M: What time shall we meet at the restaurant?
Richard: I was thinking—why don't I make a special dinner at home?
M: That sounds great!
R: And I'll pick up a bottle of "our" wine.
M: You think of everything.
R: I do, don't I? Uh…Miyuki…
M: I know, Richard. I love you, too.

I'll be right back.
中座する際の「すぐに戻ります」も覚えておくと便利なフレーズ。その前にひとこと Excuse me. と入れてもいい。

It's a matter of time.
「時間の問題だ」。ここではジェニファーとデーブの結婚を肯定的に受け入れている。

- I like this idea.
- That sounds great!
飲み会の誘い、仕事の企画など何かいい提案が出されたときのひとこと。That's a good idea.、も同じ。good の代わりに wonderful、terrific、nice、cool など状況や相手によって応用できる。

Miyuki: Good morning, everyone.
Dave, Jennifer, others: Morning! / Hi, Miyuki!
Max: Hello. *Hajimemashite.*
J: Miyuki, this is our new assistant travel consultant, Maksim… Ku—
Max: Kudryavtsev. But please call me Max.
M: Thank you! I'm Miyuki Tsukazawa. Please call me Miyuki.
Max: Thank you also. Happy to meet you.
M: Nice to meet you. If you have any questions, please feel free to ask.
Max: That is kind of you.
M: I heard you worked at a travel agency in Moscow?
Max: Yes. But I am afraid my English is… uh…rusty.
M: No, it's great! Excuse me. Hit the Road Travel. Miyuki speaking.
Moloney: Miyuki, this is Andrew Moloney. Do you have that information yet?
M: I'm sorry, Mr. Moloney, I'm still waiting. I'll call you as soon as it comes in.
Mo: Well… OK. Thank you.
M: Thank you for calling. Goodbye. Whew!
Max: Miyuki, I have a question already.
M: Yes, Max?
Max: Your English is excellent. Where did you learn it?
M: Well, from Dave and Jennifer… and our friends Joe and Anna…
D: Aren't you forgetting your husband, Miyuki?
M: I could never forget Richard. Oh, he's calling. I'll be right back.
Max: I think they are newlyweds, yes?
D: Very perceptive, Max.
Max: Uh… may I ask… You and Jennifer are married?
D: Not yet, but… I reckon it's a matter of time. Oh, hiya, Jen!
Jennifer: What's a matter of time?
D: Uh…learning to appreciate good sake. Say—let's all go to my favorite sake bar after work.
Max: I like this idea.
J: Me, too. But I don't think Miyuki can join us. Today is her one-month anniversary.

M: What time shall we meet at the restaurant?
Richard: I was thinking—why don't I make a special dinner at home?
M: That sounds great!
R: And I'll pick up a bottle of "our" wine.
M: You think of everything.
R: I do, don't I? Uh…Miyuki…
M: I know, Richard. I love you, too.

訳

ミユキ: みなさん、おはようございます。
社員: おはよう。／ハイ、ミユキ。
マックス: ハロー。ハジメマシテ。
ジェニファー: ミユキ、こちらは我が社の新しいアシスタント旅行コンサルタントのマキシム・ク……
マックス: クドゥリヤヴツェヴです。でもマックスと呼んでください。
ミユキ: ありがとう。わたしはミユキ・ツカザワです。ミユキと呼んでください。
マックス: こちらこそありがとうございます。はじめまして。
ミユキ: こちらこそはじめまして。もし質問があれば気軽に聞いてください。
マックス: ご親切にどうも。
ミユキ: 以前はモスクワの旅行代理店で働いてたって聞いたけど？
マックス: はい、でもすみません、僕の英語力は……にぶっていて。
ミユキ: いいえ、うまいわよ。失礼。ヒット・ザ・ロード・トラベル、ミユキです。
モロニー: ミユキ、アンドリュー・モロニーです。あの件の情報はもう入りましたか。
ミユキ: 申し訳ございません、モロニー様、まだ待っている状況です。情報が入り次第すぐにお電話します。
モロニー: そうか……オーケー。ありがとう。
ミユキ: お電話ありがとうございました。失礼します。フー。
マックス: ミユキ、早速質問があるんですが。
ミユキ: なに、マックス。
マックス: あなたの英語はすばらしいですね。どこで習ったのですか？
ミユキ: それは、デーブやジェニファー……それに友だちのジョーやアナ……
デーブ: 夫のことを忘れていないかい、ミユキ。
ミユキ: リチャードのことを忘れるわけないじゃない。あ、彼からの電話だわ。すぐに戻ります。
マックス: ご新婚のようですね、そうでしょう？
デーブ: とても鋭いね、マックス。
マックス: あの……お聞きしてもよろしければ……あなたとジェニファーは結婚しているのですか。
デーブ: いや、まだ、でも……時間の問題だろうな。あ、やあ、ジェニファー！
ジェニファー: 何が時間の問題なの。
デーブ: えーと……うまい酒を味わうことを覚えるのもってことだよ。そうだ、仕事の後にみんなで僕のおすすめの酒バーに行こうよ。
マックス: それはいいですね。
ジェニファー: わたしもそう思うわ。でもミユキは参加できないと思うわ。きょうは彼女の結婚1カ月記念日だから。

ミユキ: レストランで何時に会う？
リチャード: 考えてたんだけど……僕が家で特別ディナーを作るっていうのはどう？
ミユキ: いいわね！
リチャード: 「僕たちの」ワインを買って帰ろうか？
ミユキ: あなたはなんでもよく考えるわね。
リチャード: だろ？　えーと……ミユキ……
ミユキ: わかってるわ、リチャード。わたしも愛してるわよ。

Chapter 12
March

Exercises

Part A   Track 25

①リスニング、②パラレル・リーディング(音を聞きながらテキストを音読)、③プロソディ・シャドーイング (音の再現) ④コンテンツ・シャドーイング (意味を意識) の順で会話を再現してみましょう。下記の Key Phrases を意識しながら、最低でも7回は会話を聞いてみましょう。

Key Phrases:
- Please call me…
- (Miyuki) speaking.
- I'll call you as soon as…
- I'll be right back.
- It's a matter of time.
- I like this idea.
- That sounds great!

Part B

相手の語りかけや質問に対して、自分なりの答えを考えてみましょう。

1) **Stacy:** If you have any questions, please feel free to ask.
   You: _____
2) **Stacy:** I heard you worked at an American company.
   You: _____
3) **Stacy:** Have you received the fax yet?
   You: _____

今度は相手の応答にふさわしい語りかけや質問をしてみましょう。

4) 電話の相手に「返事がき次第、お知らせします」といってみましょう。
   You: _____
   Stacy: Okay, thank you. I'll be waiting to hear from you.
5) お気に入りのイタリアン・レストランに誘ってみましょう。
   You: _____
   Stacy: OK! I always wanted to try that place. Shall I make a reservation?
6) 「私の英語力はにぶっていて」といってみましょう。
   You: _____
   Stacy: Not at all. I think your English is very good!

Exercises の解答例と訳

1) Thank you. That's kind of you.
2) Yes, I worked at an American auto company.
3) I'm still waiting. I'll call you as soon as it comes in.
4) I'll call you as soon as I receive their reply.
5) Let's all go to my favorite Italian restaurant.
6) My English is rusty.

問題と答えの訳
1) ステイシー：質問があれば、気軽に聞いてください。
   あなた：ありがとう。ご親切に。
2) ステイシー：あなたはアメリカの会社で働いたことがあるそうですね。
   あなた：はい、アメリカの自動車会社で働いたことがあります。
3) ステイシー：ファックスは届きましたか。
   あなた：まだ待っているところです。届き次第すぐにお電話いたします。
4) あなた：返事がき次第、お知らせいたします。
   ステイシー：わかりました。ありがとうございます。ご連絡をお待ちしております。
5) あなた：みんなで私のお気に入りのイタリアン・レストランに行きましょう。
   ステイシー：いいですね。前からその店に行ってみたかったんです。予約しておきましょうか。
6) あなた：私の英語力はにぶっていて。
   ステイシー：そんなことないですよ。私はあなたの英語はとてもいいと思います。

コラム happy hour & 割り勘

欧米のバーやレストランにはhappy hour というものがあり、5時から7時といった早めの時間帯に行くと安く飲食することができます。

欧米人は夕方までに仕事を切り上げて、その後の時間を同僚や家族と楽しむ傾向が強いので、このような時間帯に飲みに行くのは決して珍しいことではありません。親しい仲間や同僚2〜4人くらいで行くことが多いようです。

遅くまで働くことの多い日本のサラリーマンにはなかなか考えにくい贅沢ですが、最近では日本でもhappy hour というシステムが徐々に普及してきています。

また、日本では仕事帰りに上司と部下が飲みに行くと、上司が飲食代を支払うことが多いものですが、欧米では割り勘が基本です。しかし、自分があまり飲み食いしていない場合には、フェアではないといって割り勘したがらない人もいます。

Chapter 12の 重要表現リスト

Skit A

- □ *Let's take a picture with...
  〜といっしょに写真を撮ろう
- □ *Get together.　寄って
- □ *Let me take one.
  私にも1枚撮らせて
- □ *Smile.　笑って
- □ *Could you take a picture of us, please?
  私たちの写真を撮っていただけませんか
- □ *Do you want me to take a picture of all of you?
  みなさんの写真を撮りましょうか
- □ We're lucky to...
  〜ができて幸せだ
- □ They look like...　まるで〜みたいだ
- □ Ta-da!　じゃーん
- □ How did you do this?
  どうやって作ったの?
- □ *I'll beat you this time.
  こんどは勝たせてもらうよ
- □ I won't let you!　そうはさせないよ
- □ That's not a pretty sight.
  お見せできるような光景ではない
- □ Are you sure...?
  ちゃんと〜しましたか?
- □ *Are you sure?　本当に?
- □ Gotcha!　やーい、ひっかかった
- □ What will you do when you get to (Los Angeles)?
  ロサンゼルスに着いたら何をするの?
- □ Look who's here.
  おや、誰かと思ったら
- □ I sure do.　もちろん
- □ We'll really miss...
  〜がいなくなるとさみしいわ
- □ We wish you a wonderful life in (Los Angeles).
  (ロサンゼルス)ですばらしい生活を
- □ We'll see you again, right?
  また会おうね、いい?
- □ You guys should come to (L.A.).
  (ロス)に来るんだぞ

Skit B

- □ *If you have any questions, please feel free to ask.
  何か質問があれば気軽に聞いてください
- □ Please call me (Max).
  (マックス)と呼んでください
- □ *My real name is (Kenichi), but everyone calls me (Ken).
  本名は(ケンイチ)ですが、(ケン)と呼ばれています
- □ (Miyuki) speaking.　(ミユキ)です
- □ I'll call you as soon as...
  〜し次第、すぐにご連絡を差し上げます
- □ I'll be right back.　すぐに戻ります
- □ It's a matter of time.
  時間の問題だ
- □ I was thinking...
  考えたのですが
- □ ・I like this idea.
- □ ・That sounds great!
  いいね

キャスリーン・フィッシュマン　Cathleen Fishman
ライター、エディター

カリフォルニア州ロサンゼルス生まれ。カリフォルニア大学ロサンゼルス校(UCLA)卒業。フランスに3年間滞在するなどヨーロッパ各地を旅行する。1980年代に来日し、現在、東京でライター、編集者、翻訳者として活躍中。大の日本食好きで、ほかに日本のアート、デザイン、織物、即興音楽もお気に入り。最近は日本のお笑いに興味があり、そこに日本社会の変化が反映されていると感じている。趣味は太鼓の演奏、クロスワードパズル、旅行、東京の町を散歩することなど。

坂本光代
上智大学准教授

トロント大学大学院後期課程卒。応用言語学者。近年、30年以上にわたるカナダ生活を経て帰国。現在上智大学外国語学部英語学科准教授。同大学大学院英語教授法プログラムの教員としても教鞭を執っている。最近、ずっと習いたかった書道を始めた。ほかに趣味は読書、映画鑑賞、絵画鑑賞、食べ歩き。ハリー・ポッターからヴィトゲンシュタインまで多分野にわたって読破。また、東京のおいしいレストラン情報の収集にも精を出している。

24シーンのミニドラマで口からすらすら
日常英会話。ほんとに使える表現500

2008年11月5日　第1版第1刷発行

キャスリーン・フィッシュマン、坂本光代・共著
コスモピア編集部・編

表紙・本文イラスト／松並良仁
装丁／オフィス・エヌディ

編集協力／濱崎 都

発行人／坂本由子
発行所／コスモピア株式会社
〒151-0053　東京都渋谷区代々木4-36-4　MCビル2F
営業部／TEL: 03-5302-8378　email: mas@cosmopier.com
編集部／TEL: 03-5302-8379　email: editorial@cosmopier.com

http://www.cosmopier.com/

印刷・製本／　株式会社シナノ
音声編集／安西一明
CD製作／中録サービス株式会社

©2008 Cathleen Fishman / Mitsuyo Sakamoto / CosmoPier Publishing Company

出版案内

CosmoPier

まるでマンツーマンのレッスン！
英会話 1000本ノック

話せるようになるには「話す練習」が必要。ソレイシィコーチがCDから次々に繰り出す1000本の質問に、CDのポーズの間にドンドン答えていくスタイルの本書なら、沈黙せずにパッと返答する瞬発力と、ことばをつないで会話をはずませる本物のスピーキング力が独学で身につきます。とにかく徹底して発話させるCDは画期的。

【本書の内容】
・最重要トップテン定番あいさつノック
・海外旅行中のトップテンノック
・ベイシック文型ノック＋ステップアップ文型ノック
・トピックノック［家族／天気／仕事／健康］他

著者：スティーブ・ソレイシィ
A5判書籍237ページ＋
CD2枚（各74分）

定価1,890円
（本体1,800円＋税）

本書では沈黙は「禁」！
言いまくり！英語スピーキング入門

「あいさつ程度」から脱却して中級レベルに上がるべく、描写力・説明力を徹底的に鍛える、これまでなかったタイプの特訓本。写真やイラストの「視覚素材」を使って、考える→単語を探す→文を作る→口に出すという一連のプロセスのスピードアップを図り、見た瞬間から英語が出てくるようにするユニークなトレーニングブック。

【本書の内容】
「もの」を描写／「ひと」を描写／「複数のひと」を描写／「風景」を描写／「順番・手順」を説明／「ひと」を紹介・説明／「日本的なモノ・コト」を説明／スヌーピーの4コママンガで「ストーリー」の流れを説明

著者：高橋 基治／ロバート・オハラ
A5判書籍184ページ＋
CD1枚（54分）

定価1,680円
（本体1,600円＋税）

コスモピア・サポート

いますぐご登録ください！ 無料

「コスモピア・サポート」は大切なCDを補償します

使っている途中でキズがついたり、何らかの原因で再生できなくなったCDを、コスモピアは無料で補償いたします。
一度ご登録いただければ、今後ご購入いただく弊社出版物のCDにも適用されます。

登録申込方法
本書はさみ込みハガキに必要事項をご記入のうえ郵送してください。

補償内容
「コスモピア・サポート」に登録後、使用中のCDにキズ・割れなどによる再生不良が発生した場合、理由の如何にかかわらず新しいCDと交換いたします（書籍本体は対象外です）。

交換方法
1. 交換を希望されるCDを下記までお送りください（弊社までの送料はご負担ください）。
2. 折り返し弊社より新しいCDをお送りいたします。
   CD送付先
   〒151-0053　東京都渋谷区代々木4-36-4
   コスモピア株式会社「コスモピア・サポート」係

★下記の場合は補償の対象外とさせていただきますのでご了承ください。
● 紛失等の理由でCDのご送付がない場合
● 送付先が海外の場合
● 改訂版が刊行されて6カ月が経過している場合
● 対象商品が絶版等になって6カ月が経過している場合
● 「コスモピア・サポート」に登録がない場合

＊製品の品質管理には万全を期していますが、万一ご購入時点で不都合がある「初期不良」は別途対応させていただきます。下記までご連絡ください。
連絡先：TEL 03-5302-8378
　　　　FAX 03-5302-8399
「コスモピア・サポート」係

発行　コスモピア　　　　　　　www.cosmopier.com

出版案内

決定版 英語シャドーイング〈超入門〉
ごく短い会話からスタート

シャドーイングは繰り返しが肝心。せっかく何度も練習するのなら、日常会話や旅行会話の表現を使えば、聞く力と話す力が同時に伸びて一石二鳥です。そこで、ゆっくりしたスピードの短い会話や定番表現、実感を込めて話せる感情表現をたくさん集めました。継続トレーニングを成功に導く記録手帳付き。

編著：玉井 健
A5判書籍210ページ+
CD1枚（73分）

定価1,764円
（本体1,680円+税）

決定版 英語シャドーイング〈入門編〉
聞く力がグングン伸びる！

シャドーイングは初めて、やってみたいが、そもそも英語が聞き取れないし口も回らないという方に、ゆっくりしたスピードの練習素材を提供します。スピードは遅くても、内容は充実。名作の朗読や、小学校の理科と算数の模擬授業、そしてイチオシはロバート・F・ケネディの、キング牧師暗殺を悼むスピーチです。

編著：玉井 健
A5判書籍194ページ+
CD1枚（71分）

定価1,680円
（本体1,600円+税）

決定版 英語シャドーイング
最強の学習法を科学する！

音声を聞きながら、即座にそのまま口に出し、影のようにそっとついていくシャドーイング。「最強のトレーニング」と評される理論的根拠を明快に示し、ニュースやフリートーク、企業研修のライブ中継、さらにはトム・クルーズ、アンジェリーナ・ジョリーへのインタビューも使って、実践トレーニングを積みます。

著者：門田 修平／玉井 健
A5判書籍248ページ+
CD1枚（73分）

定価1,890円
（本体1,800円+税）

シャドーイングと音読 英語トレーニング
リスニング＆スピーキングに即効あり！

シャドーイングと音読の練習素材を提供し、効率よく英語力を伸ばすステップを示すトレーニング本。シャドーイングの前段階の学習法であるパラレル・リーディングを加えた3ステップで、初心者でも無理なく取り組めるようにしました。中でも、オバマ上院議員のスピーチは挑戦しがいのある題材です。

著者：門田 修平／高田 哲朗／溝畑 保之
A5判書籍224ページ+
CD1枚（65分）

定価1,890円
（本体1,800円+税）

英語シャドーイング〈映画スター編〉Vol.1
早口のスターのインタビューに挑戦！

キアヌ・リーブス／ケイト・ブランシェット／デンゼル・ワシントン／シャーリーズ・セロン／ケヴィン・スペイシー／ダニエル・ラドクリフ＆エマ・ワトソン／ジェニファー・アニストン他『フレンズ』出演者の、計7本のインタビューでシャドーイング。興味津々の発言内容を楽しみながら、高度なトレーニングができます。

著者：玉井 健
A5判書籍168ページ+
CD2枚（74分×2）

定価1,890円
（本体1,800円+税）

英語シャドーイング〈映画スター編〉Vol.2
「高速モード」のリスニング力がつく

レニー・ゼルウィガー／マット・デイモン／ニコール・キッドマン／ジョージ・クルーニー／ジェニファー・ロペス／レオナルド・ディカプリオ等のインタビューを収録。手強いスターの英語にも、シャドーイングなら、出身地で異なる発音や心情を伝える細かなニュアンスまで、正確にキャッチできるようになります。

著者：玉井 健／西村 友美
A5判書籍168ページ+
CD2枚（72分、46分）

定価1,890円
（本体1,800円+税）

全国の書店で好評発売中！

発行 コスモピア　　www.cosmopier.com

出版案内　　　　　　　　　　　　　　CosmoPier

ダボス会議で聞く世界の英語
世界20カ国の英語をリスニング！

緒方貞子、マハティール、アナン、ラーニア王妃など、ノンネイティブを中心に20カ国、26名の政財界のリーダーのスピーチを集めました。地球温暖化、テロ、エネルギー資源といった、世界共有のテーマの多種多様な英語のリスニングに挑戦し、自分らしい英語を堂々と話す姿勢を学び取りましょう。

著者：鶴田 知佳子／柴田 真一
A5判書籍224ページ+CD1枚（64分）
定価2,205円（本体2,100円+税）

世界を動かすトップの英語
ダボス会議の発言に学ぶ！

ダボス会議の「変わりゆく力の均衡」「Web2.0の影響」をテーマとした討論を収録。ビル・ゲイツ、チャド・ハーリーや、ナイキ、コカコーラをはじめとするグローバル企業のCEOの発言を聞きながら、トップレベルの英語コミュニケーション力、時事英語力、そして国際ビジネス感覚を鍛えます。

著者：鶴田 知佳子／柴田 真一
A5判書籍217ページ+CD1枚（59分）
定価2,205円（本体2,100円+税）

VOAスペシャル やさしいニュース英語トレーナー
「シャドーイング」と「サイトラ」を導入

VOAの中でも、使用単語を1,500に限定し、1分間100語のゆっくりしたスピードで放送される「スペシャル・イングリッシュ」のニュースが素材。シャドーイングで英語の音の壁を乗り越え、サイトラで英語の意味の壁をくずすトレーニングで、はじめての人でも、流れてくるニュースをすっと理解できるようになります。

著者：稲生 衣代／河原 清志
A5判書籍170ページ+CD1枚（73分）
定価1,680円（本体1,600+税）

ゴア×ボノ「気候危機」「超貧困」
ダボス会議スペシャルセッション

2008年のダボス会議からアル・ゴアとロックバンドU2のボノの歴史的対談を収録したCDブック。ゴアの見事なスピーチ、ボノのユーモアを交えて聞き手を巻き込む発言から、地球が直面するテーマの時事英語が学べます。小冊子には英文・対訳・語注を掲載。司会は『フラット化する世界』のトーマス・フリードマン。

CD1枚（63分）+小冊子96ページ
定価1,575円（本体1,500円+税）

リーダーの英語
シャドーイングの練習に最適！

スピーチやプレゼンのみならず、交渉や会議においても、自分の考えを明確に相手に伝えるスキルは必須です。どうすれば人を説得し、動かすことができるのか。ケネディ、サッチャー、レーガン、ブレア、ヒラリーをはじめとする英米のトップのスピーチには、スピーキングにすぐに応用できるエッセンスが凝縮されています。

著者：鶴田 知佳子／柴田 真一
A5判書籍204ページ+CD1枚（70分）
定価2,100円（本体2,000円+税）

VOAスタンダード ニュース英語トレーナー
分速160語のニュースを攻略する！

手加減なしの生のVOAニュース「スタンダード・イングリッシュ」の20本のニュースが素材。シャドーイングとサイトラを中心にしたトレーニングで「音の壁」「意味の壁」「速さの壁」「長さの壁」「未知の壁」の5つを次々にくずして行きます。特に未知の壁については、予測と推論のための大特訓を用意しています。

著者：稲生 衣代／河原 清志
A5判書籍200ページ+CD1枚（60分）
定価1,890円（本体1,800円+税）

全国の書店で好評発売中！

発行 コスモピア　　　www.cosmopier.com

出版案内　CosmoPier

さっと使える英語表現1100 まるごと練習帳
映画のセリフをとことん活用しよう

日常生活のーコマからビジネスシーンまで、90場面の短い会話を作成し、その中に映画のセリフから拾った使える表現を平均12個も埋め込みました。まるで映画のワンシーンのようなイキのいい会話を楽しみながら、ディクテーションとシャドーイングで練習して、1100の表現を自分のものにしましょう。

著者：佐藤 砂流
A5判書籍224ページ＋CD1枚（74分）

定価1,953円（本体1,860円＋税）

巽先生の「主語と動詞」の英会話
全ページフルカラー、イラスト満載！

英会話のはじめの一歩は、適切な主語、続けて正しい動詞がスッと出てくること。中学1、2年までの基礎だけを使って、いろいろな場面での主語と動詞が、3秒以内に、しかも無意識のうちに出てくるように練習します。英語を文字通りゼロからやり直したい人におすすめ。カラフルなテキストで楽しく学べます。

著者：巽 一朗
A5判書籍238ページ＋CD1枚（56分）

定価1,890円（本体1,800円＋税）

この英語、日本語ではこういう意味。
ニュアンスのつかめない英語の裏事情

英語圏で昔から使われているイディオムや比喩表現には、日本人が勘違いしやすいもの、そもそもの由来を知らないと理解できないものがあります。そこで「動物の比喩」「色の比喩」「身ぶり」などの項目別に分けて、欧米圏の習慣から説明し、ネイティブの感覚を「感じ取れる」ようにしました。

著者：クリストファー・ベルトン
翻訳：渡辺 順子
B6判書籍194ページ

定価1,365円（本体1,300円＋税）

チャンク英文法
なるほどと「わかる」英文法！

文法の中で「やっかいだ」と思っていることの数々を、本書はイラスト付きでピタリと説明してくれます。ひとつずつ覚えるのではなく、文法の本質の部分が感覚的にわかるようになるのです。そして意味のかたまりである「チャンク」の仕組みをつかめば、「読む・聞く・話す」の英語の運用能力は飛躍的に向上します。

著者：田中 茂範／佐藤 芳明／河原 清志
A5判書籍256ページ＋CD1枚（38分）

定価1,680円（本体1,600円＋税）

はじめての英語日記
1日3文の日記で決定的な差が出る！

英語で日記を書くことは、自分のことを英語で話す「リハーサル」。自分に最も必要な英語表現が身につきます。毎日3文ずつ続けることの積み重ね、これは英語で何と言うんだろうと考える習慣が、英語力アップに決定的な差を生むのです。1カ月分の日記スペース付きで、その日からスタートできます。

著者：吉田 研作／白井 恭弘
A5判書籍200ページ

定価1,365円（本体1,300円＋税）

L&R デュアル英語トレーニング
リスニング＋リーディング大特訓！

L&Rとはリスニングとリーディング。2つの力を同時に、しかも一挙に高めるトレーニング法が誕生しました。シャドーイングをはじめとする数種類の学習法を組み合わせて、効果の最大化を図ります。英語のスピードについていけないとか、途中からわからなくなるといった悩みを解消し、中級レベルへとグンと引き上げます。

著者：長沼 君主／河原 清志
A5判書籍180ページ＋CD2枚（72分、63分）

定価1,890円（本体1,800円＋税）

全国の書店で好評発売中！

発行　コスモピア　www.cosmopier.com

出版案内

100万語多読入門
辞書を捨てれば英語が読める!

リーディングのみならず、リスニング・語彙・文法の総合力が、読書を楽しんでいるうちに身につく多読とは? 本書を読めば、多読の大きな効果とその理由、100万語達成までの道のりのすべてがわかります。レベル別に選定した洋書6冊と朗読CD、簡易版読書記録手帳もついて、すぐに多読をスタートできます。

著者:古川 昭夫／伊藤 晶子
監修:酒井 邦秀
A5判書籍242ページ＋CD1枚(73分)
定価1,890円(本体1,800円＋税)

ミステリではじめる英語100万語
結末が早く知りたいから、多読に最適!

犯人は? 手口は? 動機は……。読み始めたら、どうしても結末が早く知りたくなるミステリは、100万語多読には最適の素材です。日本ではあまり知られていない、英米の子どもたちに大人気のシリーズから、ジョン・グリシャム等の本格派ペーパーバックまで、多読におすすめのミステリをレベル別に紹介します。

著者:酒井 邦秀／佐藤 まりあ
A5判書籍218ページ
定価1,680円(本体1,600円＋税)

「ハリー・ポッター」Vol.7が英語で楽しく読める本
原書で読めばもっともっと楽しい!

原書と平行して活用できるガイドブック。章ごとに「章題」「章の展開」「登場人物」「語彙リスト」「キーワード」で構成し、特に語彙リストには場面ごとに原書のページと行を表示しているので、辞書なしでラクラク読み通すことができます。呪文や固有名詞の語源や、文化的背景まで詳しく解説。

著者:クリストファー・ベルトン
A5判書籍306ページ
定価1,764円(本体1,680円＋税)

●Vol.1～6も好評発売中!

大人のための英語多読入門
50代からの人生を変える!

中学高校の6年分の英語の教科書に収録されている総語数は、平均的文庫本の4分の1。本1冊も読まないで英語が使えるわけがないのです。本書は多読の効用、大人になって英語を学び直す有利な点を説き、みずからも50代から多読を始めた経験をもとに、無理なく多読を続ける方法を丁寧にアドバイスします。

監修:酒井 邦秀
著者:佐藤 まりあ
A5判書籍239ページ
定価1,890円(本体1,800円＋税)

英語多読完全ブックガイド〈改訂第2版〉
洋書12,000冊のデータを網羅!

多読に最適な、英語レベル別に語彙や文法を制限して執筆されたリーダーズのほかに、児童書、絵本、ペーパーバックなど、合計12,000冊を紹介。読みやすさレベル、総語数、おすすめ度、コメント、ISBNのデータを収録しています。次に何を読もうと思ったときにすぐに役立つ、多読必携の完全ガイドです。

編著:古川 昭夫／神田 みなみ 他
A5判書籍476ページ
定価2,730円(本体2,600円＋税)

イギリス英語で聞く「ハリー・ポッターと不思議の国イギリス」
イギリス英語の響きに浸りきる

クリストファー・ベルトン初のエッセー集『ハリー・ポッターと不思議の国イギリス』の原文を、格調高いイギリス英語の朗読CDにしました。原書から特に朗読に適した章を抜粋し、巻末には著者とナレーターの特別対談を収録。ハンディなテキストには英文・対訳・語注のほか、イラストや写真も掲載。

著者:クリストファー・ベルトン
朗読:スチュアート・アトキン
CD2枚(各72分)＋小冊子144ページ
定価1,890円(本体1,800円＋税)

全国の書店で好評発売中!

発行 コスモピア
www.cosmopier.com

出版案内　CosmoPier

基礎からの英語eメール仕事術
ビジネスeメールのマナーから実践まで

海外駐在15年の著者が、仕事を成功に導くeメールの書き方を伝授。シンプルな英語で必要事項を簡潔に伝える「ビジネスライク」な英文に「パーソナル・タッチ」を添えて、相手との信頼関係を築くメール作成のコツを学びます。現役ビジネスマンだから書けたナマナマしいケース・スタディが本書の特長です。

著者：柴田 真一
A5判書籍240ページ

定価2,100円（本体2,000円＋税）

参加する！英語ミーティング
出席するだけから、積極的に発言するへ！

英語会議を録画した膨大な記録データから、日本人の弱点を分析。会議に必要な「英語力」と、あいづち、うなずき、アイコンタクトから始まる「英語力以外の要素」の2方向から、ビジネス・ミーティングのスキルを習得します。誌面にはイラストを多用し、会議に参加しているかのようなOJT感覚で学べます。

著者：田中 宏昌／マイク・ハンドフォード
A5判書籍208ページ＋CD1枚（44分）

定価1,890円（本体1,800円＋税）

ライティング・パートナー
プロのイギリス人ライター直伝の1冊！

英文ライティングの基本ルール、注意したい文法事項から、日記・メール・ビジネスレター・スピーチ原稿・プレゼン原稿の具体的書き方までカバー。これ1冊でどんな英文でも書けるようになります。英語を書くプロが、ネイティブの目から見た日本人の苦手な部分、稚拙な印象を回避するテクニック等を丁寧にアドバイス。

著者：クリストファー・ベルトン
翻訳：渡辺 順子
A5判書籍376ページ

定価2,310円（本体2,200円＋税）

決定版 英語エッセイ・ライティング
フローチャートでよくわかる！

英文レポートや小論文作成、TOEFL受験や留学で必要となるエッセイ・ライティングの「ルール」を、わかりやすくフローチャート化して提示。具体的な練習問題を解きながら、全フローを体験することができ、自分の考えが伝わる英文、明確かつ説得力のある文章が、誰でも書けるようになります。

著者：門田 修平／氏木 道人／伊藤 佳世子
A5判書籍216ページ

定価2,100円（本体2,000円＋税）

ここまで使える超基本単語50
コアから広がる英単語ネットワーク

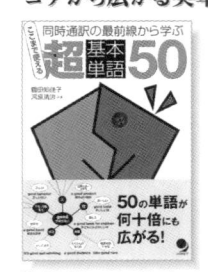

CNNなどで現役バリバリの同時通訳者として活躍する著者は、専門用語よりも簡単な単語ほど苦労すると漏らします。goodやbad、makeといった50の基本語がどんなに幅広く使われているか、同時通訳の現場から拾った豊富な実例を通して学びます。読み物としても楽しめ、英語の表現がグンと広がる1冊です。

著者：鶴田 知佳子／河原 清志
B6判書籍234ページ

定価1,470円（本体1,400円＋税）

シャドーイングと音読の科学
英語力が伸びる根拠を徹底検証する！

英語学習に王道なし。でも「ほとんど王道といえる」方法はある。シャドーイングと音読がなぜ効果的なのかを、広範な指導実験のデータをもとに、最新の脳科学の成果も交えて明快に示します。専門的な内容をわかりやすくするためにイラストやグラフを多用し、Q&A形式であらゆる疑問に答えます。

著者：門田 修平
A5判書籍280ページ

定価2,415円（本体2,300円＋税）

全国の書店で好評発売中！

発行　コスモピア　　www.cosmopie

出版案内 CosmoPier

新・最強のTOEIC®テスト入門
「見れば」すぐにポイントがわかる！

新形式のTOEICテストに完全対応し、「動作だけを聞いても正解を選べる」「最初の数行に1問目の答えがある」というように、61の出題パターンをズバズバ提示。具体的な例題に沿いながら、解答のフローをページ見開きでわかりやすく示します。初受験で500点獲得、2回目以降の人は150点アップが目標です。

著者：塚田 幸光／横山 仁視 他
A5判書籍260ページ＋CD1枚（59分）

定価1,890円（本体1,800円＋税）

わかる！はじめての新TOEIC®テスト
まずは日本語で解いてみよう！

最初の説明・例題から英語のみのスタイルが、TOEICテストのハードルを高くしている要因のひとつ。最初に日本語で解いてみることでテストの全体像を短時間で把握し、心理的障壁を取り去ります。TOEICの特徴である頻出ビジネスシーンに慣れ、ゼロから始めて12日間でスコアアップを実現します。

著者：高橋 基治
A5判書籍174ページ＋CD1枚（43分）

定価1,470円（本体1,400円＋税）

新TOEIC®テスト パーフェクト模試200
セクション別に予想スコアが算出できる！

手軽に1回分の模試が受けられます。200問すべてについて、モニターテスト参加者の正答率、各選択肢の誤答率を公開しており、自分のレベルを客観的に把握することができます。CDには米英豪加のナレーターを均等に起用し、巻末には同一ナレーションを各国の発音で順番に収録した、聞き比べエクササイズも準備。

著者：田中 宏昌／Amy D.Yamashiro 他
A5判書籍204ページ＋CD1枚（71分）

定価1,029円（本体980円＋税）

TOEIC®テスト リーディング速効ドリル
新形式のPART7はこう攻めろ！

読む量がグンと増えた新形式の長文読解で、最後の設問までたどり着くにはスピード対策が不可欠。本書のねらいは、「トピック・センテンス」をすばやく見つけて大意を把握、5W1Hに照らして要点を「スキミング」、設問で問われている情報を「スキャニング」するの3つ。114ページを割いたダブル・パッセージ対策も完璧。

著者：細井 京子／山本 千鶴子
A5判書籍264ページ

定価1,764円（本体1,680円＋税）

新TOEIC®テスト 出まくり英文法
英文法も例文ごと耳から覚える！

TOEICテストを実際に受験し、最新の出題傾向を分析し続けている「英語工房（早川幸治、高橋基治、武藤克彦）」の第2弾。PART5とPART6に頻出する文法項目64について、TOEICテスト必須語彙や頻出フレーズを盛り込んだ例文を作成し、CDを聞きながら例文ごと脳に定着させます。

著者：英語工房
B6判書籍200ページ＋CD1枚（58分）

定価1,575円（本体1,500円＋税）

TOEIC®テスト 出まくりキーフレーズ
直前にフレーズ単位で急速チャージ！

TOEICテストの最頻出フレーズ500を、わずか1時間で耳と目から急速チャージします。フレーズを盛り込んだ例文は、試験対策のプロ集団がじっくり練り上げたもので、例文中のキーフレーズ以外の単語もTOEICテストやビジネスの必須単語ばかり。ひとつの例文が何倍にも威力を発揮する、まさに短期決戦の特効薬です。

著者：英語工房
B6判書籍188ページ＋CD1枚（57分）

定価1,575円（本体1,500円＋税）

全国の書店で好評発売中！

発行　コスモピア　　www.cosmopier.com

通信講座　　　　　　　　　　　　　　　　　　　CosmoPier

新TOEIC®テスト対策、
「何を」「どれだけ」「どう」学べばいいのか……
通信講座ならその答えが用意されています!

目標スコアごとに綿密に組まれたカリキュラムで、確実なスコアアップを実現します。

新TOEIC®テスト スーパー入門コース

まずはリスニングからスタート。「聞くこと」を通して、英語の基礎固めとTOEICテスト対策の2つを両立させます。

開始レベル	スコア300点前後または初受験
目標スコア	400点台
学習時間	1日20分×週4日
受講期間	3カ月
受講料	14,700円（税込）

新TOEIC®テスト GET500コース

英語を、聞いた順・読んだ順に英語のまま理解する訓練を積み、日本語の介在を徐々に減らすことでスコアアップを実現します。

開始レベル	スコア400点前後
目標スコア	500点台
学習時間	1日20分×週4日
受講期間	3カ月
受講料	20,790円（税込）

新TOEIC®テスト GET600コース

600点を超えるには時間との闘いがカギ。ビジネスの現場でも必須となるスピード対策を強化し、さらに頻出語彙を攻略します。

開始レベル	スコア500点前後
目標スコア	600点台
学習時間	1日30分×週4日
受講期間	4カ月
受講料	29,400円（税込）

監修　田中宏昌 明星大学教授

NHK「ビジネス英会話」「英語ビジネスワールド」の講師を4年にわたって担当。ビジネスの現場に精通している。

●**大手企業でも、続々と採用中!**
【採用企業例】
NEC／NTTグループ／富士通エフ・アイ・ピー／松下電工／本田技研工業／INAX／アサヒ飲料／シチズン電子／京セラ／エイチ・アイ・エス　他
●**全国の大学生協でも好評受付中です。**

まずはパンフレット（無料）をご請求ください

＊本書はさみ込みのハガキが便利です。

教材の一部の音声をネットで試聴もできます。
ぜひ一度アクセスしてみてください。
www.cosmopier.com

〒151-0053　東京都渋谷区代々木4-36-4　TEL 03-5302-8378　FAX 03-5302-8399
主催　コスモピア

TOEIC is a registered trademark of Educational Testing Service(ETS). This product is not endorsed or approved by ETS.